THE REAL WALT DISNEY

By the same author

Non-fiction
Zanuck: The Rise and Fall of Hollywood's Last Tycoon, 1984
Marshall: Architect of Victory, 1982
The Druid, 1981
Blood Relations: The Rise and Fall of the du Ponts of Delaware, 1980
Dulles: A Biography of Eleanor, Allen & John Foster Dulles, 1978
Lindbergh: A Biography, 1976
The Reich Marshal: A Biography of Hermann Goering, 1974
Power Play: Oil in the Middle East, 1973
Backs to the Wall: London in World War II, 1971
On Borrowed Time: How World War II Began, 1969
Hirohito: Emperor of Japan, 1966
The Battle of Britain, 1965
Haile Selassie: The Conquering Lion, 1964
Faces from the Fire: A Biography of Sir Archibald McIndoe, 1962
Curzon: The End of an Epoch, 1962
The Last Days of the British Raj, 1961
The Cat and the Mice: A German Spy in Cairo (also known as
    Foxhole in Cairo), 1960
Duel for Kilimanjaro, 1959
Castlerosse: The Life of a Bon Vivant, 1956
Gideon Goes to War: A Biography of Orde Wingate, 1955
Report from Germany 1945, 1945
Downstream 1939, 1939
So Far So Good: A Fragment of Autobiography, 1934

Fiction
The Seductive Mirror, 1952
Each Had a Song, 1951
War Lord, 1950
No More Remains, 1938
So I Killed Her, 1937

LEONARD MOSLEY

THE REAL
WALT DISNEY

A Biography

GRAFTON BOOKS
A Division of the Collins Publishing Group

LONDON GLASGOW
TORONTO SYDNEY AUCKLAND

Grafton Books
A Division of the Collins Publishing Group
8 Grafton Street, London W1X 3LA

First published in the USA 1985
under the title *Disney's World*

Published in Great Britain by Grafton Books 1986

British Library Cataloguing in Publication Data

Mosley, Leonard
   The real Walt Disney : a biography.
   1. Disney, Walt   2. Moving-picture producers
   and directors—United States—Biography
   3. Animators—United States—Biography
   I. Title
   791.43'0232'0924   PN1998.A3D5

ISBN 0-246-12439-3

Typeset by Columns of Reading
Printed in Great Britain by
Mackays of Chatham Ltd

CONTENTS

PREFACE AND
ACKNOWLEDGEMENTS

No one with long and happy memories of a legend wants to have them too much disturbed, and this biography is not intended to upset or destroy the image so many people cherish of that remarkable American, Walt Disney.

Disney is regarded by millions of people, particularly in the United States, as perhaps this century's most brilliantly successful creator of screen animation, and I think I should make one thing clear right away: I share this general admiration for a man whose cinematic achievements were always so happily inspired and inspiring. But – and this is where I differ from idolators – I have to know all the facts, no matter how unpalatable, as well as all the romantic myths about any great man or woman I admire. Many of the myths that have been created by his publicists about Walt Disney are unpalatable, unbelievable and unsatisfactory because so much of the real man has been deliberately concealed.

As I have tried to show in most of my previous biographies, particularly in the one I wrote about my own special childhood hero, Charles Augustus Lindbergh, I am suspicious of a legend whose image is so artificially polished that it shows no lines or warts on the face, no faults in the interior make-up, no flaws or weaknesses in the character. In some ways I sympathize with George Kaufman who once remarked about Lindbergh that 'the trouble is all heroes are horses' asses'. By that he meant Lindbergh was often his own worst enemy, and many of the most painful episodes in his life were due to faults of arrogance and pride.

Walt Disney, though totally unlike Lindbergh, also had grave flaws in his character – and in some ways I find that comforting. I do not believe in perfect people, especially perfect heroes.

I first became aware that Walt Disney was, thank God, a human being – with all the faults as well as the virtues that such a state entails – when I went to see him at his studios in Burbank in the fifties. I was then film critic for the London *Daily Express* on one of my biannual visits to Hollywood, and the studio publicity machines had, as usual, gone out of their way to try to persuade me, as a writer for an influential British newspaper, that this was a city of flawless gods and goddesses, full of clean-living, sanitized stars. No one ever got drunk (not even Ava Gardner), no one ever beat her children (not even Joan Crawford), no one ever cheated on his wife (not even Jack Warner or Clark Gable or Darryl Zanuck).

It was even more of a deodorized world at Walt Disney Studio, where the publicity men insisted their boss was faultless – never drank too much, never swore, never lost his temper, never quarrelled with his wife or family, never let down a friend. And woe betide anyone who tried to suggest otherwise. Members of the resident foreign and local press risked their jobs if they dared to write stories implying that Walt Disney could be domineering, implacable and unforgiving (as was the case, for instance, before, during and after the 1941 studio strike). The Disney publicists were capable of exerting heavy pressure, via editors, proprietors or through the advertising pages, against anyone who hinted that Walt Disney was not the epitome of well-scrubbed and benevolent perfection.

A few days spent talking to Disney's family, directors, technicians, animators and artists soon revealed a very different picture of the great man. I even encountered one of his most gifted collaborators, whose later comments figure largely in these pages, who maintained he was writing Walt's biography and calling it: *A Great Man but . . . The Truth About Walt Disney*. I never discovered from our later conversations what happened to that project; certainly it never saw the light of day. (Pressure? Censorship?) The extracts he read me and the accounts he gave me of life working with Disney, when added to the rueful anecdotes from his other associates, helped, even all that time ago, to reassure me. Walt Disney was not, after all, the holier-than-thou character the studio propagandists made him out to be, but a remarkably talented human being who also did regrettable things. He was, in fact, far from perfect.

While not neglecting his virtues or his genius, this biography has included most of his imperfections. I hope and believe his image has been enlarged rather than diminished because of that.

This book probably would never have been written had it not been for the encouraging insistence over the years of one very close friend, the well-known screen-writer and novelist, Jack Davies, who has written scripts for most of the world's famous producers – with the exception of Walt Disney. But he knew him well and met him frequently during his long and distinguished career, and has always sensed there was much more to learn about this unique American than had been revealed by the sponsored books about him. Jack pushed me into continuing my researches even during moments of great difficulty and setbacks, and I thank him for his amiable persistence.

As I have already indicated, so far as the facts in this book are concerned, they are based on research going back to the fifties; more recently, they culminated in several long stays in Hollywood and Burbank as well as sessions with Disney alumni in all parts of the world. I cannot, for space and other reasons, name all the Disney associates and veterans to whom I have talked; some of them, for instance, have insisted on anonymity because, they point out, they still rely on the good will of the Disney organization for pensions and medical insurance. But wherever they are quoted in this book, they have seen the remarks they made to me and have had the opportunity of checking, cutting (or expanding) what they told me in the course of our tape-recorded conversations.

The Disney organization have *not* seen anything of the text. I should stress that I am nevertheless extremely grateful to them for the help they gave me in allowing me access to their records. This is unusual, for this is a non-authorized book so far as they are concerned. In such cases they normally decline all cooperation, and, in particular, refuse to allow the use of their copyright photographs to 'outside' authors unless they can see the text. After initial opposition, however, they decided to make a special exception in my case, and gave me unsupervised access over several months to the extensive archives in their Burbank studios. I have quoted from these records and oral histories with permission, but my interpretations are of course strictly my own and have been made without Disney censorship of any kind. I have also been allowed to draw from Disney's unique collection of copyright photographs; though, in this case, Disney officials have seen and corrected the captions to their own pictures. So I can honestly stress that all opinions about Walt Disney expressed by me are strictly my own, and this is an entirely independent and unsponsored book.

The chief Disney archivist, David R. Smith, who has an encyclopedic knowledge of Disney facts and figures, and his amiable staff were indefatigable in helping me track down obscure documents and early photographs of Disney's pioneering days. I also owe heartfelt thanks to Wayne Morris, manager of Disney's merchandizing and publication division for allowing me to use these and other illustrations (the Disney copyright to which is acknowledged elsewhere). I may say that I have been asked not to mention the above two officials by name, but in view of their assistance, I feel I should override their modest request for anonymity and name them just the same with my thanks.

Not only from David Smith and Wayne Morris, of course, did I receive precious help from inside the Disney organization. For instance, little of this material could ever have been uncovered had it not been for the friendship, advice and influence of Disney's most sage and successful alumnus, Vincent Jefferds, whose genius as the exploiter of Disney's immortal characters and spin-offs from the studio's most famous films was earning the company 50 million dollars a year in royalties when he retired a short time ago. A talented artist himself and an expert in the art of corporate publicity, Jefferds had some enthralling stories to tell about Walt and Roy Disney and of the making (as well as the exploitation) of such famous projects as *Peter Pan, Davy Crockett,* Disneyland and Walt Disney World. I am also grateful for the help and encouragement of his charming assistant, Queenie Osinoff. In addition, my fellow-researcher and I will long savour the fascinating evenings we spent listening to Jefferds and his wife Jean at their home in Tigertail Road, Westwood.

Perhaps the frankest and most educative of all my encounters with Walt Disney's former associates was with the artist-animator who came closest to him during their long professional life together. This was the brilliant and salty-tongued Ward Kimball, whose many imaginative cartoons and short films for Disney won world-wide fame as well as well-deserved Hollywood Oscars. Kimball's passion for locomotives and railroad lore was (and is) such that he has two full-size working locomotives and other impedimenta in his garden, a former citrus grove in the San Gabriel valley of California; it also contains tracks along which the locomotives (one wood-burning, the other coal-fired) can run, a full-scale model of a Western railroad station, and one of the world's most comprehensive collections of model trains. Kimball's enthusiasm for his hobby fired Walt Disney with the same passion and they travelled the United States together tracking down rare ancient railroad memorabilia, until finally Disney built his own train and track in the garden of his house in the Holmby Hills. I found Kimball a good example of someone who loved and admired Walt Disney while being well aware of his boss's faults and weaknesses, and he gave me a wonderfully rounded picture of one of the greatest, and yet most fallible, men he had ever encountered.

An old friend, the famous plant and orchid expert, Russell Seibert, gave me an introduction to the Californian landscape gardener, Morgan 'Bill' Evans. Now living in Malibu, Bill Evans laid out Disneyland in California and Walt Disney World and EPCOT in Florida. In doing so he created gardens and spectacular landscapes out of what before had been citrus groves and virgin swamps, and they are among the greatest transformations of raw countryside since Capability Brown 'made the desert smile' in eighteenth-century England.

Travelling north to Santa Barbara, I spent some time with the former English matte-painter, Peter Ellenshaw, and his American wife, Bobbie. Ellenshaw, who worked on some of Disney's most successful films (*Treasure Island, 20,000 Leagues Under the Sea, Mary Poppins*), is now a famous painter. He took time out from preparing a big new exhibition of his work to talk about his long association with and deep affection for Walt Disney, whose equal as man, film-maker and boss he believes he will never meet again.

David Swift (maker of many box-office hits for Disney, including *Pollyanna*) is still as handsome and as boyishly active in films as ever and still a successful Hollywood director. Like his close friend, Ward Kimball, he went through all the departments at Disney in the course of his early career, and he retains a shrewd, realistic and affectionate memory of his former boss's reactions at some of the most critical moments of his lifetime.

One of the reasons why Swift's *Pollyanna* was so successful was the heart-warming performance of its English child star, Hayley Mills. She came to see me from her home beside the River Thames in Surrey and soon made it clear that, as far as she was concerned, Walt Disney was a cherished memory, a man who was thoughtful, protective and sensitive to her childhood worries and apprehensions. So far as Hayley was concerned, he had no blemishes whatsoever, and joy still throbs in her voice as she talks about her first encounters with him.

Peter Ustinov, a tennis buff whom I saw in London between rounds of the Wimbledon championships, was, on the other hand, somewhat cooler in his enthusiasm. He found Walt Disney a remote and almost unapproachable figure, and though he made several successful films at Burbank, never really got to know him, though he did have a disturbing final meeting with him just before Disney's death.

Ustinov was much more forthcoming about and more admiring of

Walt Disney's favourite producer, the late Bill Walsh, with whom he worked on several Disney films. I have made extensive use of the oral histories that Walsh left behind; they are now in the Disney Archives, and are quoted here with permission. I also talked at some length with Mrs Nola Fishman, now the wife of a well-known Californian television anchorman, about her earlier marriage to Walsh and her stormy fight to save it from the pressures placed on it by Walt Disney.

Two other old friends, the director Ken Annakin and his wife, Pauline, talked in great detail, at their home in Malibu, in England and at my home in Florida, about their long and close collaboration with Walt Disney. Annakin made four films for Disney (three in Britain and Europe, one in the USA) and often mixed socially with Walt and his wife, Lillian, at their former home in London and at the Disney winter home in Palm Springs.

Annakin arranged a meeting for me with his producer, Bill Anderson, who took over the running of the Disney Studio when feature film production resumed after World War II. During our session at Newport Beach his wife, Mrs Virginia (Ginny) Anderson, described in colourful detail how she and Pauline Annakin 'discovered' Hayley Mills in London and recommended her for stardom in *Pollyanna*.

In Florida Julia C. Wilson, associate managing editor of the Orlando *Sentinel*, was kind enough to give me the run of the reference library of her newspaper, and its librarian, Judy Grimsley, and her staff helped me track down every clipping I wanted. It was one of the *Sentinel*'s reporters, Emily Bavar (now Mrs Emily Kelly) who first broke the story that Disney was building a great theme-park in central Florida, and she gave me a vivid account of how she stumbled on the story while talking to Walt and Roy Disney in California.

My agent, John Cushman, whose sudden and tragic death sadly interrupted work on this biography, gave me an introduction to his cousin John Nesbit, a Disney executive in Florida; and my neighbour on Captiva Island, Dewitt Jones, revealed that he too had worked for Disney for many years and gave a lively account of what it was like to be at Burbank in the great days of the company after the end of World War II.

Other present and former employees (many of whom are, alas, no longer with us) talked to me over the years. Others left behind memories, spoken and written, which have been of enormous help to me in reconstructing life as it was lived at the Burbank studios. They include: James Algar, Art Babbitt, Mary Blair, Claude Coats, Norm

Ferguson, Christopher Finch, Hugh Frazier, Hazel George, Don Griffith, T. Hee, John Hench, Milton Kahl, Glen Keane, Richmond Kelsey, Eric Larson, Rico Lebrun, Gordon Legg, John Lounsbery, Dick Lundy, Don Lusk, Ham Luske, Josh Meador, Kay Nielsen, Ken O'Brien, Bill Peet, Martin Provensen, Art Riley, Joe Rinaldi, Retta Scott, Mel Shaw, Gustaf Tenggren, Vladimir Tytla.

In addition, I have relied for a great deal of my information about animation on that Disney-sponsored splendidly illustrated monster tome by Frank Thomas and Ollie Johnston (two of Walt's most brilliant ex-animators) *Disney Animation: The Illusion of Life*, although I have been refused permission to quote or use pictures from it. I have also been helped in my research by two books which Peter Ellenshaw gave me: a hardcover volume of his collected works 1929-1983 (Hammer, New York, 1983), which includes some of his work for Disney, and *Walt Disney's Fantasia* by John Culhane (Abrams, New York, 1983). Other books which have proved invaluable are *The Art of Walt Disney* by Robert D. Field (Collins, London and Glasgow, 1945), *The Art of Walt Disney* by Christopher Finch (Abrams, New York, 1975), and Richard Schickel's *The Disney Version* (Weidenfeld & Nicolson, London, 1968), a realistic look at Disney's character.

Extremely helpful were two other previously published biographies of Walt Disney in which I found nuggets of information that I could not resist quoting (again with permission). One is *The Story of Walt Disney* by his only daughter, Diane Disney Miller, based on long conversations with her father and written in collaboration with Pete Martin (Henry Holt and Co., New York, 1957). In a conversation with me while this acknowledgement was being written, Mrs Miller told me how much she loved and admired her father, and it shows in this book. The other is the splendidly written and researched *Walt Disney* by Bob Thomas, the veteran Associated Press correspondent in Hollywood (Simon and Schuster, New York, 1976).

My thanks to them all for fascinating conversations, reminiscences and reading matter.

And, once more, my gratitude to my fellow-researcher, beloved fellow-traveller and wife, Deirdre, for her constant encouragement and help.

Prologue

COMEBACK

In the autumn of 1966 Walt Disney, aged sixty-four, made a drastic decision about his future: he would cheat death and have himself frozen for eventual resurrection. It was the opinion of a panel of doctors in Burbank, California, which caused him to make up his mind. He had gone to them that summer for a clinical examination, confident they would do some tinkering with his body and then give him a clean bill of health. Instead, to his great indignation and astonishment, he had been told he was likely to die soon.

Until that moment Walt Disney had assumed he had at least another decade of productive life before him. He had found that comforting. He knew he would need every moment of the time he had left to complete the plans he was setting in train for the development of the Disney organization. Ten, fifteen, even twenty years would be necessary to finish them all, but he was sure God would give him the time to carry out the necessary tasks. But now, suddenly, the medical men had handed him what amounted to a death sentence. He did not have years left but days, and those days were numbered. Walt Disney just could not believe it, and took second and third and fourth opinions until he had to admit that it was probably only too true. And then he became not just devastated by the news but angered by it too, by the monstrous injustice of it, its sheer untimeliness, and by his grim awareness of the appalling havoc it would wreak on his carefully-constructed plans.

It was true that even before he received the doctors' verdict Walt Disney had begun to suspect that all was not physiologically well. For some time he had been enduring an agonizing pain in his neck, the result of a bad fall he had taken from a horse during his polo-playing days. But his concern about that had been cleared up. On the recommendation of his friend, Floyd Odlum, he had been to see a specialist and had been told he had better learn to live with it. Rectifying the condition would necessitate a major operation on the spinal cord, and the risk was greater than the probability of the cure.

1

Since the specialist assured him he was otherwise in good physical condition, he was persuaded to go away and try to make the best of his aches and pains. And this he had done. He had given a permanent job at the Burbank studios of Walt Disney Productions to a remarkable character named Hazel George, who was a trained nurse and a qualified masseuse.

Walt Disney had great faith in the soothing power of Hazel George's hands, and every evening at seven o'clock, after the day's work was over, he went across to the clinic he had had installed for her. While he was stripping off his shirt, she would mix him a strong Scotch on the rocks and let him take a couple of gulps before she motioned him on to the rubbing table. Then, with magical fingers, she massaged away the physical pains and the nervous tensions that had built up during the day. At the end of thirty minutes he would finish the remains of his drink, and, while he made another for himself and one for her, they would talk. It was usually going on eight o'clock by the time he drove home to Bel Air.

Walt Disney confided in Hazel George as he did in no one else, including his wife, his daughter and his brother. It was as if he sensed that, unlike anyone else around him, this down-to-earth and practical woman not only liked and admired him but was never afraid to tell him the truth, especially about himself. He took remarks from her he would never have accepted from anyone else, even allowing her to mock him about what she called his 'ostrich-egg-sized ego'. One night, when a thunderstorm was raging over Burbank and he expressed doubts about what it was going to be like driving home through it, she said: 'Well, why don't you just go out and tell it to stop?' When he laughed over the way some of his employees hero-worshipped him, and added 'Peter Ellenshaw, for instance, thinks I can walk on water,' she looked him straight in the eye and said: 'Well, can you?' Most of his employees were afraid of him, and she was constantly counselling him to be kinder and less irascible with them, sarcastically adding that he had to learn to live with them and accept the fact that 'most of us are just ordinary people, not geniuses like you'. She urged him to be more understanding, especially with his son-in-law, Ron Miller, and his nephew, Roy E. Disney Jr, who worked in the studio and were always getting the rough edge of his tongue. 'But *they're* not ordinary people!' he would protest. 'They-re —' he struggled for a word, and then blurted out, 'mediocrities!' But he did watch his tongue in future, and stopped abusing them for incompetence – at least in public.

After several months of massage sessions, Walt Disney had taken to drinking steadily during as well as before and after his treatment, lying on the rubbing table sucking Scotch highballs through a straw.

'You know,' Hazel George said one night, watching as he refilled his glass, 'if you go on like this, you're in danger of becoming a lush. What does Lilly say when you get home smelling of all that booze?'

Walt shrugged, grinned ruefully and said he kept out of his wife's 'breathing space'. He added that he knew what Hazel thought of his drinking, but he pointed out he didn't touch a drop in the office all day, and he didn't drink when he got home to Bel Air. By the time his working day was over, he was desperate for a Scotch.

Catching the disapproval on her face, he went on: 'Don't think I'm not aware of what they're saying about me around the studio.'

He knew he was a grouch, he said, that his fuse was short and growing shorter, that he blazed up and got mad at nice people who hadn't done anything wrong and didn't deserve it. It was all true, and he hated himself for it. He held up one of his specially rolled black cigarettes – he consumed anything up to seventy a day – and said that they used to calm him down, but they didn't seem to do anything for him any longer.

'My nerves are all shot to hell,' he admitted, 'and nowadays,' he put his hand gingerly on the back of his neck, 'this fucking pain here is driving me nuts!'

'Don't the rubdowns help any more?' asked Hazel. 'Have I lost my magic touch?'

Sadly, he nodded. The nightly massage didn't seem to help him any longer, he said. 'Frankly, the only reason I come here nowadays is for the booze.'

He swallowed the last of his Scotch and reached for the bottle. Hazel got there first and moved it away, locking it in the closet. Then she began talking to him softly, earnestly, persuasively.

If the pain in his neck was now so bad, he just had to go back to the doctors, and do it soon, she told him. He should also try to cut down on all the Scotch he drank when he came to see her. There were already rumours around the studio that he was drunk every night when he climbed into his car. She feared he was going to have a nasty accident on the way home, and the highway patrol would pull him in for DUI (driving under the influence). He mustn't let it happen. 'That's one of the scandals this studio can do without,' she said.

On the recommendation of Vince Jefferds, his marketing expert, Walt Disney went to see a Beverly Hills orthopaedic surgeon named Theodore Lynd. Lynd took X-ray pictures of his neck and back, and found the reason for the increasing pain: calcium was clustering so thickly in Walt Disney's neck it was cutting off the spinal column and making the slightest movement of the head, neck or shoulders an agonizing ordeal. Then he looked at the other areas covered by the X-rays and noticed the appearance of the lungs. For years it had been a joke among Disney employees that they always knew when their boss was coming along the corridors, for his continuous cough (which they called Walt's Warning Signal) would herald his approach. Walt himself considered he suffered from no more than a mild smoker's cough and thought it the least of his troubles. But Theodore Lynd strongly recommended that his patient should be examined by a lung specialist.

Walt promised to make an appointment straight away, and that was when he got the first warning that something was badly wrong with him.

At the hospital they told him he had a threatening case of emphysema, and treatment for it should be undertaken without further delay. At which point Walt Disney's confidence in his future collapsed.

For the moment, the doctors were not being straightforward: they told him only that if he didn't do something about himself soon, it *could* be fatal. But the more he studied their reports, the more he realized what they were predicting between the lines: he was going to die.

For years Walt Disney had been philosophizing about the inevitability of death.

'Like most of us,' said one of his associates who asked not to be named, 'once he reached his sixties, he became vitally concerned about when and how he was going to die. But there was this difference. With him you knew it wasn't just a personal matter. Don't forget that Walt Disney in 1966 was already the most famous man in the world. He truly was a phenomenal guy. He was no longer simply the genius who had created all those famous cartoon characters like Mickey, Donald, Goofy and the rest. He'd gone beyond that. He was now the most powerful entrepreneur in history. He controlled a multi-million-dollar leisure organization that attracted hordes of people from all parts of the world. And he spent every waking moment thinking up new ideas for them and for this enormous money-making leisure and entertainment complex he controlled. So what Walt Disney worried about was not just how his own death was going to affect him – though he

wouldn't have been human if he hadn't been bothered about that too
– but what it was going to do to his future projects and present
obligations. To the Disney organization. Millions of people and
millions of dollars were tied up in this man and his future, and they all
would be drastically affected when he died. What was going to
happen to them all – *after he was gone?*

On the advice of his lawyers, Walt Disney had already made a will
and taken steps to minimize taxes. He left behind the Walt Disney
Foundation to take care of an art school and charitable works. (The
Chouinard Art Institute, Los Angeles, was originally an independent
school to which Disney sent his young animators [see page 142]. Later
he brought a Chouinard art master to the studio to give lessons, and
formed the Disney Art School; later still he rescued the Chouinard
from financial disaster.) But that was routine. Until the summer of
1966, he hadn't seriously considered the possibility of an early death,
in spite of the pain in his neck. He had convinced himself he would
survive until he was at least seventy-five or eighty, which would give
him time to finish all the plans he had in mind for Walt Disney
Productions and WED (Walter Elias Disney) Enterprises and, as he
believed, for mankind.

Over the years, he had gradually been divesting himself of the
activities which he considered were no longer important to him. He
was now, for instance, methodically turning over all film production
at the Burbank studios to his son-in-law, Ron Miller. He had lost his
taste for animated cartoons.

'I've grown out of that phase,' he said to his daughter Diane. 'Don't
ever let it be repeated publicly, because it will sound like heresy. But
quite frankly, I don't care whether I ever see or hear Donald Duck
again. Nowadays, I find it hard to laugh at the little monster.'

Having turned away from the movie studios, he now concentrated
on very different priorities: theme-parks, for instance. At Anaheim,
California, he had built a complex called Disneyland which had, for a
time, provided unique entertainment for children of all ages from all
parts of the world. For years he considered it his proudest
achievement, but rivals had copied and improved on his conception,
Disneyland was facing competition from newer and flashier places,
and he had grown bored with it. He was much more concerned at that
time with two new projects which would make the Anaheim complex
look like the tawdry fairground it had become. One was the
completion of Disney World (later called Walt Disney World) near
Orlando, which was in the process of wrenching a massive leisure

complex, bigger than the principality of Monaco, out of the Florida swamps. The other was the monument he wished to leave behind for posterity as the crowning achievement of his life. It was a project for which, he hoped and believed, he would be remembered long after Mickey Mouse, Donald Duck and Goofy had been forgotten. In 1966 it was still a concept on his drawing board, and there was much work to be done before construction began. He desperately needed time to bring it to reality. He called it EPCOT.

Next to the vast playground of Disney World in Florida he planned to build the Experimental Prototype Community of Tomorrow (EPCOT). It was to be his final gift to the world: a gloriously self-contained city of the future into whose design he had poured all his hopes, dreams, talents and know-how. Faced by mankind's suicidal impulse to destroy itself by nuclear war or by poisoning from toxic wastes Walt Disney had envisaged EPCOT as the community of the future from which all the blights and blemishes of twentieth-century civilization had been banished. EPCOT would be a metropolis which would control its own climate, recycle its own waste, feed, preserve and nurture its citizens and do so in conditions from which disease, hunger and nagging want would be eliminated for ever. It would be his masterpiece, the culmination of his thinking. It would demonstrate that if people would only learn from this example how to live properly in an enlightened and sanitized environment, they would be able to cheat not just war and disease but death as well, and enjoy life, health and happiness everlasting.

He had spent the last two years designing Disney World, but it was planned neither to elevate nor enlighten, just to amuse. From the vast profits he was convinced Disney World would earn, he planned to pay for his dream city of EPCOT, through which he intended to edify and enlighten people – and, perhaps, save them from themselves.

So it was that in 1966, when death suddenly appeared on his horizon, EPCOT and Disney World were the only things which meant anything to him. Was it too much to expect that he be given the time needed to complete them? But now suddenly, from what the surgeons had discovered, not only did he not have another decade of productive life left, but maybe not even a year. True, the doctors who had tested his lungs had been reassuring about his condition, and Walt had pretended to his wife and daughter, as well as to his brother, that he had believed them. All was not lost, he cheerfully told them. A little operation would take care of everything.

But he was not really deceived by bland reassurances. He guessed what sort of a mess the doctors had found inside his body. Since he had never found it easy to talk to his intimates about himself, Hazel George was the one who heard how he felt about it. From her he did not conceal how devastated he was at the thought of dying, how appalled he was at the prospect it could happen any time now. What, for instance, would happen to EPCOT once he was gone? There simply wasn't anyone in the Disney organization who could fulfil what he had set out to construct and create. There would be chaos if he disappeared from the scene. The unimaginative characters with whom he was surrounded would be sure to ruin everything.

He scoffed at the suggestion that if he left precise instructions behind, his heirs and relations might be able to carry through his ideas. Who was there who was capable? He had no son, and he had made it plain, in the studio and out of it, that his son-in-law was no substitute. He was contemptuous of the abilities of his nephew, Roy Disney Jr, whom his brother admired and had appointed his heir. His wife, Lilly, did not have the boldness or the vision, and his daughter, Diane, did not have the brains. As for his partner and brother, Roy O. Disney, who had helped found the Disney organization with him, and who was the one man he loved and trusted above all others because of the faith and loyalty he had shown him over the years, what would Roy do to EPCOT if he got his hands on it? He was good, reliable, dull, unimaginative and, above all, a money man. What did he care about the city of the future? Nothing but its potential profit would interest him.

What was he going to do?

It was almost certainly Hazel George who put the idea into his head that there might be a way of cheating death. For a long time she listened to her boss's complaints, and then startled him by saying there was surely no reason why he couldn't 'come back later and clean up all the mistakes your relatives might be making with Disney'. Walt stared at her as if she'd gone mad. Was he talking about *reincarnation*? But she was not thinking of reincarnation. She later told Bob Thomas (who quoted her in *Walt Disney*) that once, during one of their sessions, Walt had said to her: 'After I die, I would hate to look down at this studio and find everything in a mess.'

'What makes you think you won't be using a periscope?' she asked.

'Smartass!' he had muttered. But the remarks had stayed in her mind. She had read all the notes Walt had written when he had first outlined his concept for EPCOT, and had been fascinated. He had, for example, forecast not simply longevity for EPCOT's citizens, but maybe even ever-lasting life for those born and raised in the city of the future's germ-free environment. It had even been predicted that there could be a second chance at life – resurrection from the dead, no less – for those who succumbed before the processes for the achievement of immortality had been perfected. Providing their bodies had been preserved, that is. Did Walt really believe there was something in it? Could dead people be brought back to life again?

No one will ever know if Hazel George was simply comforting him, giving him hope at a particularly grim moment; but she certainly struck a chord. He had begun to believe, after consulting medical experts about the promises of EPCOT, that resurrection was both medically and surgically feasible. Even while he had been preparing his preliminary studies and making consultations, California newspapers were carrying stories about the new pathological processes with which doctors in the state were experimenting. *Cryogenesis* it was called, or what one of the newspapers had termed 'the freeze-drying of the human cadaver after death for eventual resuscitation'. A newly-dead body was first treated and operated upon to eliminate the diseased organs which had ended normal life. It was then stored away in a refrigerated container until such time as it could be thawed out, organs and blood vessels brought back into action, and life restored. From his own researches into the process, Walt Disney had never had any doubts about its feasibility – one day. Since the original studies had been written, it was rumoured that at least a hundred people had already instructed their executors not to allow them to be buried or cremated after legal death but ordered them instead to deliver their bodies to a clinic for cryogenesis. There were stories around that at least a score had already died and been surgically 'cleaned up' for eventual treatment. There were not only sperm-banks in the United States now, it was said, but refrigerated body-banks in California and plans for others in Florida, North Dakota, Texas and Alaska over the next few years. However, there was one thing that the researchers had not made clear: how long would the cadavers have to wait before the surgeons had perfected the cryogenic process? And what about the preservation of the organs, especially the brain?

In the final weeks of his life, particularly between 6 November and 6 December 1966, when he was in and out of hospital and more convinced than ever that his days were numbered, Walt Disney searched for the answer to the unsolved problems of cryogenesis.

Several of his closest colleagues and advisers, including Oscar-winning cartoonist and animator, Ward Kimball, and Ken Annakin, the director of many of his films, are confident that he was closely studying cryogenesis as a viable medical process, and persuaded that, even in 1966, it was possible for a human being to have himself brought back to life after death. According to them, the chief problem that troubled Walt was the length of time it might take the doctors to perfect the process. To be brutally practical, could it be guaranteed, in fact, that he would be brought back in time to rectify the mistakes his successors would almost certainly start making at EPCOT the moment he was dead?

Walter Elias Disney died in Burbank Hospital – across the street from the Walt Disney Studio – on 15 December 1966, ten days after his sixty-fifth birthday. He had undergone an operation on his lungs which entailed the cutting away of his ribs. When he last visited the studio just before his death, he was skeleton-thin, but those who talked to him noted that he was amazingly cheerful. In fact, never had a mortally sick man seemed more confident and contented on the eve of his death.

On the last afternoon of his life, back in hospital again, he had a visit from his wife, Lilly. She telephoned her daughter Diane later and was full of optimism because Walt had seemed so contained and self-confident.

'He got out of bed,' she recalled in a conversation later repeated to Bob Thomas. 'He kept putting his arm around me and his grip was so strong. I know he's going to get well! I know he's going to be all right!'

The last relative to see him alive was his brother, Roy, later that same evening. He came away convinced Walt was going to recover. Like everyone else, he was amazed at his calmness, his equanimity.

But in the early hours of the following morning, the doctors were urgently summoned to his bedside and worked on him all night to avoid a circulatory collapse. They told his wife at 9.35 A.M. that he was dead.

And this is where the mystery begins.

If ever there was an occasion for a public announcement, this was surely it. Walt Disney *dead*? It was like the death of a king or a president. Surely the world had to know at once that such a famous figure was no more. Yet hours passed and no word leaked out. First came radio announcements of his death, followed by a statement that there would be no funeral. The great man had already been cremated, the announcement said, and his ashes interred in the Forest Lawn Memorial Park at Glendale, California. Only immediate members of his family had been present.

It was a shock in many ways and raised immediate questions. Where, for instance, had the great man been interred at Forest Lawn? And could the public visit the spot? Undoubtedly, it would become a place of international pilgrimage. At first no information was forthcoming. Then an official announcement from the cemetery authorities revealed that Walt Disney's ashes had joined those of his father, mother and sister in what was known as the Disney Memorial Garden somewhere in the grounds. But, it was further pointed out, it was against Forest Lawn rules to specify exactly where the Disney Memorial Garden was located or to allow any public visits.

In the weeks that followed, reporters did find their way into the Forest Lawn park, and so did some members of the public. But it was not entirely satisfactory for those who wished to see exactly where their hero had been buried. Even those who did find the Disney Memorial Garden had no way of telling from it which were Walt Disney's ashes and those of his parents and sister.

In the circumstances, it seemed a shabby end to the passing of America's most famous character. There were millions of Americans and many more from around the world who would have wished to pay their last respects and now would never have an opportunity to do so. They could be excused for feeling cheated.

Unless, of course, the whole rigmarole was a hoax – a ruse – and Walt Disney was planning to come back one of these days . . .

Part One:

SHAPING

Chapter 1

ROOTS

HALF a dozen times a year, even this long after his death, journalists and researchers contact the archives at the Disney Studio in Burbank, California, to try to confirm stories they have been given of where and under what conditions Walt Disney was born. They are convinced they have discovered a skeleton in the Disney cupboard, and that Walt Disney was in fact Spanish – and born out of wedlock, too. It is one of those ironies so often associated with the lives of famous men that there should not only be a mystery attached to the circumstances of Walt Disney's death, but also a myth surrounding his birth.

Perhaps this is inevitable. Given the measure of international fame and the universal affection in which he was held, both during his life and after his death, millions of non-Americans refuse to believe the USA could have produced such a phenomenon. There is a story that Walt Disney was, in fact, originally a Spanish citizen, and researchers arrive at the Disney archives seeking confirmation of what seems a most remarkable set of circumstances, deliberately concealed until now.

Stories about his Spanish birth have, in fact, now become so established that a small town in the mountains behind Almeria, in southern Spain, once carried a plaque on the road leading to the town square announcing:

MOJACCA
Birthplace of Walt Disney

Jane Wyatt, the former Hollywood film star, noticed it some years ago during a trip into the mountains while she was making a film in Almeria.

The story in Mojacca itself is that one of the village maidens, Consuela Suarez, became engaged at the turn of the century to a local boy who was killed in Morocco before they could be married. She was already pregnant when news of his death reached her. Thanks to the efforts of the local priest, the baby son Consuela subsequently bore

15

was taken to the United States by an American couple, and Consuela presently followed. There she signed the papers which enabled her son to be formally adopted and made a US citizen. Only when she came home to Mojacca to die did she reveal that her secret son was now named Walt Disney, the famous father of Mickey Mouse.

One of the unwritten functions of the Walt Disney Archives is to keep the image of its founder polished and sanitized, and to prevent any word of scandal from attaching to the Disney name and reputation. In this case it has no difficulty in clearing up the Mojacca myth, since it is a pure fantasy. Walter Elias Disney was indubitably a native-born American as his birth certificate, a copy of which can still be obtained in Chicago, will testify.

On the other hand, like a snobbish Englishman who boasts that his ancestors 'came over with William the Conqueror', Walt Disney too could legitimately claim to have had Norman forebears. Generations ago, his ancestors were French peasants in a Norman cheese-producing town, and took their name from their place of residence: d'Isigny.

According to family accounts, most of the d'Isignys were a lawless and loose-living farming clan, their menfolk reputed to have a weakness for brawling and wenching. In 1066, several members of the d'Isigny family crossed the Channel as part of the invading army of Duke William of Normandy. At the decisive Battle of Hastings, the arrows from their arbalests rained down on the defending forces of King Harold (who was struck in the eye and killed by the first volley), and put the enemy to flight.

William ascended the English throne. His mercenaries, including Jean-Christophe d'Isigny and several others of the same clan, were encouraged to settle in the conquered territories, and they were given title to English lands and properties. They married English wives, and, anglicizing their name from d'Isigny to Disney, they became rich and prosperous gentry. Not that they lost entirely their taste for fighting and women. One of them ended up as a disreputable, corrupt and womanizing Lord High Sheriff of London. The rest lived comfortable, if unbuttoned, lives working the rich farmlands of the English Midlands; until, in the seventeenth century, they supported the Duke of Monmouth's unsuccessful rebellion against the English throne of King James II. They were ordered to be arrested and incarcerated in the Tower of London, and their lands were confiscated by the Crown, but they narrowly missed being tried and hanged for treason by making their way to the safety of Ireland. They settled in County

Kilkenny, where, to give themselves a cloak of respectability, they took up the Roman Catholicism they had allowed to lapse in Protestant England. But the land they rented was poor, taxes were high and the pickings meagre. They soon began looking around for opportunities outside Ireland to restore their shattered fortunes.

In 1834, the Disneys moved again, first to the United States and then to Canada, where they had heard there were fortunes to be made out of new land developments around Lake Huron. They joined an immigrant community mostly consisting of Scottish, German and Dutch families, and it is typical of the easy-going attitudes of the Disneys that they quickly reconverted to Protestantism once they realized their nonconformist neighbours were hostile to and suspicious of Catholicism.

It was in Huron County that Elias Disney, the father of Walt, was born in 1859.

Most of the early records of the Disney family have now been collected and assembled in the studio archives at Burbank, and these seem to confirm that they were, on the whole, an amoral and easy-going lot, much given to dancing, drinking and periodical hell-raising.

Elias Disney seems to have been the exception. He was the one member of the clan who had picked up stern religious (and later political) beliefs along the way, and by the time he was sixteen years old he could recite whole passages from the Bible, had resolved to adopt a God-fearing way of life, and looked down on self-indulgence in any form as sinful. In 1878, his father, Kepple Disney, announced he was leaving with his eldest sons, Robert and Elias, to seek a fortune in the California goldfields.

To his father and his brother the journey was a joyful excuse to relax after the hard labours of Lake Huron farming, and they made their way westward in a succession of drunken celebrations. Elias was shocked at their rowdy, blasphemous behaviour which reached its climax in a bordello in Ellis, Kansas, where his brother hired one of the girls to initiate Elias into the secrets of sex while he watched through a peephole. Horrified at the girl's shamelessness, outraged at the obscene laughter of his drunken brother (who had hidden himself inside a closet), Elias first drove the weeping whore out of his room and then informed his sheepish father that he was dropping out of the party. He could no longer associate with such sinners. Kepple Disney was so ashamed of himself that he agreed to allow Elias to stay on in Ellis, and gave him half his money as a stake to tide him over until he came back to collect him.

Kepple and Robert travelled on to California where they spent several weeks panning (in vain) for gold. On his way back, broke and disillusioned, Kepple expected to find his son in similar straits. On the contrary, Elias had not only found himself a job but he had also used the money his father had given him to buy a tract of Kansas land. It was good land, too, suitable for a small farm. Kepple, to whom Kansas seemed a much kindlier climate than Canada, especially in winter, decided to stay put in Ellis and telegraphed his wife Maria to sell up their Lake Huron small-holding and join him and their son in the United States.

It was in Ellis, Kansas, that they subsequently swore fidelity to the flag and thus became American citizens.

If he differed from his kin in being so strait-laced, Elias Disney had inherited the family inability to stay put. 'Pa always had ants in his pants,' said his third son, Roy, later. 'He could never stay in one place long enough to warm a seat.' Elias quickly tired of Ellis, Kansas, and got himself a job helping to build the railroad between Kansas and Colorado; he was finally paid off in Denver after two years. Home again in Ellis, he fell in love with a neighbour's daughter named Flora Call, but he was too shy to court her and it was four years before he realized how much she meant to him. By that time she and her family had moved to Florida, and her departure left such a gap in his life that he resolved to go after her and propose – but so shy and uncertain did he feel about his prospects that he was willing to make the journey only if his parents agreed to accompany him and support his suit. They needed a break from farm chores and so they consented to go with him, even briefly considering selling up and moving south once they got there; but they quickly discovered they hated Florida and became tired of waiting for their son to pluck up enough courage to ask Flora to marry him. Only when Kepple told his son they were going back to Kansas was Elias finally emboldened to propose.

Flora had been in love with Elias since she was fourteen, and thought he would never get around to asking. Now she was nineteen and he was twenty-eight. The wedding took place in Akron, Florida, in January 1888, after which Kepple and Maria took the train back to Kansas and Elias and his bride went off for their honeymoon at Daytona Beach.

Elias, who had started out sharing his parents' antipathy to Florida, told Flora on their honeymoon that he had changed his mind and shortly afterwards he bought some land near Kissimmee where he proposed to raise cattle. Unfortunately, the terrain, which was normally underwater for most of the year, dried out in a prolonged drought; moreover, unused as he was to the problems of hot-weather farming, he allowed his cattle to become diseased and die, forcing him to put the farm up for sale. To earn some money to pay his debts, he persuaded the owner of the Halifax Hotel, Daytona Beach, where he and Flora had spent their honeymoon, to let them move in and manage it, and they took it over for the season. But when the last guest moved out to go north for the summer, the hotel closed and they were told by the proprietor to find other work and accommodation until the next season. It was vital for Elias to find another job because by this time Flora was pregnant, and he gladly accepted an offer from the postmaster in Kissimmee to take over one of the rural mail routes.

At the end of 1888, just prior to her twentieth birthday, Flora gave birth to their first son, Herbert Disney. She hoped the fact that they had now started a family would persuade Elias to settle down. Suspecting that he was unhappy in his mail job and looking around for something else to do, she drew her savings out of the bank, appealed for financial help from her parents, and bought them a citrus grove outside Kissimmee.

Unfortunately, Elias had already made other plans for himself. The newspapers were full of rumours of the approaching war against Spain, and he came home one day to tell his wife he had volunteered for the militia and, though the war was still years away, said he expected soon to be fighting in Cuba. When she told him about the orange grove, he swore that it was too late to back out now, and added that he refused to let down his country if it was going to be involved in a war.

Instead of the action he craved, however, he found himself undergoing strenuous basic training in the sticky heat of a boot camp outside Tampa, and he hated it. Weeks went by. Flora, unable to look after her young baby and take care of the citrus grove at the same time, was soon writing Elias desperate letters telling him he just had to come home. So one day he simply walked out of boot camp and took the train back to Kissimmee. He was in the orchard spraying his orange trees when the military police arrived to arrest him for desertion.

Angry and indignant, Elias summoned a local lawyer who pointed out to the M.P.s that since his client had freely volunteered for the militia he could just as freely elect to discharge himself. It was such a simple and plausible-sounding argument that the astonished police

19

said they would have to go back and consult with the military authorities and, in the meantime, demanded that Elias hand over his uniform. This he refused to do on the grounds that he had bought it himself. Baffled, they finally retreated, promising to return. But they never did.

Elias's defiance did not do him much good as far as orange-growing was concerned: that winter a record frost hit central Florida, the crop was ruined and so was he.

Elias did not seem to be worried. The good Lord would provide, he told his wife. He had heard things were booming in the growing new metropolis of Chicago, so they moved there in the spring of 1889. Flora Disney was by this time pregnant with their second child, but her husband refused to be rushed into taking any old job. Instead, he enrolled in a local nightschool for a course in carpentry and discovered that he had a natural gift for furniture-making. While still studying he began taking commissions, and his flair soon attracted many orders. With the money he earned from making chairs, tables and wardrobes, and from selling his designs to local stores, he saved enough to buy a plot of land on Tripp Avenue in Northwest Town, a Chicago suburb. Flora drew up the plans for the house and Elias built it, single-handed. It was so much admired that they bought land next door, built two more houses, sold them, and made a considerable profit.

It seemed as if Elias had found his niche at last, and Flora began to think the house on Tripp Avenue would become their permanent home. Her second son, Raymond, was born there at the end of 1890, and a third son arrived in 1893.

There was a brief family struggle over the third son's name. He was born in the year of the World Columbian Exhibition in Chicago. Elias had received several commissions to make furniture and provide designs for the fair, and he made so much money from the exhibition that when his third son was born he considered naming him Columbus, as a gesture of gratitude. But Flora would not hear of saddling her son with such an outlandish name, and finally they christened the new arrival Roy Oliver Disney.

Three sons. That, both Elias and Flora decided, was enough. For the next few years there were no more Disney children and Elias and Flora seem to have settled down into solid, comfortable, middle-class respectability in suburban Chicago. They became regular worshippers and valued parishioners of St Paul's, the local Congregational church in Northwest Town, and close friends of its incumbent, the Reverend

Walter Parr.

Revd Parr knew he could always rely upon the Disneys when the church was in need. He launched an appeal to build a new church in 1898, and Elias not only dug into his savings to help find the funds but put on his overalls and helped build the edifice. The new St Paul's was consecrated in 1900 with an elaborate double celebration, since the arrival of the twentieth century was being hailed at the same time. The Revd Walter Parr informed the congregation he had appointed Elias Disney deacon of the new church and smilingly indicated the loft where Flora Disney, a passable pianist, was installed as the new organist.

It had been nine years since her last child had been born, but when, in the spring of 1901, Flora shyly announced that she was pregnant again, Revd Parr revealed that his wife was also. He gleefully pointed out that the births looked as if they might happen at the same time, and said to Elias: 'If your wife has another son, you must call him Walter, after me. And if my wife has a son, I will christen him Elias, after you.' And that was what happened.

The fourth Disney son was born on 5 December 1901, in the family bedroom of 1249 Tripp Avenue, Chicago. A short distance away, Mrs Walter Parr was also in labour, and delivered a baby boy the following day. The children were known locally as the Consecration Babies, and presents for them poured in from the congregation. There was a joint christening ceremony just before Christmas 1901. True to his word, Revd Parr christened his new son Elias, and the other infant Walter Elias Disney.

It was the baby's nine-year-old brother, Roy Disney, who shortened his first name to Walt.

Five years later Walt Disney's father, Elias, succumbed to the itch to start travelling once more, and by that time the first and only girl in the Disney family had arrived: Ruth Flora Disney was born in 1903.

Chicago in the first years of the century was a raw, brawling, rambunctious city which was constantly growing and changing. When the Disneys first arrived, Northwest Town had been a quiet suburb of law-abiding, middle-class citizens, but as the Middle West grew and prospered, immigrants from Italy, Ireland and central Europe swarmed into the city. Soon they began to take over the inner suburbs, transforming the once-quiet streets into gaudy, raucous bazaars that sometimes looked, especially on weekends, like areas of Naples, Ennis or Bratislava. Criminals moved in, too, and crooked local officials seemed to welcome the influx. The police, well bribed to look the other way, preferred to ignore their sometimes violent lawlessness. One of Northwest Town's suburban neighbours was Cicero, later to become the bailiwick of gangsters like Al Capone; already it had developed into a 'safe' area for petty crooks, racketeers, pimps and prostitutes. The bars and brothels they patronized began spilling over into Northwesttown. A state law forbade the opening of saloons within half a mile of a church, which protected St Paul's, but there were plenty of rowdy establishments just beyond the boundary lines. Their drunken patrons rolled home along Tripp Avenue and often brawled beneath the Disney windows until the early hours. Elias, who was a total abstainer, would have objected had the saloons been run with impeccable obedience to the law, but he was shocked by the deliberate laxity of police superintendence. Moreover, since these were the days of ever-open bars and cheap spirits, he was horrified to discover how widespread was the drunkenness and even more appalled to find how many of the drunkards were women. Elias galvanized his fellow parishioners into accompanying him as a delegation of protest to the police, but they scoffed at his demand that the saloons be shut down or cleaned up, and that the streets be patrolled for drunks. Angry and frustrated, Elias told Flora the only way to preserve the sanctity of his family was for them to move out of Chicago.

Elias Disney still thought of himself as a man of the soil and dreamed of having a viable farm of his own. He and Flora began looking around for a suitable agricultural holding out of the orbit of sinful Chicago. Finally they found what they wanted in Marceline, a quiet community of 3,000 people 120 miles north-east of Kansas City, practically in the centre of Missouri. It was a mixed fruit and stock farm of forty-eight acres, and they bought it for 35 dollars an acre. They signed the purchase papers on 5 March 1906, and they moved to Missouri in the spring of the same year.

It was there, in Marceline, that Walt Disney spent the happiest and best years of his childhood.

Walt Disney was five years old when he first saw the farm. Elias had arranged for his two older sons, Herbert and Raymond, to help him with the final packing in Chicago, so he sent Flora on ahead to their new home. She took with her the three younger children – Roy, now thirteen, Ruth, three, and Walt. One of their new neighbours met the train and gave them a lift from the railroad station to the farm. All three children were immediately enchanted with their first sight of their new home.

'It was set in green rolling countryside,' said Walt later, 'and the apple and plum orchards were just starting to blossom. I thought it was a beautiful place. Coffman, the neighbour, pointed out acres of grape and raspberry vines and strawberry beds, and reminded us it was all ours. He added with a grin at us kids that even after we'd picked and shipped the crop off to market, there would still be enough left over for us to eat berries until they ran out of our ears. We started to slaver there and then.'

These early impressions made such an impact on him that he often recalled them in later life. This and other quotations are reconstructed from later conversations (as told to the present author during interviews) with directors and animators like Ken Annakin and Ward Kimball with whom Walt frequently reminisced.

The farmhouse was roomy, with a parlour, living rooms, a good kitchen, lots of pantries and storerooms, and three bedrooms. A tall elm grew just outside the front door and its leafy branches threw a welcome shade over the shingle roof and the porch. For the first few days, while waiting for Elias and the two older boys to arrive with the furniture, Flora and the youngsters camped in the empty house.

Flora, with Ruth tagging along, got down on her knees to scrub the floors. Too busy to bother about the boys, she shooed them out of the house and told them get off and explore their new territory. Farmer Coffman had indicated the jack-rabbits gambolling in the fields when they arrived, and, after warning them they were a pest and would eat up the berry and vegetable crop unless they were controlled, advised them to start the culling process right away, adding 'jack-rabbits is good eating'.

Now, crawling through the fields, the boys were able to observe the animals at their spring mating games, the females provocatively waving their scuts in the spring air, the males standing on hind legs to signal them. Walt was thrilled and excited at the rituals and in the next few days, scribbling in crayon on a square of packing paper, made his first drawings – a whiskered rabbit waving frantically to another concealed in the grass. He was appalled at the idea of harming such delightful creatures. Roy was more practical. On their way to Marceline, they had stopped with their mother at Fort Manson to visit Flora's married sister, and just before leaving Roy had been presented by his uncle with an air-gun 'to keep down those thieving grackles you're going to find around the farm'. Now Roy put the gun to his shoulder, fired, and brought down a magnificent jack-rabbit as he was posturing above the scrub and signalling to a potential mate. The beautiful creature was still alive and squirming when the boys reached it, and Walt burst into tears as his older brother reached down and casually broke its neck. He refused to eat the rabbit stew that Flora subsequently made for supper.

It was a week before Elias arrived, and Walt enjoyed every moment of it. Like his brothers and sister, he was afraid of his father who never laughed, never played with them, and scared them with his permanent expression of frigid disapproval. It was a relief not to have his icy presence around for a time. Even Flora was much calmer and more relaxed with the children, laughing and playing with them.

'It was no hardship at all sleeping on the hard floor of that empty house,' Walt said later. 'Mom read us to sleep by candlelight and reassured us when we shuddered at the eerie hooting of the owls outside. She made us feel like pioneers and it was a great adventure. I remember we laughed a lot and were sorry when Father and my brothers eventually arrived.'

Elias, Herbert and Raymond had travelled rough from Chicago in a boxcar containing not only the furniture but two work-horses that Elias had bought just before his departure as well. It was on one of them, called Charley, that Roy later learned to ride. The horse was too big for Walt's tiny legs to straddle, so Walt stayed a non-rider until the day Elias came back from Marceline with a herd of hogs and a load of ducks, hens and pigeons. Walt later boasted that at the age of five he became the youngest hog-herd and the smallest poultry-keeper in Marceline County. Each day, after feeding the pigeons and chickens and scattering bread on the duck-pond, he would unlock the doors of the pigsties and, through a succession of whistles and strangled cries ('I was a helluva poor hog caller,' he said later), he would assemble the herd and drive them out to snuffle for old vegetable roots in the fields. Later in the day he would call them in for their afternoon feed of steaming swill, which he and his mother had boiled up from bran, potato peelings and old vegetables. But one day, after enviously watching Roy ride by on Charley, he decided to mount a charger of his own, and picked Porker, the biggest sow in the herd. Leaping on her back, he grabbed the frightened and snorting animal by the ears, and was carried on a wild and noisy ride across the farmyard. Two minutes later, the indignant sow ploughed into the duck pond and tossed him contemptuously into the mud.

'I never did learn to stay on Porker's back,' said Walt later to his daughter Diane, 'and I always ended up the same way, covered in duck feathers and mud. I think Porker got as much of a kick out of it as I did. She used to stand there in the pond after she'd tossed me in the slime, her curly tail whirling away like a watch spring and her piggy eyes streaming with water and what looked like tears – tears of laughter, I always used to think. She just loved throwing me off into the mud. Once when I got chicken pox and had to stay in bed for a few days, she came up to the porch and honked the house down. "What's Porker want?" I asked Mom. "You," she said. She did, too. Later, when I recovered, Porker practically invited me to climb on her back, and stayed as peaceful as pie while I crawled aboard. No tantrums, no protests. She was as proper as a show-horse as she cantered me across the farmyard. I was convinced I had tamed her, and she was really glad to see me back. But I should have known better and guessed she was only biding her time. We ended up in the same way. She waded me into the pond, stood quite still for a few seconds, and suddenly tossed me like a tadpole into the deepest and slimiest part of the pond. Then she splashed back to her sty, snorting and snickering in triumph. For the rest of the evening, I could hear her honking away between snores – with smug satisfaction, I suspect.'

Paper was scarce around the Disney household, and when Walt discovered he wanted to draw the domestic animals with which he was now surrounded, he resorted to toilet paper. He later gave that as the reason why his earliest drawings were never preserved.

'You can guess what I did with them, especially as I ate a lot of green apples in those days,' he said. 'Anyway, that's all those drawings were really good for – and that's where they went, down the can. Childish scribbles, that's all. The only interesting thing is I did them at all. I suppose I did them because just about everything around me at Marceline excited me. Even the chores with the birds. Feeding them every day, I got familiar with the shapes and the habits of ducks, chickens and pigeons. I can't remember I ever made a real pet of any of them, though I did learn their language and I think they learned to understand me. What I mean is they'd come when I called them, even individually when I summoned them by name. There was one pullet I called Martha who used to come over when I shouted her name and lay an egg right in my hand.'

On the other hand, none of the birds meant as much to him as Porker who became both a challenge and a close friend.

'I used to horse around with her a lot. I guess I really loved that pig. She had an acute sense of fun and mischief and when she wanted to be, she could be as naughty as a puppy and nimble as a ballet dancer. She liked to creep up, nudge me up the rear, and then sashay off squealing with delight, especially if she'd tipped me over. Do you remember the Foolish Pig in *The Three Little Pigs*? Porker was the model for him. I did the preliminary sketch from remembering Porker, and I was practically weeping with nostalgia by the time I had finished.'

In many ways, the animals around the farm, young, noisy and playful as they were, gave him more companionship than he found in his father and brothers. Elias was too forbidding and had absolutely no sense of fun. His brothers were all so much older than he was, and his sister Ruth was too young. On the other hand, the barnyard stock in all their different moods fed his need for affection, and he gave them names, carried on conversations with them and made up stories about them. His brothers jeered at him and scoffed when he walked through the farmyard raising his hand and saying, 'Hi, Effie!' or 'Hallo, Elmer!' or 'How're the old feet this morning, Mortimer – frozen?' to a pullet or a cockerel or a duck. But though they made him feel sheepish and ashamed, they never really stopped him because he felt the birds would have been hurt if he had failed to say hallo.

The only human being with whom he had a real rapport and with whom he shared his fantasies in those days was his father's brother Ed, who often came to visit them on the farm. In appearance he was small and slightly hunched, with a lined, tanned face that made him look, Walt later said, like a cross between a leprechaun and a prune. He usually sported a battered derby and someone's cut-down suit, and he would turn up unexpectedly with his few belongings in his carpetbag, brightly announcing to his brother and sister-in-law: 'Well, now, here I am again. Could you take me in for a few days?'

There was never any hesitation. Ed could always be sure of a welcome. Even Elias seemed sunnier at the sight of him. As for Walt, he would greet Uncle Ed with such unalloyed pleasure it was as if Father Christmas had suddenly arrived. By a slip of the tongue, but not inappropriately, he always referred to him as Uncle Elf. Ed looked and behaved like an elf, too. He would park his bag in the spare room and then scamper down the stairs to join Walt on an expedition into the fields. He adored the boy and was inordinately proud of the fact that Walt obviously looked up to him and admired him. Sometimes the others were a shade patronizing in their manner, and the older Disney boys, though always pleasant and polite, seemed to regard him as something of a freak and an object of pity. Not Walt, though. He thought Uncle Elf was the most wonderful person he had ever met.

Ed was so much at home in the fields that birds, animals and insects seemed to know instinctively that he would never harm them. He was expert at catching grasshoppers and frogs. Fieldmice liked to creep up his arm and snuggle into his pockets, where he always kept bits of cheese. He could imitate birds so realistically that they would fly around his head and perch on his shoulder; he taught Walt how to tickle fish and unhook catfish from his line without being injured by the spines. He liked nothing better than to squat in a field munching muddy turnips, or to lead a raid on a neighbouring farmer's orchard. Remembering the stern prohibitions of his brother, Elias – who not only disapproved of liquor and cigarettes for grown-ups but sweets for small boys as well – Uncle Ed always brought bags of boiled sweets with him to satisfy the cravings of Walt's sweet tooth. Once he even produced a particularly forbidden luxury in the shape of a packet of chewing gum, sticks of which his nephew munched delightedly for hours and then parked under the railing of the front porch, for use on the morrow.

Uncle Ed never overstayed his welcome. One day he would creep out of the house before dawn and tramp off down the dusty road, on his way to visit yet another of his relatives. He never left behind a note of thanks or warned anybody he was leaving, but had always made his bed and tidied up the room before he crept away. The family would be sorry that he had gone, and Walt would be devastated. But every six months or so he came back, and the woods and meadows at Marceline once more echoed to Uncle Elf's whoops and whistles and bird calls and the happy laughter of his young friend.

Then one day Walt came home from school to learn that Ed had been 'taken bad' while staying with another relative and had had to be sent to a home for the retarded near Chicago. Elias and Flora sometimes went to visit him but, as if sensing it would be too distressing, never took Walt with them. In fact he never saw him again. It was years later that a message was received that Ed Disney was dead, and by that time Walt's memory of him was fading. Yet he never really forgot him. Many years later, when his animators at Walt Disney Studio were experimenting with new characters for *Pinocchio*, Ward Kimball came up with some spritely sketches of a top-hatted, half-human grasshopper. Everybody liked it, even Walt Disney who pored over Kimball's drawing, half frowning, half smiling. Then he took a brush and pen and played with the facial features until someone remarked that he now 'looked like a prune'. And like Uncle

Elf, Walt might have added. Kimball went back to his drawing board and Jiminy Cricket saw the light of day.

If Walt Disney was happy at Marceline, his father, mother and two older brothers were not. Elias was soon having trouble turning the holding into a viable farm, and the weather was no help to him. The hogs got swine fever, and there came the terrible day when even Porker had to be shipped off and destroyed. Two years in a row the crops failed, and Elias was forced to raise a mortgage on the farm. Bad times made him short-tempered and even more tyrannical than usual, and he railed at his sons when they failed to turn up at breakfast for early morning prayers or when he caught them reading 'frivolous books' instead of the Bible at night. In return for their labour, he had promised Herbert and Raymond that in lieu of pay he would turn over several arable acres of his land to them so they could begin farming on their own. They were eager to get away from their domineering parent and took it badly when he was forced to explain to them that, because of the mortgage, he could now no longer carry out his pledge. There was a bitter quarrel, and in the early hours of the next morning the two older boys ran away from home.

Herbert was now nineteen years old and Raymond seventeen. They left a note for Flora saying they were tired of being treated by their father like wicked children. They kept in touch with a weekly letter, and reported to her that Herbert had found himself a job at Sears, Roebuck and Company in Kansas City, while Raymond worked in a local bank. Shortly afterwards, they began sending parcels of their old clothes home to Marceline to be cut down and adapted for Roy and Walt. Considering their youth and their rebellious mood, they both stayed remarkably free from the temptations of the big city. But they still smarted at the treatment they had received from their father and could not resist pretending to that stern and unforgiving man that they had gone to the dogs. They would fill the pockets in the old clothes they sent with the odd stub of a cheroot or cigarette, or with torn scraps of newspapers and magazines showing scantily clad women, knowing how deeply he abhorred smoking and images of licentious women. Elias never realized it was all a joke and was convinced his two older sons had sold their souls to the devil. He told Flora he would never allow them to set their sinful feet inside his house again.

Shortly after the departure of Herbert and Raymond, disaster struck the rest of the Disney household. The family and the livestock got their water from a well on the farm, which, they had been assured by the previous owners, was one of the purest in the county. But shortly after swine fever hit the hog herd, Elias went down with a bad case of diphtheria. The authorities who came to analyse the well announced it was questionable whether or not it was suitable for animals, and definitely unfit for human consumption.

Luckily, Flora, Roy and Walt all remained untouched by the tainted water, but Elias had to be shipped to hospital, where he was seriously ill for several weeks.

Meanwhile, Roy, as the eldest male in the household, took over the farm chores and the remaining livestock, and laboured manfully to keep things going. But it was soon clear to Flora that even with her help and that of Walt, he could not manage and still keep up his schooling. When Elias finally returned from the hospital, it became obvious he would need a long convalescence and be unfit to undertake any strenuous work on the farm in the meantime. Flora persuaded him that there was only one thing to do: sell up the farm and return to the city.

It was mid-winter, 1908-9, and the Midwestern plains were subjected to an even more bitter winter than usual. While the frail and sickly Elias Disney huddled in his chair near the stove, Roy and Walt trudged through the snow nailing signs to trees and fences, announcing the forthcoming auction of their farm. The local doctor, Caleb Sherwood, would drive by making his rounds in a beautiful cutter drawn by a magnificent stallion called Rupert. Often he would see the boys struggling through the snow and would give them a lift into Marceline. Walt, who hated the cold, always remembered the joy of snuggling under the thick fur rugs draped across the front seat of the sleigh and peeping out at the round rump of Rupert steaming in the frozen air.

Walt was nearly eight years old at this time. Flora had bought him a book for his drawings and Dr Sherwood liked what he had seen of Walt's sketches of the lamented Porker and Martha the hen. When Walt tearfully told him that Porker was dead and Martha had been put into the family pot, he took the boy home and down to the box in his yard where Rupert was stabled when his day's work was over. Handing him cardboard and crayons, he told Walt to make him a picture of the horse. After he had inspected the finished drawing, Dr Sherwood announced himself satisfied. He handed the boy a 50-cent piece and said he would buy it. It was Walt Disney's first commission, and the first time he was ever paid for a picture.

The Disneys received a good price for the farm at the auction – enough, at any rate, to pay off the mortgage and the debts and have something left over with which to start again.

Elias began to make plans to move the family to Kansas City and find himself a job, but Flora would not hear of leaving right away. Now they had a little money in the bank, she said, she was determined to see that the two boys finished their education. She didn't worry too much about Ruth – girls' education did not get the same consideration in those days. Shrewdly, she maintained that taking the boys out of a small-town school and plunging them into a big city educational establishment without careful preparation might well prove too much of a psychological wrench. She persuaded Elias to find a temporary home for them in Marceline while the boys finished their school year. So although the family farm was sold in 1909, it was not until 1910 that they finally moved to Kansas City.

That summer, after the boys had passed their exams, they rented a house on East 31st Street in Kansas City, and a few months later moved again to 3028 Bellefontaine Avenue. It was not a happy period for any of them. Elias Disney had improved in health, but not in temper: failure had turned him into even more of a tyrant.

Chapter 2

ROY RUNS AWAY

Elias Disney had his fifty-first birthday shortly after they all arrived in Kansas City, but the family did not celebrate the occasion, knowing how much he disapproved of such frivolities. In any case, Elias was not in the mood to salute another milestone in his life. To be over fifty could be the beginning of old age in those days, and Elias was already behaving like an old man. Towards his family he was as strict as ever but he had become mean-tempered as well, querulous with his wife and overbearing with the children. The years and his recent illness had not just sapped his strength; his viewpoint on life had soured as well. In earlier days he had been interested in left-wing politics, and had always closely related his religious with his ideological beliefs. During his service with the militia in Tampa he had caused concern among the staff (some of whom denounced him as a 'trouble-maker') by making fiery speeches to the other soldiers in boot camp denouncing capitalism and the seven deadly sins in the same breath, equating them as exploitations of the innocent and the work of the devil. He fervently preached that one day the sinful crime of capitalism would be wiped out because Jesus Christ would reappear on earth and change the system, and he made it clear the change in the system the reborn Jesus would bring to the poor people of the earth would be socialism.

Now, though he still professed faith in his religious and political standards, still abhorred the sins of drink, tobacco and the flesh, still attended church and spoke at left-wing meetings, and regularly continued to vote for the socialist leader Eugene Debs, his glowing vision that a brighter new world would soon be dawning seemed to have dissipated and bitter pessimism had taken its place. When he fell on his knees to pray, as he still often did, there were those who now felt he was praying for himself rather than for them as he had done in the past. There was a tone of resignation – and even contempt – in his voice when he spoke, as if he had decided his listeners were now hopelessly beyond redemption. People began to be repelled rather than stirred when he addressed them.

Walt was unhappy but mostly because he missed Marceline, Uncle Ed and the farm. He had always been too much afraid of his father to realize he had now got worse. It was his brother, Roy, who made Walt aware of the change, and how deeply he resented it. Roy complained to Walt that their father had become a hypocrite. Back in Chicago, he pointed out, while it was true Elias had seen no contradiction in being a Christian socialist while running a prosperous capitalist enterprise at the same time, he had at least given some of his money to worthy causes. But now all he seemed to think of was making money for himself and doing it by exploiting everyone around him. His father had become a fraudulent windbag, Roy told his brother: all his religious and political talk was now merely hot air. He was nothing but a ruthless capitalist exploiter, just like all the others. Especially, he added, where his own sons were concerned.

In one way it was true. Physically too frail to do manual work any longer, Elias put his sons to work for him – and, in Roy's view, cheated them. After looking around Kansas City for a way of making money, Elias had decided his best bet was with the circulation people of the local newspaper group, the morning Kansas City *Times*, and the *Evening* and *Sunday Star*. For 45 cents a customer per week the newspapers were willing to sell a delivery franchise for a roster of 700 subscribers in the city suburbs. These 700 subscribers would then pay the franchise owner three dollars a week each for the delivery of their newspapers, giving him a tidy profit of 1,750 dollars a week – minus his outlays for labour and other expenses.

The circulation manager of the *Star* group was not too eager to turn the franchise over to Elias, however, since he looked too old and ill and was palpably not up to the job. Elias, however, swore he would prove a better delivery contractor than any they had already franchised if only the newspaper group would give him a chance to prove himself.

Roy was out of school by now and was immediately recruited as a delivery boy. Soon afterwards so was Walt, though he was only ten years old. When the boys asked about pay, Elias told them they would receive no actual wages, but he swore he would reward them more lucratively by investing a regular sum for each of them for every week's work they did for him. And there is no doubt that, being an honest man, that is what he intended to do.

From now on their father made both boys get up at 3.15 each morning in order to go downtown and collect copies of the *Times* from the *Star* offices, deliver them to the customers, after which Walt would snatch a quick breakfast and race off to school. When school was over for the day he had to rush back to the newspaper office to collect the afternoon *Star* and once more make the delivery rounds. Sundays brought no respite. In fact, both boys found it a particularly hard day because the Sunday edition of the *Star* bulged with advertisements and was heavy and awkward to lug around. But when the boys grumbled about it, Elias gave them a solemn lecture, saying they should give thanks for being so usefully occupied on the Lord's day, and glad that they had only one newspaper to deliver and only church services and Sunday school classes to attend afterwards.

Walt Disney remembered that he was always so tired that he sometimes fell asleep while making the rounds, napping in doorways or outhouses. So anxious was Elias to prove to the *Star* people and to the customers that he was well up to the demands of the franchise, he refused to let his sons deliver in the manner American newsboys have made famous – by riding down the street on their bikes and hurling the rolled-up papers on to the porch or the garden paths of the customers' houses. Elias insisted the papers be kept impeccably flat and delivered, unrolled, on the customers' doorsteps. In addition, they must be anchored down by a brick or stone to prevent them from blowing away.

It was mid-winter when the boys' chores began. Elias, of course, was too frail to do the rounds regularly with them; he did accompany them occasionally, but only to keep a hawk-like eye on them to see they were obeying the rules he had laid down. Roy and Walt had to crawl painfully out of their warm beds every morning, slog their way through the dark, snowbound suburban streets loaded down with papers, slipping and stumbling as they mounted the icy steps to the customers' houses. Almost invariably double storm doors confronted them, one of which had to be prised open and the newspaper securely anchored inside. It was dreadfully hard work, especially for a ten-year-old boy, and Walt had a terrible time trying to remember which customers took the *Times* and not the *Star*, or vice versa. Sometimes he had to retrace his steps and rescue a paper he had delivered to the wrong house, wasting precious time and missing his breakfast, and he was often beaten for arriving late at school.

It was obviously impossible for the two youngsters to do the job all by themselves, and eventually even Elias realized this and recruited a team of newsboys to help them. On Saturdays, after their morning rounds, they were all dispatched to collect the three dollars due to them from their clients. It wasn't always easy. Often customers made excuses for not paying, or doorbells weren't answered, and the boys came back empty-handed. It was always Walt who was then sent back by Elias to keep on ringing until someone answered the door and the customer could be cajoled into handing over three dollars to this small pathetic-looking boy who seemed just about to burst into tears. Elias had to pay his newsboy team the going rate of two dollars 50 a week, but he still kept his purse shut tight when it came to his own sons. He reminded them he was investing their wages – in what he said was a thriving jelly factory run by a friend of his in Chicago, and that one day they would thank him for providing each of them with a nest-egg. But when Roy finally insisted on being given at least some of his back pay, there was a showdown. Elias explained to the boys that he couldn't give them anything because the factory was having 'a little money trouble', and though their nest-eggs were safe, they couldn't be touched for the moment. 'Don't worry, there's 20 dollars invested over there for each of you,' he told his sons, 'and one day you'll thank me for it.'

Since Roy had now left school and was earning money doing odd jobs, he could get along without his father's money, though he refused to believe his father and insisted they were being 'cheated'. But Walt wanted pocket money, if only to keep up with the other kids in school. He got nothing from Elias and only the occasional dime or quarter slipped to him by his mother. He was always hungry and he loved sweets, and he envied the way his classmates could raid the local candy store and stuff themselves. In the end, without telling his parents, he got a job working in the candy store during recess time at school, and this enabled him at least to satisfy his sweet tooth and earn a quarter or so a week from the proprietor.

Then one morning someone not on his list of regular newspaper customers stopped him and mentioned he would like to become a subscriber, so Walt went down to the *Star* offices and ordered extra papers. Other new customers followed, and each time Walt would pay the *Star* an extra 45 cents a week from the money he earned in the candy store and start delivering to the new customer – collecting the extra three dollars each Saturday and keeping it for himself. He now had a extra newspaper round of his own, the existence of which he concealed from Elias. It meant getting up at 3 A.M. instead of 3.15 and he was even more often late for school and so exhausted when he got there he dozed through the lessons. But, as he said later, 'I had inexhaustible energy in those days, and I didn't mind being scolded by my parents for bad marks and beaten by my teachers for inattention. In any case, I needed the money. I ate candy like a mad fool.' On one occasion during this period, while walking home from his evening round, he found a 20 dollar bill lying in the middle of the road. He had never seen one before, and he went into the corner drug store, where the delivery boys gathered to eat chilli and beans, to ask them if it was genuine.

A particularly belligerent newsboy took a look at the note and pronounced it a phoney, but added that since he collected phoney money he would take it off Walt's hands for a dollar. He tried to snatch it off him, but Walt held on and went over to the storekeeper to check. The storekeeper assured him it was the genuine article, and said he would break it into small bills for him.

At this the bullying newsboy broke in and declared Mr Disney was a God-fearing man who would be shocked if he found his son had failed to return the bill to the one who had lost it. It was as bad as stealing. Walt pointed out he couldn't return it since he had found the bill on an empty street, but the boy still threatened to tell Elias unless Walt handed over five dollars to keep quiet. Reluctantly, Walt paid him the hush money. At least, he comforted himself, he had 15 dollars left.

In the next few days he spent six dollars on a wild orgy of candies, beans, hamburgers and a pair of roller skates. He hid the remaining nine dollars under a floorboard in his bedroom, the beginning of a little stake he planned to hoard for next summer when school was out and he could buy himself a camera.

But the following Saturday, when he came home after collecting the weekly three dollars from three of his customers, he found he had mislaid the purse in which he carried the money, and though he retraced his footsteps and looked everywhere, he failed to find it. Frightened of his father's rage if he told him what had happened, he reluctantly dug under the floorboards and brought out his precious nine dollars and handed it over to Elias. 'I came nearer to tears that day than I ever did later when I nearly went bankrupt,' Walt said. 'I really hated giving him that lovely money.'

It was just about this time that Roy finally decided he had had enough. One night he confided to Walt that he was getting out, and by morning he was gone. Flora Disney wanted to report her son missing to the police, but Elias forbade it and told his wife and Walt he never wanted to hear Roy's name mentioned in the house again. When a letter came a week later from Elias's brother, Will Disney, to say Roy had turned up at his farm in Ellis, Kansas, and was helping with the harvest, Flora fell on her knees and began saying a prayer of thankfulness until her husband sternly ordered her back on her feet.

In fact, Roy Disney never did go back home to his parents. In 1913 he took a job as a clerk in a bank in Kansas City at 19 dollars a week, and when, in 1917, rumours of American involvement in World War I began to sweep the country, he volunteered for the Navy and was posted to the Great Lakes Training Camp nineteen miles north of Chicago.

About the same time, Herbert Disney, the oldest son who had run away from home with his brother Raymond some years earlier, now turned up again. He brought with him a wife and daughter and asked for help because he was out of a job. After he had humbly apologised to Elias for his previous transgressions, he was grudgingly given accommodation in the family home on Bellefontaine Avenue.

But Elias was restless again, and Herbert's arrival seemed to act as a catalyst to the itch to get moving. He announced to his family that he was selling off the newspaper round, turning the Bellefontaine house over to Herbert, and that they were moving back to Chicago. This, he explained to Walt, would give him a chance to keep a closer watch on 'our investment'. He had been offered a job in the Chicago jelly factory run by his friend. In addition to making jelly, it seemed, it was about to expand and would soon begin turning out a new soft drink called Ozell, which was going to make their fortune. In return for investing a further 16,000 dollars in the factory ('Part of it was the money he'd squeezed out of Walt and me,' Roy said later), Elias would run the operation and wait for the profits to roll in.

Once more Flora Disney put her foot down. Walt and his sister Ruth were still in school in Kansas City and she was determined that Walt should not be taken out of school until he had got his diploma. Elias was adamant in refusing to let her stay behind with her son, so it was finally arranged that Walt should lodge with Herbert and his family in the Bellefontaine house until his school exams were finished.

Walt was delighted. It enabled him to carry on with his bootleg newspaper round until the summer term at school came to an end; then he sold it to the man who had bought his father's franchise and took a holiday job as a newspaper-seller on the Pacific railroad running between Kansas City and Jefferson.

'What more could a young boy want?' he asked later. 'I was seeing the world and earning money while doing it! In addition, I didn't have my father always hovering over me, badgering me. I don't want anyone to think my father was a tyrant, but he did have a terrible temper and he was always trying to make you do things for which you weren't suitable. For instance, I was only fifteen then but I already knew I wanted to draw. But when I told my father, he just scoffed at me and said if I was foolish enough to want to become an artist I should learn the violin, and then I could always get a job in a band if I was in need of money. He tore up my drawings, brought out his own violin and forced me to saw and scrape at it for hours every day, although he must have known from the squawks I was making I was tone-deaf and would never be any good at music.' He added: 'It was good to get away from him – and from that fiddle. Even I hated the sounds I was making.'

It was not until the end of the summer of 1917 that he finally moved to Chicago. His family was now living at 1523 Ogden Street and he enrolled for his final year in school at McKinley High School on Adam Street. The main attraction of McKinley for Walt was that it had a school magazine called *The Voice* and it printed drawings. He persuaded the editorial committee to let him be junior art editor, and he not only went around soliciting drawings from the pupils but did a lot of the illustrations himself. They were crude attempts to imitate local cartoonists and humorous drawings he saw in *Judge* and *Life*, America's leading humour magazines, and the jokes he appended to them were poor; but at least he was aware of his lack of expertise and was not afraid to work at the job of conquering his amateurishness.

While still in school, Walt enrolled as a night student at the Chicago Academy of Fine Arts, though he did not tell his father and paid the fees out of his savings from Kansas City.

The academy was a private institution run by a dedicated teacher named Carl Wertz, and what differentiated Wertz from the other art teachers in the city was that he encouraged his pupils to draw from live models, hens, cats, chickens, dogs, human beings. It made all the difference to Walt in improving his technique, and Wertz particularly liked the comic, almost satirical line he put into his caricatures of birds and animals, though he didn't do so well with the human model.

Some of the teachers at the academy worked as cartoonists on Chicago newspapers, and it was because of one of them, Leroy Gossett of the *Chicago Herald*, that he became interested in learning cartooning techniques. On one occasion the most famous Chicago cartoonist of the day, Carey Orr of the *Tribune*, came in to take a session and he asked young Disney to show him some of his work.

Under Gossett, Walt had improved a lot. He was beginning to

concentrate his ideas and get flair and humour into his work. Orr was impressed, so much so that he invited Walt to visit him at the *Tribune* office and introduced him to the rewrite editors and the reporters. Walt came away filled with the ambition to be a newspaper cartoonist like Carey Orr.

However, before he dared ask for a job he needed to put in more time at the academy, and that meant finding more money for the fees because his Kansas City hoard had been used up. The moment he graduated from McKinley High he began to look around for jobs, and found one doing part-time work as a watchman on the Chicago El (the elevated railway). He worked there every Friday, Saturday and Sunday from six until midnight. In the early hours of every morning he would turn up at the main Chicago Post Office and fill in for any postman who was away sick or on vacation. Then he would set off with a sack of mail to cover a so-called 'short route' delivering letters and packages inside the city limits, after which he would dash back to the main office, start sorting mail again and then go out with a second delivery. He was paid 40 cents an hour for this work, and did it until the middle of the afternoon, when he would ask the assistant postmaster if there were any special deliveries to be made. These he delivered to their recipients either in a post-office horse and buggy or a brand-new motorized mail-van, which he had secretly learned to drive in his spare time. Then, with his fees in his hot and eager hand, he would go off to the academy for an evening of lessons and concentrated drawing, the only time of the day when weariness was forgotten and the minutes sped by in joyous concentration.

Despite the gap in their ages, Walt missed Roy whose practical views on life he had grown to admire and respect. But, except that they knew he was now fighting in the war, it was hard to get news of him, because any of his letters arriving at Ogden Avenue were burned in the stove by the unforgiving Elias. It was not until he celebrated his sixteenth birthday that his mother revealed what Roy was doing. News had secretly reached her by way of her brother-in-law Will Disney, in Kansas, that Roy was now on active duty with the US Navy. He was serving on a destroyer convoying merchant ships between America and Europe.

How Walt envied him! He was suddenly desperately eager to see his brother again and also longed to emulate him and serve with US forces in the war. For the moment this ambition drove all thought of a cartooning career out of the boy's head, and he began haunting army and navy recruiting offices in an attempt to enlist 'before it's all over'.

He was turned away for being under-age and underweight but, like many another patriotic American in those days, he was determined to get into the war somehow. So he added a year to his age and persuaded a Red Cross recruiter in Chicago to let him join up with one of the units due to be shipped to France. He pointed out he could drive a van, and the Red Cross desperately needed ambulance drivers.

After persuading the recruiter, he had to go home and argue his parents into letting him go. Flora was reluctant, but once she was convinced of his determination she went to work on Elias. He didn't approve of the war in any shape or form, and withheld his consent for weeks. There were many fierce arguments before Flora won the day.

By the time Elias had grudgingly signed Walt's passport application and the Red Cross induction formalities were completed, it was 1918 and World War I was all but over. Walt sailed for France aboard the S.S. *Vaubin* in October 1918 with the last batch of fifty Red Cross volunteers to be shipped to the war.

He missed Roy who was being invalided out of the service at that very moment, and he missed the fighting. But he would at least see the devastated lands over which the so-called 'war to end all wars' had been fought. Moreover, he would be fulfilling a long-cherished ambition to see something of the world beyond Missouri and Chicago; an exciting prospect for a sixteen-year-old.

Chapter 3

YANKEE DOODLE KID

A girl named Su Pitowski had been in Walt Disney's class during his last year at McKinley High, and he thought she was the most beautiful but also the most unattainable girl he had ever seen. Bright-eyed, glowing with energy, vocal and intelligent, she had so many beaux hanging round her after school that he could never get near enough to catch her eye, and decided she would never notice him even if he did. Nevertheless, he tried everything to attract her attention and win her esteem. He took up tennis because she played the game, but since the sexes were segregated on the courts, he never did succeed in playing with her. However, as he said later to his daughter Diane: 'The thought she might be watching me did enormously improve my backhand.'

Then he discovered Su had a brother who was in the army and fighting in France, and this explained why she was so madly patriotic. She took part in school plays in which she wrapped herself in an American flag and declaimed passionate verses about the gallantry of our boys 'over there'. She also wrote pieces in the McKinley High newspaper, *The Voice*, exhorting readers to do more for the war effort.

The fact that she was one of the members of the editorial committee of *The Voice* was an added incentive to volunteer for the job of junior art editor, and it spurred his ambition to make a good job of it when he realized he would be reporting regularly to Su about the kind of drawings that went into its pages. To catch her interest, he started a section called 'The Tiny Voice (McKinley's Smallest Paper)' which he filled with a series of cartoons, almost all of which he drew himself.

He may well have sensed that what would stir her interest most in his drawings would be their patriotic content, because most of his cartoons exhorted his readers to rally round and help win the war. There were caricatures of Uncle Sam with a sickle in his hand surveying a vast farm and saying: 'I have the land. You furnish the help.' There was a marksman winning a prize for shooting the steel helmet off the German Kaiser, with a caption declaring: 'Volunteer! You may hit the bull's eye too!' There was a cartoon of a plump citizen saying complacently: 'I am too fat to fight and I guess there is nothing I can do to help win this war.' At which a small figure pipes out from the side of the drawing: 'Why don't you stop eating so much and save food for the boys over there! *And* you will reduce so you can fight.' The fat man looks surprised. 'I never thought of that,' he says. At the bottom of the cartoon page was a strapline saying: 'Buy savings stamps and help win this war' followed by a credit line: 'Walt Disney, Editor' and then 'With apologies to Orr'. Orr was, of course, Carey Orr, the *Tribune* cartoonist to whom he owed the inspiration for many of his cartoons.

They certainly weren't strikingly original cartoons, but what they lacked in expertise they made up in flair and panache; and, in any case, Su thought they were wonderful. She began to take an increasing interest in this shy, solemn, fair-haired kid who shared so much of her fervour for 'our boys', and when Walt told her he wanted to improve his technique as a draughtsman and had signed up for night classes at the academy she did likewise, mainly to stay close to him. Soon they were sharing class rings and going to patriotic meetings together. She was tremendously proud of him when she heard he had volunteered for the Red Cross and she greeted the news of his acceptance with an impulsive kiss. Emotion burning in her bright brown eyes, she faithfully promised to write to him 'at least twice a week' while he was serving his country overseas.

She was true to her word, too, and once he reached France the letters began to arrive regularly, and were even more frequently answered. He kept her picture under his pillow in camp in France and dreamed of the bliss awaiting both of them when he returned at last from doing his bit for his country. All he worried about was whether or not he was good enough for her.

The fifty-strong intake of new Red Cross personnel was shipped first of all to a camp behind the headquarters of the famous French military school, St Cyr, and it was here, on 5 December 1918, that one of his comrades enticed Walt into a bar, promising to buy him an innocuous drink called grenadine. But once he was inside, the rest of the unit suddenly appeared and began singing 'Happy Birthday' to hail the fact that he was now seventeen years old. Some of them drank their toasts in grenadine, and others in white and red wine, but then the drinkers among them began changing to pastis and cognac, and at the end of a raucous session Walt found himself stuck with a whopping bill, which he didn't have the money to meet. His first pay-cheque from the Red Cross was overdue.

Someone suggested that he go outside and sell his spare pair of service boots to a local Frenchman, pointing out that what with leather and other shortages, local footwear was scarce and he shouldn't have much trouble making a sale. He came back with a sheaf of francs and paid off his debts. He realized he had been conned by his comrades, and while he didn't resent them taking advantage of his youthful naïvety, he had already spelled out a rule for himself: never repeat a mistake, and never let anyone con you twice. He didn't intend to be caught without money again, and pending the arrival of his first pay-cheque (he was due 40 dollars a month, later raised to 52), he looked around for ways of raising cash.

For 15 francs a week, paid out of unit funds, he agreed to do some signs around the camp to show personnel where things were. With the aid of his crayons and drawing paper, he plastered the camp with simple, funny and effective posters pointing the way to the canteen (an arrow over a huge steaming mug), the bath-house (a knobbled and mud-spattered foot dipping a grimy toe into a steaming tub), toilets (a pair of hairy legs, pants around the ankles, dangling from a giant water closet, with a line underneath saying: 'And DON'T Steal the Toilet Paper!').

Even at St Cyr, far away from the trenches and the fighting, they had, when they first arrived, heard the thud of the big guns thundering over the Western Front. But by the time the unit was posted closer to the actual battlefields, the war was over and the armistice signed, and everything was strangely quiet. Their new location was the small town of Neufchâteau, which was on the railway connecting the rear areas with what had been the main battlefronts of the Marne only a few weeks before. Already the first troops were coming back down the line from the trenches on their way to the demob centres, and new shipments of draftees, although too late for the fighting, were still being sent up to the front as temporary replacements. Since every train that came through stopped at Neufchâteau, the unit's job was to meet the weary veteran troops and see that they were greeted as returning heroes and given plentiful food, sweets and hot coffee.

It was from the influx of new recruits that money was to be made. Walt formed a friendship, and then a partnership, with a Red Cross comrade who was, because of his Southern accent, known to everyone as the Cracker. He was in fact a streetwise kid from New Orleans, and there was nothing he hadn't learned about how to make easy money from dealing with the tourists in his native city.

To the Cracker, the recruits now arriving on the Western Front were just the same sucker breed as the trippers disembarking from the buses in the French Quarter. He saw in their eager eyes the same willingness to hand over their surplus cash in return for souvenirs. The moment they smelled the acrid reek of the battlefields, growing stale though it now was, they began clamouring for war mementos. The Cracker set out to give them what they wanted, and more.

Whenever he and Walt had a day off, they would borrow a Red Cross ambulance and drive up to the front line and scour the trenches for the flotsam and jetsam of the fighting. Mostly they would load up the ambulance with German steel helmets, which they would then sell as genuine souvenirs of the fighting. The most popular items among the troops were what the Cracker termed KSDs, or 'Kraut Sniper Derbies', which usually meant steel helmets with bullet-holes in them, and these were so eagerly sought that the dough-boys fought among themselves to get hold of them and didn't mind what they paid. Unfortunately, and not unnaturally, genuine KSDs were few and far between, since there had only been a limited number of German snipers in the front lines and quite a few of them had survived. So it was difficult to keep up with the demand.

Then Walt had an idea for exploiting his artistic skills in pursuit of the plentiful money he and his partner were now being offered. He would take a limited number out of each load of helmets and set to work adapting them, firing bullets into them, treating the holes so the burn marks stayed but didn't appear too new, and generally doing a job on the helmets themselves until they looked as if they had just fallen into the mud straight out of a sniper's nest. As both demand and prices soared, he grew more skilful at dressing up his souvenirs, coating the inside of the bullet holes with grease, hair and even stains of dried blood, to make them appear as if they had been ripped from the heads of the dead or wounded snipers.

'You'd be surprised how popular they were,' Walt said later to Diane. 'Some of the boys would hand over every cent they had to get them, and the gorier they looked the more they'd pay.'

When you are only seventeen, money and success rapidly go to your head and Walt Disney was soon the cockiest kid in the unit. He hardly touched his Red Cross pay, and sent home over half of it each month for his mother to bank for him. He learned how to drink and smoke and got himself a girlfriend, a sympathetic American auxiliary who helped out at the Red Cross. He took her out with him to the local *estaminets*, and she taught him how to dance the tango and the bunny-hug. They sometimes sneaked into the station waiting room and 'canoodled', as they called it, after their evening out. But that, he confessed later, was as far as his youthful love-life went. He hadn't the courage to snatch anything more than a fumbling embrace from the American girl. There were plenty of French girls available, of course, but he didn't speak their language; and he was, quite frankly, scared of 'catching something' from them. He was very conscious of one of the posters he had drawn after arriving at Neufchâteau to warn the personnel of the dangers of disease. It had turned out to be one of his most graphic and effective efforts, since he had crammed all his own fears into it. Done in bold red and black, it showed a half-undressed dough-boy staring down in horror at a loathsome bug crawling up his leg, while a shapely female limb decorated with a red garter was visible behind. The caption warned: 'Beware The BUG! Don't let it bite you! Keep Clean! Keep PURE!! Beware VD!!!' Venereal disease was rife in that part of France and not even the professional prostitutes in the bordellos were said to be immune. His comrades were willing to risk both the disease and the court martial the army ordained if they caught it, but he was so scared of both he never dared to accompany them when they went off for a night in the brothels of Neufchâteau and Nancy.

He spent a lot of time in camp drinking and gambling. The Cracker taught him how to play a smart game of poker, and in one all-night session he won 2,000 francs. He went to the bank next day, had half of it converted into dollars, and wired it home to his mother. With part of the remainder he bought himself a young collie pup which he called Carey, after the *Tribune* cartoonist, and until the dog grew too big he carried him around in his military musette bag wherever he went. Carey barked to waken him at reveille every morning and learned to dig out his spare underwear and shirt and hand it to him in his teeth. Walt liked to draw him in his more playful moods, and sent a number of the drawings back to Flora. The one she liked best was a sketch of Carey as a puppy peeking saucily out of her son's musette bag. She kept it in her kitchen drawer and liked to take it out and look at it, but it was unfortunately destroyed many years later.

Carey in turn adored his master. Sleeping at the foot of his bunk, ever-watchful to defend him from enemies or intruders, he liked wearing Walt's forage cap and showing off the many tricks he learned to perform. He could even stand on his hind legs and salute with his right paw whenever 'The Stars and Stripes' or the 'Marseillaise' were played.

Back in Chicago, Walt had made friends with a young man called Russell Maas, who came from Waukegan, Illinois, and who had joined the Red Cross with him. Russell also had a pet dog and they were planning to spend part of their demob leave together. Walt always knew he would go back to Chicago and renew his association with Su Pitowski, with whom he was still keeping up a warm and, on his part, increasingly passionate correspondence. But before settling down to life with Su and the job he hoped to get in the cartoon department of the *Chicago Tribune*, he thought it would be exciting to see a little more of the world.

Both boys dreamed of adventures of the kind they had read about in books, their favourite being *The Adventures of Huckleberry Finn*. They decided it would be a great adventure to build a raft and float down the Mississippi to New Orleans, and when they mentioned their project to the Cracker, he enthusiastically invited them to visit and stay with him at the end of their journey. They would take the dogs with them, naturally, to ward off any suspicious characters who might try to board their raft en route.

It never worked out, and Walt Disney always regretted it didn't – and never really forgot about it, either. Instead, Russell heard from Waukegan that his mother was ill and he applied for compassionate leave. He was told he was being shipped home and terminated instead. Since he had to go through the formalities of shipping home his own dog, he arranged to take Carey with him too, and said he would look after the collie until Walt came back for him.

He tried to persuade Walt to ship home too; after all, he pointed out, the war was over and there was no reason to stay on. But by that time Walt was thinking of volunteering for a Red Cross unit going to Albania, where forces were still fighting and casualties were dying for lack of medical help. Volunteers were being sought by the Red Cross and offered 150 dollars a month, and Walt was tempted by the money. So he said goodbye to Carey and watched his beloved pet and his best friend leaving to go home. He was so lonely and miserable after they had gone that, after hesitating for a few weeks, he decided to apply for a discharge too. Once his mind was made up and the formalities completed, he happily sent a cable telling Su Pitowski the goods news that they would soon be together again.

Suddenly everything around him in France seemed strange and

foreign, and he could hardly wait to get back home to familiar places, to his reunion with Su and with his collie dog, Carey.

But, from the moment he landed back in America, everything was an anticlimax. When he staggered out of the train in Chicago, loaded down with bottles of perfume, boxes of delicate underwear, yards of lace and other expensive presents for Su (including a 'genuine' pair of German sniper's binoculars which he had bought from the Cracker after being assured his comrade had personally taken them from the neck of a fallen German marksman), he made his first discovery of the deviousness of women. Su had married someone else three months earlier – and had gone on writing while neglecting to tell him of her wedding. He was so angry at first that he was tempted to throw his gifts away, but was finally persuaded by his frugal-minded mother to pass them on to some of her friends.

Harder to bear was the news he received when he journeyed alone to Waukegan that weekend. Russell met him and took him on a street-by-street tour of the city in his brand-new Model T Ford, proudly showing off both his skill as a chauffeur and his new fiancée, a brassy blonde who shared the front seat and giggled loudly at every remark Russell made.

When, after more than an hour, Walt finally managed to interrupt his friend's boasts and the girl's raucous laughter long enough to ask when he was going to be reunited with Carey, the girl burst into more fits of giggles. Then Russell, almost casually, informed him the dog had died of distemper some months earlier, shortly after his return to Waukegan.

'I'd have written you about it,' Russell said, 'but I'm not much good at letters. And anyway, what did you care what happened to that scruffy little mutt? As Ellie here says, you can always buy another dog.'

At which she sputtered with renewed giggles and Russell went on to talk about something else, as if the death of Carey was the most unimportant thing in the world.

'If we hadn't been in a car with a girl,' Walt said later to Diane, 'I'd have punched him in the nose.'

In truth, his dog's death hit him harder than the betrayal by his girl. In a way he was relieved that Su had let him down. It was as if he had never been emotionally involved with her. He didn't care if he never saw her again, and he didn't hate her either – but the incident turned him against the female sex, and the only woman he would trust for the next few years was his mother. On the other hand, he felt bitter and sad over the death of Carey. He had really loved that dog and he realized now he had been the only real friend he had made during his service in France. It was devastating that he was no longer alive and waiting to greet him. He would never forgive Russell Maas for letting him die.

He asked his mother to let him have one of the drawings of Carey he had made during his sojourn at Neufchâteau, but she had thrown all of them away with the exception of the one of the puppy in the musette bag, and she refused to part with that. It so happened that he had plenty of pictures of Su Pitowski, but that was no compensation. When he took them out of his wallet they no longer meant a thing to him and he tore them up without a qualm.

Chapter 4

K.C. BLUES

ONE of the ambitions Walt Disney had carried with him to France was to become a newspaper cartoonist on his return home. He pinned his hopes for the future on Carey Orr who had practically promised to find him a job in the art department of the *Chicago Tribune* when he came home from the war.

A couple of weeks after his return from France, he went down to the *Tribune* office to show Orr his latest work. But if he expected to come away with a job, he was disappointed. Orr received him hospitably enough and made it plain he was glad to see him back. He listened with grins of appreciation to the tale of his adventures in France and nodded in sympathy at the woes which had greeted him on his return. Then he began to leaf through Walt's drawings. He was disappointed with what he saw. The drawings were good, there was no doubt about that, and the techniques had improved beyond measure. He laughed at some of the sketches and thought most of them were fun and remarkably cute. But where was the bile a cartoonist needed to possess if his work was to make an impact on the reader? As Orr well knew, good cartoonists use prussic acid in their pens and scorch the paper with their feelings. Cartoonists must be editorialists with their own deeply felt, and peculiarly individual, point of view. It was fortunate there were genuinely no vacancies at that moment in the *Tribune* cartoon department, or else Orr might have been forced to tell Walt Disney that he lacked the cartoonist's principal qualification: not just artistic talent and burning ambition but fire in the belly and a livid prejudice against the powers that be. Walt wasn't really biased against anyone. Even war and personal rejection hadn't left him angry or bitter. His recent experiences hadn't driven him to his drawing board to get back at the world by distilling his venom into devastating cartoons; his way of getting back at the world was to draw something that made people laugh.

The way Carey Orr saw it, that attitude might well turn Walt Disney into a splendid artist one of these days, but it wasn't going to make him into a cartoonist. So he let him down lightly and told him to take another job until conditions were more propitious. As he sent him away he had a shrewd suspicion it would not be the last he heard of him.

Flora Disney was secretly pleased at her son's rejection, since she hoped it would persuade him to forget his artistic aspirations and settle down to something more practical. Besides, it would keep him at home. Meanwhile, Elias Disney reminded him that there was a 25 dollar a week job waiting for him at the jelly-making factory, and why was he dragging his feet? There was a blazing row when Walt contemptuously spurned the proffered job and insisted that he was going to be an artist, no matter what the setbacks. His father, scoffing at such lofty ambitions, angrily told him he had grown swollen-headed over his experiences in France and that it was time for him to face facts. The result was that both father and son used words Walt, at least, later regretted, and it ended with the last of the four Disney boys – despite the pleas of an unhappy Flora – walking out of the family home.

It was just as well he rejected the job offer. Not long afterwards the jelly factory went into bankruptcy and its principal owner was charged with embezzlement and sent to prison. Elias lost all his investments in the enterprise.

Fortunately, Walt had somewhere to go now he too had walked out on his parents: Roy would help him.

Walt had always had a distant, almost hostile, relationship with his two older brothers, but Roy was different. It was true there was a ten-year gap between their ages, and temperamentally they were completely opposite, but if Walt had sometimes found Roy dull and unresponsive to his whims and sudden enthusiasms, at least Roy had tried to understand them – which was more than could be said for Elias. In many ways Walt had come to regard Roy as a substitute father who would respond when he needed him. And Roy did not fail him now.

In fact, Roy was far from well, having been discharged from the US Navy with a disability pension as a result of his overseas service. For the moment he was back in his pre-war job in the Kansas City bank, and living with Herbert Disney and his wife and children in the old family home on Bellefontaine where he paid rent for a sitting room and bedroom in the back of the house. He persuaded Herbert to let Walt sleep on the settee for an extra three dollars, and he told his kid

brother that he would be glad to share his living quarters with him –
and temporarily pay his rent. They had an affectionate reunion, for
they had not seen each other since Roy himself had walked out of the
family home.

Roy Disney was a much more business-like, more practical person
than Walt, and less commonplace and unimaginative than most
people, including Walt, suspected. Already he sensed something
special in Walt, guessing he was the most gifted – and most vulnerable
– member of the family. He felt protective towards him.

As Walt spilled out the sorry story of all that had happened to him
since he had come back from France, Roy guessed that of all the
setbacks his brother had suffered in the last few weeks, his rejection
by Carey Orr was the one which had most sorely injured his pride and
self-confidence. Gently, he set out to probe what was going on in
Walt's mind. What did he most want to do now he was in Kansas
City? Did he still want to work as a cartoonist? He did? Then Roy
was all for helping him achieve his ambition.

Roy took time off to accompany him to the offices of the Kansas
City *Star*, where they had both once worked as delivery boys, and they
hung around the city room for several days trying to persuade the art
editor to give Walt a job. Walt brought along his catalogue of wartime
drawings and, each day, before arriving, he would do a sketch to
illustrate one of the main stories on the *Star*'s front page, to show how
he might be used as a news-sketch artist. But it did no good. There
were no jobs available or offered.

There was also very little money. True, Flora Disney was still
holding on to the hoard of dollars Walt had sent her out of his pay
(and poker winnings) with the Red Cross in France, but leaving home
had been painful enough, and so long as he didn't have a job Walt
hated to admit failure by wiring home for funds. It is a measure of the
rapport between the two brothers that Roy never complained and
continued to support Walt with free board and lodging. But there
were some irksome moments. Roy had a fiancée named Edna Francis
who also worked in the bank. A willing and accommodating woman,
Edna patiently put up with the fact that whenever she met Roy his
brother would be there too. There were times when she longed to have
Roy to herself, but it was never possible. Even in the privacy of Roy's
own quarters, Walt was there; he didn't seem to go out like other
boys, but stayed home to read books about drawing or sit in a corner
making sketches, all the time saying: 'Don't mind me.' But, of course,
they did. And even on the rare occasions when he wasn't there, he

made sure they thought of him by playing one of his practical jokes: he would leave notes around saying, 'No canoodling!'; or he would draw pictures of two soppy-looking love-birds cradled in a nest, beak to beak, and once he shocked Edna by drawing her actually laying an egg. She finally lost her temper when he slipped under the sofa a toy duck he had specially designed so it squeaked only under the weight of two bodies. Edna was deeply embarrassed and annoyed when she was pressed down on the sofa by Roy's passionate embrace, and the duck set up a violent squawking – at which Walt peeked round the door and, grinning broadly, wagged a reproving finger at them.

All this increased Roy's determination to find Walt something that would get him out of the house, bring in a pay-cheque and satisfy his artistic aspirations. It so happened that two of Roy's clients at the bank were in advertising, and Roy plucked up courage to ask if there were any jobs going for a young and promising artist. He was lucky. The two clients ran the small Pesmen-Rubin Agency which provided illustrations for the advertisements and catalogues put out for its customers by the bigger Gray Agency, and it turned out that they were looking for an apprentice.

Roy told Walt to apply, he rushed round with his portfolio and was hired on the strength of his wartime caricatures. He was so delighted at getting a job that he not only promised Roy five dollars a week for his bed and board but also splurged on a long-distance phone call to his mother and told her the good news. He had to confess it was a temporary job and diplomatically did not add that the pay was only 12 dollars a week. This was just as well since Elias reacted sceptically to the news, refused to congratulate him on his good fortune and prophesied he would soon be out of a job again.

Walt worked for the agency for nearly two months and said later that he picked up more technical skills in that time than he had learned at the academy in Chicago in a year. The two illustrators, Louis Pesmen and Bill Rubin, thought up the layouts and did the principal drawings for the Gray Agency, which chiefly produced advertisements for farm instrument manufacturers. After making rough sketches they passed them over to Walt and another apprentice to add the final touches. The other apprentice was Ubbe Iwwerks, the shy and tongue-tied son of a Dutch immigrant family. He was already a quick, smooth and efficient draughtsman; he had picked up all the tricks of the trade and was generous in showing Walt professional short-cuts in drawing technique. He taught him how to spruce up and enliven a drawing by the deft use of razor-blade marks on white paint

51

and the practical uses of a pentograph to increase his output. He was also full of ideas for brightening up Pesmen-Rubin's often mundane sketches for their clients, adding crowing cocks, barnyard animals and cloud-flecked skies as background to the sketches of the ploughs and hoes and carts they were advertising. Walt respected his talent and was grateful for his help, but found it difficult to resist the temptation to play tricks and make fun of his fellow apprentice, who was intensely shy and naïve, and quite unsophisticated.

Walt Disney at nineteen still bore traces of the cocksure young veteran who had learned to play poker and sell fake souvenirs to the troops in France. He had a sunny disposition and, when things were going well, a tendency to boast about himself. There was nothing he liked better than to tell tall tales which he did not mean to be taken seriously. Few people did take him seriously but Iwwerks was so credulous that he believed everything Walt told him, and brooded, in resentful disillusion, when he realized his fellow-apprentice had been taking advantage of his gullibility. Though he never gave any signs of anger or irritation, he hated being made fun of, and was deeply mortified when he found himself the butt of Walt's often crude and juvenile practical jokes. This was a pity, because his resentment was to have unfortunate consequences for both of them later.

Walt had been hired in October 1919 because it was the busy season, what with all the Christmas catalogues to prepare as well as the brochures for the January sales. But after that business sagged and he was let go at the end of November. He was not too downcast; he had learned a lot of new skills, thanks mainly to Iwwerks's tutelage, and was confident he could now go out and make a living as a commercial artist.

In the meantime, to build up his funds, he did what he always had done before when he was short of cash – he went down to the central post office in Kansas City and got himself a temporary job sorting and delivering the Christmas post. It was after one session of tramping the Kansas City streets with his heavy load that he came home to his lodgings, and found the forlorn figure of Ubbe Iwwerks awaiting him on the outside steps. Iwwerks too had been sacked, and for him it was much more of a catastrophe. It took Walt some time to get the truth out of him, but he finally extracted from the reluctant Iwwerks the fact that his father was a hopeless inebriate, his mother was an invalid, and there were several younger children in the family. All of them had relied on the 15 dollars a week Iwwerks earned to pay the rent and keep them clothed and fed, and now they were in danger of being thrown out on to the streets to starve. What was he to do?

Walt took him inside, gave him a meal, and, after some thought, decided the only solution was for them both to go into business together as freelance illustrators. He tucked a ten-dollar note into Iwwerks's pocket and sent him back home to pick up samples of his work. Combining them with his own, he went to see a man named Jake Carter who ran a fly-by-night publication called *Restaurant News* in downtown Kansas City. It was one of those news-sheets distributed free in cafés and restaurants that advertised in its twelve flimsy pages.

Carter was already running his throwaway sheet on a shoestring and had no money to spare to buy illustrations. But even in those days, at nineteen, Walt Disney had a line of talk capable of charming blood out of a stone, and it did not take him long to persuade the reluctant editor that he and his partner would be good for business. He showed Carter a picture he had drawn of Gloria Swanson, the most glamorous film star of the day, seated at a table sipping champagne and seductively smoking a cigarette in a long, long holder. Walt had actually adapted the drawing from a publicity still of the big film then showing in town, Cecil B. deMille's *Male and Female*, but he had added some familiar potted palms and Roman urns featured at a well-known local restaurant, and the caption had Swanson saying: 'I always dine at Alfredo's when I'm in Kansas City.' Walt promised that he and his partner could provide similarly attractive come-ons for every eating place in town, and Carter could sell advertising space on their illustrations alone.

Carter was won over to the extent that he promised to pay them ten dollars a week, and to provide them, rent-free, with a work room in his small suite of downtown offices. Actually, it turned out to be the spare bathroom, containing nothing but a wash-basin and a toilet, but Walt was not in the least abashed. He decided at long last to send home for the money Flora Disney was guarding for him, and asked her to wire him 500 dollars at once.

Unfortunately, all letters arriving at the Disney household in Chicago, no matter to whom they were addressed, were still opened by Elias if he was at home when the post was delivered. He read Walt's letter to Flora and sternly forbade her to send any money at all until she had first learned exactly what he proposed to do with it. Anxious not to make trouble for his mother, Walt explained that he needed to pay for furnishing the new office he was setting up with a partner in Kansas City. His mother, on Elias's instructions, wired him 250 dollars only and with this sum he bought desks, easels, drawing boards and airbrushes. He also arranged for a sign to be posted on the door with the name of the new firm. He had already persuaded Iwwerks to drop some letters from his name, so that he would henceforward be known as Ub Iwerks, and, at Ub's suggestion, he had officially shortened his own name from Walter Disney to Walt Disney (which was what his family already called him). The sign-painter was instructed to put IWERKS-DISNEY on the door, but then Carter came past and complained that it looked like a dentist's sign. Finally, they decided on: IWERKS & DISNEY, Commercial Artists.' They were in business.

In no way could they live on the ten dollars a week Jake Carter was paying them, not even with free office space, and it was imperative to find other clients without delay. Iwerks was no help at all. He was struck dumb in the presence of other people and although Walt openly acknowledged he was a brilliant illustrator, he also realized his talents as a salesman were nil. So it was left to Walt, a born promoter, to drum up prospects likely to pay them money. He decided his best plan was to seek business from all the printers in town. He designed and produced a flashy-looking contract which pledged Iwerks & Disney would become the 'official art department', producing on demand all the art work needed by any printer who signed an agreement to pay them 30 dollars a month. Most of them were shrewd enough to know a bargain when one was offered. After looking over the samples, they signed up. By the end of their first month in business, the partners were making twice what their combined earnings at Pesmen-Rubin had been.

The first client was a printing firm which sent them a promotional prospectus from an oil company and asked them to illustrate it. The oil company wanted investors' money. Walt, always the inspired visualizer, designed and Iwerks drew an oil well from which gushers of 20-dollar bills were raining down. It was startling and effective. Both printer and promoter were delighted.

The partners soon had enough in the bank to move out of Carter's bathroom and rent themselves an office near the railway station. One day, Ub told Walt that as a result of his new-found prosperity his father had signed the pledge, his mother had been seen by a doctor, and all members of the family were eating as much as they wanted. He would like to have added how deeply grateful he was to Walt for what he had done for him, but he was tongue-tied when it came to showing his emotions. Then, too, each time he made a special effort and summoned up sufficient courage to express his heartfelt thanks, Walt would spoil everything by playing some crude practical joke on him or making fun of him in front of other people. The words would freeze in his throat and he would find himself again feeling resentful towards him. Although he had grown to love and admire Walt Disney, appreciating his talents and envying him his cheerful and happy-go-lucky attitude towards life, there were moments when he hated him and was as jealous of him as ever Iago was of Othello.

In the spring of 1920, Iwerks read an advertisement in the *Star* for a cartoonist for the Kansas City Film Ad Company. For some time, they had both been fascinated with the cartoon features that were now frequently shown in local movie houses, and Walt had begun experimenting with comic strips which he dreamed of one day animating for films. Iwerks, who had some lively ideas of his own, saw the ad in the *Star* as a great opportunity to fulfil their ambitions. Well aware of his own inarticulateness, he urged Walt to answer it for both of them and try to sell their joint services for the job, which they could easily do in addition to their work for the local printers.

Walt went along to the offices of the Film Ad Company and was offered the job as soon as he showed his portfolio, but the moment he mentioned doing it part-time in collaboration with his partner, he was crisply informed this was a full-time position for one person only. Moreover, though the advertising man apologized for offering only 40 dollars a week for the job, he did add that there were good prospects for advancement. This was more money than Walt had ever dreamed of making. He would be rich! But what was he going to say to Ub? He knew Ub would be devastated if he told him he was going to take the job and split up the partnership. On the other hand, how could he possibly turn down the offer? Now that he had seen the kind of work the Film Ad Company were doing, he knew this would be the fulfilment of a dream. In a sudden flash of revelation, he realized this was the kind of art work he had always wanted to do – animating cartoon characters on a screen. Fancy being paid 40 dollars a week for the realization of your dreams! But what about Ub?

For once, Iwerks took the words out of his mouth. Seeing the expression of suppressed excitement on his partner's face, he hastily interjected: 'I know. They offered *you* the job and not the partnership. How much are they paying?'

'Forty dollars a week!' said Walt Disney, trying to keep the wonder out of his voice.

'Why, it's a fortune!' exclaimed Iwerks. He was silent for a long time while he struggled with his emotions, and then he burst out: 'You just have to take it, Walt. There will never be another opportunity like it!'

'But what about you – about *us*?' said Walt, doubtfully.

'Why, I can always go on running Iwerks & Disney on my own,' Iwerks said. He looked anxiously at Walt. 'Provided you'll turn the assets over to me, of course, and let me carry on with the firm – and the name.'

It was what Walt had been going to suggest as the solution, and he was relieved that it was his partner who had proposed it. In the end, it was arranged that all the good will and assets of Iwerks & Disney would be transferred from their joint names to that of Ub Iwerks alone. Only the air-brushing equipment, which Walt had purchased personally and still owed money on, was sold to Iwerks on an instalment basis. They shook hands on the deal. Then, not looking at each other, wished each other luck in their future ventures.

Any feelings of guilt Walt Disney might have had over his desertion of Ub Iwerks were soon dissipated. He was suddenly conscious of a lift in his spirits, and he knew it had as much to do with the break in the partnership as with excitement over his new job. It was as if responsibility for his erstwhile partner's welfare had been a troublesome burden from which he was now free. He was quite sincere later when he swore he always loved Ub like a brother and admired his talents tremendously, no matter what subsequently passed between them. But there was no denying the fact that Ub was a problem when he was around, and Walt had not only played tricks on him but worried about him too. But no longer.

'Don't think I won't miss Ub, worry about him, feel I have to keep an eye on the guy and make sure he isn't in trouble,' he later confessed to his brother Roy. 'But for the moment I'm darned glad to be rid of him. And frankly I don't care if I ever work with him or worry about him again.'

But if he truly believed Ub Iwerks had disappeared from his life, he was mistaken. He would be back, as brooding, resentful and burdensome as ever.

Chapter 5

AN ANIMATED LIFE

In the spring of 1920, Roy went down with a bout of influenza and was so seriously ill it was decided to transfer him to hospital. His recovery was slow and painful and the doctors confessed they were worried about him. He went back to work in the bank, but it was obvious he was not getting any better, and when he and Edna came back to Roy's quarters now, Walt could hear them muttering together urgently, as if they had something other than 'canoodling' on their minds.

Frequently he caught his own name being mentioned and once he overheard Edna whispering fiercely: 'But he'll soon be a grown man! You can't look after him all his life!'

At which Roy whispered back: 'But he's family! I feel responsible.' As indeed he did, and the knowledge of it did nothing to help his physical recovery.

One day he went to a local surgeon for a cut-price tonsillectomy and collapsed on the way home. He was rushed to hospital where they cured the haemorrhage but discovered a patch on his lungs, and told him he had a serious case of tuberculosis. He was advised to leave Kansas City right away for a drier, warmer climate.

It is a measure of Roy Disney's regard for his brother that while he worried about what effect the news of his condition would have on his fiancée, he was almost equally concerned about what it could do to Walt. How would the kid manage if he was left to fend for himself?

It was true his eldest brother, Herbert, would still be around with his family. But Herbert was too wrapped up in his own affairs to keep a benevolent eye on Walt and besides, Roy knew both Herb and his wife objected to the boy's breezy manner and rather patronizing attitude towards them; if they sensed he had any special qualities, they resented rather than appreciated them. What he had to do, Roy decided, was to make sure that Walt was safely settled in a good job before his own physical crisis came to a head. So in his spare time, aware that his health was deteriorating, he worked on his younger brother's future security. Finally he came up with a touching, if ironic, gesture: he succeeded at last in procuring for Walt the offer of a job as a cartoonist in the Kansas City *Star* group.

While Walt was toiling in the cramped bathroom of the *Restaurant News*, drawing pictures of glamorous film stars to drum up ads for local bistros, as well as slogging around the city's printers in search of contracts for himself and Ub Iwerks, the ailing Roy had gone through the lists of the bank's customers and set his sights on any of them who worked for the *Star* group. One by one he cultivated them, simply in order to show off his brother's drawings and sing his praises as a potential newspaper illustrator.

Early in 1920 his efforts were rewarded when a call came from one of the editors of the *Star*'s morning paper, the *Times*, to say a cartoonist was leaving, and if Walt was ready to start the following week, there was a job for him as an assistant. But this happened about a month after Walt had been working at the Film Ad Company, and his outlook had changed radically.

Absorbed in his new work, Walt was hardly aware of the tremendous effort his brother had been making on his behalf. So he had no compunction in saying flatly that he was no longer interested in a newspaper job. 'Of course I'm not going to take it!' he said bluntly. 'It's too late. They had their chance months ago when we offered my services, and they kicked us out.'

The strength of Roy Disney's affection was such that he showed not the slightest resentment at Walt's rough rejection of what his brother considered a tremendous opportunity. And Walt's tone of voice was enough to convince him he really needn't have worried, after all. His kid brother had found his niche.

Walt Disney went to the movies at least five times a week and, unlike most young men of his age, it was not simply to drool over sirens like Mae Murray or Betty Blythe or Nazimova, but to study the short films which were an integral part of the programme in those days. He was an admirer of the Hollywood comics who figured regularly in the short-feature programmes: Charlie Chaplin, Buster Keaton, Ben Turpin and the antics of the Keystone Cops. He watched their techniques closely, scrawling notes in the dark about their facial expressions, body language and the methods they used in the construction of their gags. But he was particularly interested in the animated cartoon shorts which were becoming a popular feature of cinema programmes at the time. He was both fascinated by and dissatisfied with them, and was already convinced that he could do better himself.

Thanks to Ub Iwerks, who had lent him books about art and the cinema, he had taken to patronizing the Kansas City public library where he read every book and magazine article about cartooning and cinematic animation he could lay his hands on. Not that there was much material available at the time. But he did discover that the idea of putting animated drawings on the cinema screen had attracted artists and illustrators from the earliest days of the movies, and names like Georges Méliès and Winsor McKay began to figure largely in his consciousness and his conversation.

Méliès was a French magician and illusionist who had made a short film, using live actors and sketched backgrounds, called *Trip to the Moon* in 1902. McKay had been one of the great newspaper cartoonists of his day, principal cartoonist for the *New York Herald*. He had fallen in love with the movies when he saw an early work of Thomas Edison, starring D. W. Griffith, called *Rescued from an Eagle's Nest*, and felt that many of its amateurish flying sequences could have been vastly improved by graphic animation.

McKay had begun experimenting by making his own animated cartoon films using animal characters, and they were remarkably life-like in appearance – so much so that, after their first public showing, critics accused him of tracing his cartoon characters from photographs. To demonstrate how wrong they were, he invented a character called Gertie the Dinosaur. Quite fortuitously, McKay gave Gertie something which had been missing from his previous cartoon animals, and from other animated films. To stress Gertie's originality, both as a drawing and as a personality, he gave her a character of her own; she smiled seraphically when she sniffed (and then ate) spring flowers on a hillside; she writhed, danced and opened her great mouth to sing; she cringed when she accidentally trod on a friendly mouse and wept, tears rolling down her pendulous cheeks, when she surveyed the tiny animal's broken body.

It was the first time anyone had given a personality to a cartoon character, and if Gertie had been anything but a great mountain of an animal, she might have caught on with the public. But no one was interested in the antics of a dinosaur, even one with feelings, and Gertie died at the box-office.

McKay laboured on for the next ten years but, by 1921, found himself no longer able to afford his animated cartoons, nor could he persuade anyone in the film world to finance his work. He went back to salaried cartooning with the *New York Herald*. His early work was forgotten until movie researchers discovered it and marvelled at his technique fifty years later. Ub Iwerks had caught one of the Gertie the Dinosaur films in a small downtown movie house and raved about it to Walt when they were still working together at *Restaurant News*. But when he dragged Walt back to the cinema to see it, the cartoon had already been taken off, and one of the popular Felix the Cat series had been substituted. Felix the Cat was the invention of an illustrator-animator named Pat Sullivan (with Otto Messmer), and, as Iwerks pointed out, it had no personality of its own but relied entirely on action, situation and fast-moving gags to give it character. The two young men spent hours dreaming up characters for animated cartoons of their own. What they envisioned was a cartoon animal who would become as real to anyone watching it on the screen as humans like Chaplin, Turpin or Larry Semon. After all, Walt pointed out, human or not, these comedians were only celluloid characters too. Why couldn't he and Ub create an animated cartoon animal whose appearance and foibles would be appreciated in the same way as Chaplin's moustache, winsome smile, battered bowler, cane and funny walk – remembered not simply for its gags and unlikely situations but for its personality?

Convinced this was the way ahead for any newcomer to animated cartooning, Walt openly scoffed at the creations featured on the screen. One of the particular objects of his contempt was the most popular animation series of the day, Max Fleischer's 'Out of the Inkwell'. Walt maintained that the Inkwell characters, no matter how ingeniously they were drawn, were forgotten moments after they spilled on to the screen because Fleischer never thought of them as anything but quaint creatures involved in comic situations.

However, for the moment, it was mostly talk. Involved as he was in his new job at the Film Ad Company, Walt did not have the time to do much creating. In any case, he was too busy completing his education in the basic skills and techniques of animated cartooning.

The Film Ad Company derived most of its income from publicity shorts for local shops and businesses. The clips lasted anything from thirty seconds to two minutes and were shown in local movie houses between the short subjects and the main feature. Most of them used animated characters, but the technique was old-fashioned even for the twenties. Walt and the other artists (there was a staff of sixteen) drew animal and human characters which were then pasted on to cardboard and painstakingly cut out and fixed to a drawing board, with their legs, arms and bodies separated and pinned so they could be moved. A cameraman photographed the cut-outs in stop-motion, then moved the limbs and body and photographed them again and again, so that when projected the series of pictures gave the impression of motion.

Even a beginner like Walt Disney knew that in New York and other big movie-making centres, they had already gone beyond these techniques and were using drawings instead of cut-outs. In Kansas City public library he had found two books which now became his teachers: one was a volume by Carl Lutz on the art of animation; the other was a book of stop-and-go photographs taken by Eadweard Muybridge of animal and human motion. After poring over the text and the illustrations, Walt began making a succession of drawings in which the characters fractionally changed (or 'moved') in each different frame, and could be photographed in stop-motion without being cut out and clumsily manoeuvred on the drawing board. When projected on the screen the movements appeared much smoother and more realistic, and would be even more so, Walt decided, if he increased the quality of the technique and the number of drawings.

Walt Disney was always realistic and honest with himself about his own talents, and he was aware his drawings had more flair than polish. So far as draughtsmanship was concerned, he knew there were many others – Ub Iwerks, for instance – who could surpass him in quality. So although his employers were impressed with the results of his experiments, he was dissatisfied. He knew he did not have the patience to complete sufficient drawings to eliminate all jerkiness from the projected images, nor did he have the expertise to make the movements of the characters in each frame blend smoothly with the next. He needed and badly missed the technical help which had always been at hand when he and Ub Iwerks had worked together. So he was pleased, if hardly surprised, when he came back to his rooms one night in 1920 and found Iwerks forlornly waiting for him on the doorstep.

With shamed apologies, Ub confessed that the firm of Iwerks & Disney was on the verge of bankruptcy. Since he had assumed sole direction of the company, his lack of ideas and salesmanship, his timidity and ignorance of business know-how, had brought the company to a standstill. A once thriving enterprise was on the verge of disaster – and once more he had come to Walt, the man he both loved and resented, to plead with him to save him from ruin.

Walt made a few inquiries and quickly came to the conclusion that Iwerks & Disney was beyond saving. He advised Ub to start bankruptcy proceedings without delay and not to worry.

Walt had by this time acquired enough prestige with his new employers to be able to ask them to hire his erstwhile partner, and so Ub Iwerks came into his life again – at a crucial moment in his professional career. Henceforward, it was Walt Disney who provided the rough drawings and brilliant ideas at the Film Ad Company and Ub Iwerks who took them in hand and smoothly executed them.

They resumed their close collaboration, but Ub Iwerks was, if anything, more sensitive than ever to slights, more vulnerable to assaults on his *amour propre*, while Walt Disney, now twenty years old, had grown into a bouncy and self-confident young man. Though never deliberately cruel, he could be thoughtless and never seemed to understand the weaknesses and hidden resentments of his friend.

Walt's salary was now 60 dollars a week, which was enough in the Kansas City of those days to finance a life-style of some affluence for an unattached young man. He patronized the best tailors in town and became a flashy dresser, with sharp suits and bright bow ties. He was seen in the best restaurants, and his name figured in the society columns among those who went to charity fancy-dress balls. He was even photographed at one such party doing rope-tricks dressed in cowboy costume complete with ten-gallon hat.

He was still as much of a practical joker as ever. He was never vindictive about it, as some famous practical jokers of the time – the name of Alfred Hitchcock comes to mind – could be. Nor did he get a kick out of making people feel humiliated or inferior, as Charles Lindbergh, for instance, used to. It was just that he was always unable to resist an easy mark. And Ub was still an easy mark. Fortunately, most of the tricks he played on him were harmless enough and easily forgotten. For instance, he would lock Ub in the office toilet until he was forced to hammer on the door to be freed by one of the girls Walt had let in on the joke. He sent him saucy postcards at the office signed 'Lulu' or 'Fifi', because he knew he was terribly embarrassed about girls. But sometimes his thoughtlessness caused pain – and, as it turned out, a deep determination to get even.

Ub was quite hopeless with girls. There was a pretty girl in the office named Margaret Metzinger whom he adored, but he was far too shy to ask her for a date. Actually, Margaret had a crush on Walt, which he did not reciprocate. So one night he persuaded her to meet him in a downtown restaurant and then sent Ub instead. The situation might have caused them only temporary embarrassment had not Walt also persuaded one of the staff cameramen to make a secret film of the rendezvous, with close-ups of their expressions when they realized they had been tricked. Walt screened the film next day in front of the rest of the office. Amid the jeers and laughter, Margaret Metzinger threw a pot of ink over Walt and ruined his jacket. But Ub walked out of the projection room without saying a word, and Walt realized that this time he might have gone too far.

Inevitably, Walt's success and self-confident manner aroused a certain amount of jealousy in other quarters at the Film Ad Company, and one of those who openly resented him was the head of the art department. Aware of Walt's inability to draw life-like human faces, the art director decided to draw his boss's attention to it. He ordered Walt to execute a series of ads for a local hat merchant, insisting that each hat illustrated be drawn with a face beneath it. Walt realized that the art director was setting him up. So he turned in a series of drawings in which each hat was perched on an electric light bulb or an egg, with eyes, nose and mouth crudely but comically sketched in underneath the brim. The art director triumphantly marched into the boss's office to demonstrate Walt's incompetence, and was mortified when the boss laughed out loud and praised the young man's ingenuity. The ads were prominently displayed in the Kansas City papers and drew a lot of favourable comment.

Meanwhile, after only a momentary pang of conscience over his friend's discomfiture, Walt was back at his old habit of teasing Ub Iwerks. He put mice in his pockets, guinea pigs in his desk, and once found an African macaw in a downtown pet shop that talked in Afrikaans, the nearest he could get to Dutch. He smuggled it into Ub's locker, and, when he opened it, the bird came out squawking: *'Dod, waar is de prickel? Scrabble op de beestjes!'* – roughly translatable as 'Death, where is thy sting?' and 'Mount your horses!' He still found his friend an irresistible butt for his jibes and crude schoolboy tricks, and continued to be unaware of how much Ub resented them.

At twenty Walt Disney seethed with energy, ambitions and ideas. He spent every waking hour working out characters and situations for animated cartoons, and the art director began to complain that he was using too much office time and space on his own preoccupations. Walt's reaction was to march into the boss's office and persuade him to lend him one of the agency's cameras, so he could continue his experiments at home.

Roy was getting paler, thinner and sicker every day, but he insisted on helping Walt and Ub rig up a makeshift studio in the garage of

Herbert's house on Bellefontaine. There Walt began making a series of animated shorts. They were slickly made and smartly drawn, and they were funny, but they didn't incorporate any of the new ideas Walt had been discussing with Ub who would have preferred him to do something more original. For the moment Walt needed money and a reputation, and he decided the only way to get them was by playing safe. So in imitation of Max Fleischer's Out of the Inkwell series, he drew a picture of his own hand on the screen sketching comic gags about local situations. The first featured an open car filled with a family out for a Sunday picnic. As it proceeded down Kansas City's main streets, which were full of potholes, it shook itself to pieces. The false teeth of father and mother flew out and did a dance together on the pavement. Kids bounced in the air and fenders, hub-caps and rear wheels came off creating havoc all around them. The condition of Kansas City's streets was notorious.

Walt had no difficulty selling his cartoon to Milton Feld who ran a chain of movie houses in the city known as Newman Theaters. It was such a success and caused so much talk that the city actually got around to voting money for road repairs.

Feld decided that Walt's cartoons would work best as advertising films and contracted for twelve more, which he named Newman's Laugh-O-Grams. It soon became clear that the audiences liked them, too. So did local merchants, who queued up to have Walt do Laugh-O-Grams about their products.

By 1921, Walt felt confident enough to begin introducing some of his new ideas into the cartoons. They demonstrated that his wit and ingenuity more than made up for any shortcomings he might have as a draughtsman. For instance, in subsequent Laugh-O-Grams he never showed the telephone number of a client simply as a set of letters and figures, but gave each letter and number legs and arms, and had them scurrying around and jostling each other for place until he got them in the right order. He did an ad for a company which fitted new tops on open cars, and had a proud purchaser being asked, as he drove a slick-looking vehicle out of the garage: 'New car, old top?' to which he smugly replies: 'No, new top, old car.' For another cartoon, Walt's hand on the screen drew a huge and elaborate birthday cake from which, in a burst of fireworks and flames, the images of Gloria Swanson and Mae Murray spilled out, plus all the other stars of the new films coming to the Newman Theaters.

The bane of a moviegoer's life in those days was the sound of other members of the audience reading the subtitles of the silent films out loud. To curb this disturbing habit, Walt invented a crazy professor who was seen on the screen stalking through the audience flattening with a huge mallet anyone caught reading the subtitles out loud.

Soon everyone was talking about Newman's Laugh-O-Grams, and Walt Disney's success was such that, in 1922, he resigned his job with the Film Ad Company and formed his own production company, called, inevitably, Laugh-O-Gram Films, Inc. Lack of business experience on Walt's part prevented his cartoons – even the Laugh-O-Grams he had already finished – from making the profits they deserved. When Milton Feld had first asked him to name a price for his shorts, Walt had asked 30 cents a foot of film, which was exactly what the cartoons cost him to make. It was accepted and he was given a contract for the amount he named. But he had completely forgotten to add a profit margin. The result was that he had no capital to spare when he incorporated his production company and branched out into new ventures. Fortunately, he had already acquired a reputation in Kansas City for his skills and resourcefulness, and a number of local citizens clubbed together to contribute a capital of 15,000 dollars in 250 dollar shares, and with this he was able to put a number of new films into production. He made two seven-minute films, both based on well-known fairytales, one called *Puss in Boots* and the other *Red Riding Hood*. In both of them he used live actors and then added cartoon characters drawn directly on to the film. The live actors were unpaid students who were learning the art of animation at the small school of movie cartooning he had now started in the Bellefontaine garage, and as part of their tuition they were expected to double both as actors and technicians.

The two cartoon shorts did sufficiently well locally to persuade Walt to hire salesmen to sell them nation-wide, and both *Puss in Boots* and *Red Riding Hood* were soon being seen on cinema screens in New York, Chicago and Philadelphia. But none of the salesmen ever came back with receipts from these showings and, by the end of 1922, Laugh-O-Gram Films, Inc. was desperately short of money. Not only were the salesmen withholding the receipts but they were pocketing the profits too, and shareholders in Laugh-O-Gram shied away when they were asked to provide further capital while the situation was straightened out.

All might have been well had Walt had the help of his brother, but Roy had aggravated his lung condition by remaining in Kansas City and towards the end of 1920, army doctors sent him to convalesce at a veterans' hospital in Arizona, and said they were going to keep him there for at least a year.

As a farewell gift to Walt, he paid a year's rent in advance for lodging and use of the garage-studio at Bellefontaine, and he gave him 100 dollars to tide him over emergencies.

Walt went down to the depot to see him off and only the presence of Edna Francis, who was weeping bitterly at her fiancé's departure (Roy's illness had interrupted their marriage plans, and she would have to wait another five years until they were reunited) prevented him from bursting into tears himself as the train pulled out.

Roy asked his fiancée to keep an eye on Walt, and she faithfully discharged her responsibilities. Edna Francis, in fact, proved to be both tactful and understanding. She often slipped round to Walt's lodgings to do his laundry, to make sure his bed sheets were changed regularly and he had food in his larder. But motherly and attentive though she proved to be, he still missed Roy badly. His brother had come to mean much more to him than Elias, and he would always regard Roy as his real father. He couldn't bear to think that Roy might not recover. From the moment he departed for Arizona, he began bombarding him with 'get well' cards, and Roy wrote back to him almost every day.

By 1923 Walt was desperate because everything was going wrong. He felt the only chance he had to restore his fortunes was to risk everything. So he pooled his resources and managed to raise enough cash to tackle his most ambitious venture so far. It was a film called *Alice's Wonderland*, which was based on the Lewis Carroll character and used a real-life Alice – a six-year-old moppet with blonde corkscrew curls – whom he surrounded with animated cartoon animals. He drew them with the help of Ub Iwerks and a small band of student-animators. Walt was convinced the successful launch of Alice would save him from disaster but, worthy though the production proved to be, it came too late to save Laugh-O-Gram Films, Inc. from ruin. There were too many creditors, and they were closing in. Only one of the original shareholders still had faith in him and continued to send a weekly cheque for a modest sum which helped to keep some of the creditors at bay.

From his convalescent hospital, first in Arizona, then in West Los Angeles, Roy kept mailing blank cheques to his young brother telling him to 'fill them up for any sum you like up to 30 dollars'. They were welcome, but they were not enough to pay off the debts, nor enough to keep Walt in lodgings and food.

Trouble, in fact, was now coming at him from all directions. Herbert, who still worked for the post office, had been transferred to Portland, Oregon, and departed with his family. Elias and Flora Disney then arrived to take up residence again. Following the collapse of the jelly factory in Chicago in which Elias had invested all his money, his father was now looking around for a carpentry job. When he failed to find one, he put the Bellefontaine house on the market, told his son he would have to find other accommodation, and departed for Oregon to join his eldest son.

Walt no longer had a bed or a studio. He found himself a small downtown office into which he crammed his camera and equipment, and dossed down in a chair or on the floor at night. Once a week he went down to Union Station where, for a dime, he got a towel, soap and the use of the depot's bathing facilities. The cartoon school had long since collapsed along with all his other ventures, and the students had departed. Ub Iwerks, who had worked without salary when business turned sour, had used up his savings and reluctantly gone back to work at the Film Ad Company. He sometimes lent Walt a couch at his own lodgings when his erstwhile associate could no longer bear the hardness of the office floor. But Ub, who was owed 1,000 dollars in back wages by Laugh-O-Gram, needed every dime he could lay his hands on. He was still keeping his family and had no money to spare for Walt.

'It was probably the blackest time of my life,' Walt said later. 'I really knew what hardship and hunger were like. I remember a couple of Greeks who ran a restaurant below my office gave me credit to run up food bills for a time, but even they grew hard-hearted in the end and though they never really let me starve, they always made sure I got the cheapest food in the house and fed me on left-overs. It was a pretty lonely and miserable time of my life.'

Another recollection of what it was like was later provided by a local dentist, Dr Thomas McCrum, who had seen some of the Laugh-O-Grams in the Newman Theaters and thought that Walt could make a cartoon film for the Kansas City Dental Institute, teaching young people how to take care of their teeth. He went to see Walt at his downtown office and was surprised at the seediness of the surroundings. There was a half-eaten can of corned beef with a jack-knife in it on the desk, and no staff visible. Walt told the dentist an animated cartoon could be made for around 500 dollars and Dr McCrum said he would go back to consult his colleagues at the institute. A few nights later he telephoned to tell Walt the project had been approved, and if he would come round to his surgery he could sign the contract and be handed the money.

There was a long pause, and then Walt said: 'I can't come. I haven't any shoes. They were falling apart and I left them with the shoe-mender round the corner, and I don't have the dollar and a half to collect them.'

'Stay where you are,' said Dr McCrum, 'I'll be right over.' He paid for and picked up Walt's shoes and arrived with them thirty minutes later. Then they drove back to the dentist's office, where they signed the deal for the film. Walt made it single-handedly and called it *Tommy Tucker's Tooth*. In McCrum's words it was 'a little comic gem. The kids loved it.' He added: 'Later on, when I met Walt again in Hollywood, I said that must have been the worst moment of his life, having to eat corned beef out of a can. Walt shook his head vigorously. "Oh, no," he said. "I'm nuts about corned beef." '

Tommy Tucker's Tooth notwithstanding, it was obvious that it would not be long before Laugh-O-Gram – or Walt – collapsed entirely.

Roy Disney wrote from Los Angeles: 'Call it quits, kid. You can't do anything more than you've already done.'

Walt filed for bankruptcy in the spring of 1923, and persuaded his creditors to allow him to hold on to his camera and to a copy of *Alice's Wonderland* which he intended to use as a sample for soliciting future work. But all his other equipment and the few tangible assets he possessed were seized. He wrote his brother that a local Kansas City moviemaker had offered him a job making animated cartoons, but he had decided to make a completely fresh start and planned to leave for either New York or Hollywood. Roy wired him to come out West.

In order to pay off his personal debts and raise the money for his fare, he got himself a job as a stringer for the Universal and Pathé Newsreel companies, and found it an exhilarating experience. Using the camera his creditors had allowed him to keep, his cap rakishly worn back-to-front and his camera perched on the back of a hired open Ford car, he soon became a well-known figure in the city as he cruised the streets looking for stories. Pathé paid him a bonus for his work, and it was enough to enable him to quit Kansas City. Tired of skimping, desperate for a little luxury, he went down to Union Station and bought himself a first-class one-way ticket to Los Angeles. He wore a check jacket, blue trousers, a bright red bow tie, and he carried a small suitcase with two spare shirts and a spare set of underwear.

Ub Iwerks and Edna Francis came to see him off, and they all wept as the train pulled out, Walt included. He was convinced he was going out of their lives for ever, and for the moment, at least, it seemed a devastating thought. Then he cheered up. It was July 1923. He was twenty-two years old and had 50 dollars in his pocket, plus his camera. By the time the train had picked up speed and was flying across the flat Kansas plain, life was full of promise again. He had California to look forward to, and a new world to conquer.

Part Two

OF RABBITS
AND MICE

Chapter 6

NEW WORLD

WALT was fortunate in having an uncle, Robert Disney, who had retired to Los Angeles after a successful career in mining. He lived with his second wife, Charlotte, in a house on Kingswell Street in Edendale and, since he had always been close to Elias, he felt an obligation to do what he could for his brother's sons. He and Charlotte regularly visited Roy Disney in the Sawtelle Veterans Hospital in West Los Angeles, where he was still convalescing; and when Walt turned up with his shabby suitcase at Kingswell Street one morning in July 1923, he was taken in without question and given a room.

When Robert asked Walt what he intended to do for a living now that he was in California, the young man loftily replied: 'I'm going to direct films.'

He explained to Roy when they celebrated their reunion at Sawtelle the following day that he had decided to abandon his career as a maker of animated cartoons. For one thing, he had no staff and had lost his equipment. Besides, all the newest techniques in cartoon films were being developed in New York, which was the heart of the industry. Hollywood was too preoccupied with filming live action epics, and had neither experts nor interest in animation. In any case, he had developed new interests. Working as a newsreel-cameraman in Kansas City had given him a taste for making pictures about human beings. He proposed to look around and then start visiting the studios to offer his talents and ideas to the Hollywood moguls.

Roy, always prudent, warned Walt that directing jobs in Hollywood were not all that easy to come by, even for bright kids, and counselled him not to throw away the experience as an animator he had so painfully accumulated in Kansas City. But after a time he realized that Walt had made up his mind. He told Walt that the government was now paying him a pension of 85 dollars a month, of which he was saving over half, and promised to be good for a loan when Walt's 50 dollars ran out.

Of Rabbits and Mice

The early twenties were good days in Hollywood. The movie industry was booming and bustling with new stars and talent, and the film city was still small and parochial enough for its most famous personalities to be unafraid of mixing with ordinary people. A star-struck newcomer who strolled along Hollywood Boulevard on a Sunday morning could be sure of catching a glimpse of celebrities such as Ramon Novarro, Adolphe Menjou, Mae Murray or Clara Bow on their way to a rendezvous at one of the nearby restaurants. Everyone from Lionel Barrymore to Zasu Pitts and Slim Summerville came out on their free weekends to show themselves off. But for Walt Disney, who seemed impervious to the beauty and sex-appeal of famous female stars – and of beefy male stars too – the magnet that drew him into Hollywood at the weekends was the possibility that he might sight one of the film colony's great comedians.

He had hovered in vain outside Charlie Chaplin's studio, hoping to catch him as he came out at the end of the day, only to be taken by his uncle and aunt to Musso's Restaurant on Hollywood Boulevard for Sunday brunch, where he found himself sitting at the next table to the great man himself. For once, he was overawed and did not dare ask for an autograph, but it was an experience he continued to savour years after the event. His ambition was to direct comedy films, and one of the first things he did was to go to the studios where the Keystone Cops reigned, after which he went on to the lots where Mack Sennett produced and Harold Lloyd operated, hoping to get inside to watch them at work and then perhaps cajole someone into giving him a job. But at every studio he was refused admittance and told to apply at the employment office, where he was curtly informed there were no jobs going.

He still held on to the press-card Universal had given him when he had worked as a newsreel stringer in Kansas City, and in desperation he used this one day to bluff his way into Universal City and on to the set where Lon Chaney was starring in *The Hunchback of Notre Dame*. But then another watcher, arrogantly surveying the scene from the sidelines, put a monocle to his eye to examine the youngster at his side and decided he didn't belong. Haughtily calling on a couple of crew-members, he demanded Walt's instant removal, and it gave the young man no comfort at all when he discovered later he had been thrown off the set by none other than the great Erich von Stroheim.

It took Walt over a month to use up the remains of his 50 dollar hoard, and he stretched it over another two weeks when he exploited his riding skills and earned eight dollars as a cowboy extra at Warner Brothers. But that was the only money he made, and even his Uncle Robert began to hint that he was wearing out his welcome and that it was time he found himself a place to live and a job. In the meantime, he asked Walt to start paying five dollars a week towards his room and board. That was the moment Walt decided he had been wasting his time, and it would perhaps be wise, despite his qualms, to begin exploiting his know-how as an animator.

He informed both Roy and his uncle, much to their relief, that he was going back to making cartoon films, if necessary even financing himself by making the Laugh-O-Gram type of advertising film he had pioneered in Kansas City. In that case, said his uncle, he could have the use of his garage as a workshop for an extra dollar a week. Roy lent him ten dollars to get himself some letterheads announcing that 'Walt Disney, Cartoonist' was back in business. And with the new sense of realism hunger always induced in him, he began the well-worn task of peddling his wares and ideas. He didn't have much luck.

In the meantime, he had written to a well-known New York film booker he had met when she visited Kansas City, to let her know that he was still in business. Her name was Margaret Winkler and she had always been an admirer of Walt Disney's work. She had recently written to point out that he had never, as he had once promised, shown her a copy of his last animated feature, *Alice's Wonderland*. He wrote back to her, disingenuously concealing the extent of the disaster he had suffered in Kansas City.

Dear Mrs Winkler,

This is to inform you that I am no longer connected with the Laugh-O-Gram Corporation of Kansas City, Mo., and that I am establishing a studio in Los Angeles for the purpose of producing the new and novel series of cartoons I have previously written you about [a series based on the adventures of the Alice of *Alice's Wonderland*].

The making of these new cartoons necessitates being located in a production center that I may engage trained talent for my casts, and be within reach of the right facilities for producing.

I am taking with me a select number of my former staff and will in a very short time be producing at regular intervals. It is my intention of securing working space with one of the studios, that I may better study technical detail and comedy situations, and combine these with my cartoons . . .

I have written you about *Alice* in the past, but you never did see a copy of it. I send you one now. It remains the property of Laugh-O-Gram Films, Inc. but I have the permission of my successors to let you see it to give you an idea of the characters and situations I propose to use in the new series.

It seems unlikely that Mrs Winkler was ignorant of the fact that Laugh-O-Gram Films, Inc. had gone bankrupt, and that Walt Disney was not being entirely frank about his professional situation. But, working in the film industry, it could scarcely have surprised her.

Mrs Winkler had *Alice* screened and liked what she saw. She already knew Disney's previous work with *Puss in Boots* and *Red Riding Hood*, and recognized that here was someone who might lack expertise but was certainly rich in talent. She sent back a telegram dated 15 October 1923 from New York saying:

BELIEVE SERIES CAN BE PUT OVER BUT PHOTOGRAPHY OF ALICE SHOULD SHOW MORE DETAIL AND BE STEADIER. THIS BEING NEW PRODUCT MUST SPEND LARGE AMOUNT ON EXPLOITATION AND ADVERTISING, THEREFORE NEED YOUR COOPERATION. WILL PAY $1,500 EACH NEGATIVE FOR SIX, AND TO SHOW MY GOOD FAITH WILL PAY FULL AMOUNT ON EACH OF THESE SIX ON DELIVERY OF NEGATIVE. THIS PROVIDING SAME ALICE AND CAST BE USED. LETTER AND CONTRACT FOLLOW. WINKLER.

Walt Disney opened the telegram in front of his uncle and aunt, let out a whoop of triumph, and dashed from the house without informing them of its contents. He rushed down to the trolley-car and began the long journey out to the veterans' hospital at Sawtelle to let his brother Roy in on the good news.

He badly needed his brother's advice. What should he do now? In his search around Hollywood for openings, he had had an offer from Alexander Pantages, who owned a cinema chain in south-west California, for a series of one-minute reels. Should he take it up? Or should he accept Mrs Winkler's offer and plunge into big-time animation with the Alice project? Together they discussed the pros and cons of the situation. Roy wanted to know if Walt could deliver the Alice films for the price Mrs Winkler was offering.

'For half of that,' said Walt, confidently. 'We'll make 750 dollars profit on every one of the series!'

'*We?*' asked Roy.

'Yes, *we*,' repeated Walt. 'I can't possibly do it unless you come in with me. I need your help, Roy. You've just got to get out of here and join me. Please say you'll do it.'

There was a long pause while Roy tossed and turned in his bed, going over the pros and cons of the situation. He was unable to make up his mind until, according to Walt's later account of that evening, the patient in the next bed rolled over and growled in exasperation: 'Say yes, for Christ's sake, and then we can all get back to sleep!'

Next morning Roy Disney discharged himself from Sawtelle and went to Los Angeles, where Walt had already found a cheap apartment. Roy's doctors had warned him that his tuberculosis was far from cured, and that he must spend most of his time in bed and sleep at least every afternoon. But, in fact, he was never troubled by his illness again, and lived and worked to a lively old age.

There was one big problem. In the contract that presently arrived from Mrs Winkler, what had been suggested in the telegram became a stipulation. In the film the part of Alice was played by a lively six-year-old schoolgirl named Virginia Davis. Mrs Winkler thought she was marvellous and insisted that the same girl be used in the series of six films. Unfortunately, the little girl lived with her parents in Kansas City. How on earth could he get her to California, and what would her parents say if he proposed it?

Roy, now filled with enthusiasm, got in touch with Edna Francis who was still working in the Kansas City bank and waiting faithfully for her fiancé to send for her. Edna was charged with the task of visiting the little girl's parents and persuading them to allow their daughter to come out to California and star in the series at a salary of 100 dollars a month. To Walt's amazement and delight, Edna's depiction of the glamour of California and the potential of Hollywood stardom for their daughter so dazzled Mr and Mrs Davis that they decided to leave Kansas City themselves and accompany Virginia. The family drove to Los Angeles, and Virginia was delivered to Walt at the makeshift studio he had established two doors up from Uncle Robert's house on Kingswell Street.

Meanwhile, Robert Disney had been approached by his nephew for a loan to help set them up in business. He demurred at first, but in the end gave the two brothers 500 dollars and wished them well. With Roy's savings, which amounted to some 300 dollars, this was enough to rent equipment, hire extras, and start rolling.

Their first cartoon, entitled *Alice's Day at Sea*, starred Virginia Davis and a dog that performed cute tricks, and with the embellishment of some animated cartoon characters and backgrounds, it came out looking fresh and funny. Walt did the direction and all the animation himself, aided only by two girls who inked and painted the celluloids for 15 dollars a week. It had cost exactly 750 dollars to make. Walt shipped it to his booker in New York and Mrs Winkler was so pleased with it she sent a telegram saying: 'DAY AT SEA RECEIVED TODAY. SATISFACTORY. MAILING TODAY DRAFT ON LOS ANGELES BANK WITH DETAILED LETTER.' A few days later 1,500 dollars arrived together with a contract for a further six films. Mrs Winkler's only criticism of the first effort was 'unsteady camera work' and the jerkiness of some of the animation.

Walt was only too well aware of these faults and the reasons for them. To save money, he had used the camera he had brought with him from Kansas City and it was not really suitable for studio work. In addition, he had brought in Roy to work the camera, but he did not have the even rhythm of a professional operator, so the pictures were jumpy and sometimes out of synch. So for five dollars a day he rented a studio camera which Roy found easier to use. But then, as rumours of Walt's initial success swept around the makeshift studio, those involved in the series who had accepted 50 cents a day for their services began to feel they might have sold themselves too cheaply. The parents of the child extras used in the film demanded prevailing Hollywood rates for future productions. Then the performing dog used in the first film – Uncle Robert's German shepherd, Peggy – went sick and a professional pet had to be employed and paid for. Moreover, Virginia Davis's father failed to find a job in Los Angeles. He decided to leave Virginia behind with her mother and go back to Kansas City in the family car. Meanwhile, he demanded, and got, accommodation expenses for his daughter and Mrs Davis, plus the doubling of her monthly salary.

All this drained the company's resources, and quickly exhausted any funds they had built up. Once more they needed money, desperately. But who could they tap this time?

Walt tentatively suggested that Roy should approach his fiancée, Edna Francis, since she must have accumulated a little nest-egg over the years in anticipation of her marriage. Indignantly, Roy refused to do any such thing, but Walt wrote to her secretly, begging her to help and pledging her not to say anything to Roy about it. She sent back a cheque for 25 dollars, all she could afford, and it arrived just in time to pay off creditors who were beginning to besiege the studio.

This time they weathered the storm. More help began to come in. Carl Stalling, organist at the Isis Theater in Kansas City, sent 275 dollars. Walt had once made a cartoon film for one of Stalling's sing-alongs, and charged a special low rate; now he wrote reminding the organist of the favour he had done him, and asked for a gesture in return. The money enabled Walt and Roy to finish film number six of their contract.

They had barely wrapped up the project when in walked Mrs Winkler with bad news. She announced that although there had, as yet, been no public showings of the films, sales of the first series of Alice films to the renters had been very disappointing, and she attributed this to the fact that Walt had seemed to lose the fun and fresh quality which had been such a feature of his first film. She said she was doing so badly on the rentals she had decided she did not need the next series. She wanted the contract cancelled there and then. Roy seemed resigned and ready to accept this disastrous news without protest. But not Walt.

'Oh no you don't!' he said to Mrs Winkler. 'We have a contract with you for six more films, and we're sticking with it.'

When Mrs Winkler started to get angry, he went on: 'OK, I know about some of those earlier films. They missed out. We played safe with them – because we were too worried about money to take risks – and I agree that some of them might have been dull and boring. But just you have a look at film number seven, which we've just finished. I've changed my style, and said to hell with playing safe. Because we're now in such a bad way, we don't have anything to lose. Just let me set up the projector and look at the new film. It's a whole new ball game.'

As, indeed, it was.

Number seven of the Alice series (*Alice's Spooky Adventure*) though it still lacked 'flow' in some of its sequences, had all the old originality and sense of fun which Walt had pumped into *Alice's Day at Sea*. In addition, it had expensive production values not usually seen in shorts in those days – and these, Mrs Winkler surmised, were probably the reason why the Disneys had used up the last of their money. But she recognized that they made all the difference to the film. She was so delighted that she was more than willing to keep to her contract and even improve on it a little, if this was what Walt was going to give her. She wrote out a cheque for 2,000 dollars there and then, and departed with the cans of film under her arm.

Back in New York, after receiving number eight of the Alice series, she expressed her satisfaction in an even more tangible way, by offering Walt a contract for a new series of twelve Alice films, after the present series was finished.

'I am very optimistic about the future and believe we have

something here of which we will all be proud,' she wrote, adding that the first public showing of the very first film, *Alice's Day at Sea*, would open in New Jersey, Pennsylvania and Washington, DC, in March 1924, to be followed by *Alice's Spooky Adventure*. In another letter she wrote: 'But do try to get a livelier quality into your cartoon characters. Everyone around here agrees the ideas are brilliant but your execution lacks something.'

Walt Disney knew exactly what she meant. Always aware of his own inadequacies as a draughtsman, and of his tendency to skimp, he had hired the services of a professional animator to help him get out the required number of drawings of the right quality. But first-class animators were still scarce in the cartoon business, and the one he had hired lacked the requisite flair. Walt knew the answer to his problem, but felt uncomfortable even thinking about it: Ub Iwerks. More than ever, he needed Ub's sensitive genius, his patience, persistence and magic sense of line.

Ub was still slogging away for the Film Ad Company in Kansas City, his salary having risen to 50 dollars a week. But Walt hesitated to ask for his help. He felt guilty about Ub. When Laugh-O-Gram Films, Inc. had collapsed, Ub had been owed 1,000 dollars in salary, and though sales of Laugh-O-Gram's assets had since realized enough to reimburse him in part (400 dollars), he was still badly out of pocket and still needed every dime he could earn to keep his family from starvation. How could he possibly appeal to Ub to come out here and help him now, when he couldn't even afford to pay his fare? Even Walt Disney, never a shrinking violet where his own interests were concerned, didn't have the sauce to do it. How could he guarantee to Ub, whose only interest was in job security, that disaster would never confront them again?

Roy Disney knew all about the situation between Walt and Ub, and he urged his brother to forget his scruples and write to Ub about his difficulties. When Walt was still reluctant, Roy wrote the letter in Walt's name, going so far as to suggest that if Ub would make the move to Los Angeles, there was the prospect that he would be offered a partnership in the new company.

Walt subsequently denied such an offer was ever made, and cited the letter (dated 1 June 1924) he wrote back once Ub had expressed interest in making the move:

Everything is going fine with us and I am glad you made up your mind to come out. Boy, you will never regret it – this is the place for you – a real country to work and play in . . .

I can give you a job as artist-cartoonist and etc. with Disney Productions, most of the work would be cartooning. Answer at once when you want to start. The salary is $40 a week. At the present time I have one fellow helping me on the animation and three girls that do the inking etc. while Roy handles the business end.

Ub Iwerks and Walt Disney settled on the 40 dollars a week salary and Disney Brothers Studio (as they were now known) did not even have to pay Ub's expenses from Kansas City, since Mr Davis was coming out to see his wife and daughter, and gave him a lift in his car.

Ub Iwerks's arrival revolutionized the operations of the Disney Studio. Ub was not a great draughtsman, but he had a special feel for animation. The early work was crude, but Ub turned out 600 drawings a day, could stage a whole picture for both layout and attitude, contribute gags, train the new help and, an expert mechanic, could keep the company car running. Ub had not been trained by any experienced animator, and had just picked up what he needed to know as he went along. But he was a genius – with flair and panache.

Walt was delighted to see his old collaborator back with him, for he was genuinely fond of him. But he still did not understand how sensitive and vulnerable Ub really was. To everyone in the studio he always seemed the most gentle and helpful man, ever willing to halt his own work in order to encourage others. And when Walt thumped him on the back, or tripped him up, or directed him to open a cupboard door only to have a bucket of water spill over him, he never complained, while everyone else roared with laughter. He just sighed, sucked in his gut, and went away in silence. 'What a good sport he is!' everyone said, and failed to divine how much he hated the way his boss treated him, and how he longed to get back at Walt Disney for continually making him look like a fool.

There were more ups and downs for the Disney Studio, even after Ub rode in to the rescue. For one thing, Mrs Winkler suddenly remarried, retired from business, and let her new husband take charge of the distributing company. And, like the death of a close adviser, that made a change for the worse. The new head of the agency, Charles Mintz, had never met nor been charmed by the bright and cheerful Walt Disney, as Mrs Winkler had. She had seemed to understand instinctively that the more money Walt could lay his hands on, the more he would pour into his films, for he was a perfectionist who would never cease trying to do better. So she had always made sure he was paid promptly. Her new husband, on the other hand, was a renter of the old school who never paid up until he was all but sued for what he owed. Walt was soon calling him 'Mister Mingy', because he dodged sending the full fee when a film arrived and tried to fob off the brothers with a half payment. The Disney files at Burbank are filled with letters to 'Mister Mingy' from Walt complaining about the late delivery of money they were due.

We need money [he wrote in August 1924]. We have been spending as much as you have been paying us . . . in order to improve them and make them as good as possible, and now that we are receiving only $900.00 from you [in part payment] it puts us 'in a 'ell of a 'ole.' I am not kicking about that, however, I am perfectly willing to sacrifice a profit on this series, in order to put out something good, but I do expect you to show your appreciation by helping us out. As you know, if we haven't the money to spend on them, we will have to skimp, and at this time, it would not be the best thing to do that. So please, for our sake as well as your own, give this more consideration and instead of sending us $900.00, make it the full amount excepting a fair discount which will enable us to pull through this period.

'Mister Mingy' replied pleading poverty because of delay in his own rental receipts, and, perhaps deciding the best defence was offence, launched into a sharp criticism of the latest Alice films because of their lack of comic gags. Back came a hot reply from Walt announcing the delivery of a new film, which, he acidly pointed out, was 'nothing but gags, and the whole story is one gag after another'.

Fortunately, at this juncture the film trade press began reviewing the Alice films and hailed them for their wealth of 'imagination and cleverness'. They described the last one, *Alice and the Cannibals*, as 'a corker'. Either those notices or the influence of Mintz's wife (to whom Walt had, in desperation, written secretly) produced a change in the renter's attitude. At the end of the series he offered a contract for eighteen more Alice films at 1,800 dollars a time plus a share of the profits.

In the next three years, Walt later told his daughter Diane, they averaged a profit of 2,000 dollars a film and at last began accumulating capital. But they were so afraid of new disaster that solvency made no difference to their way of life. They continued to live very frugally in their one-room apartment, and drew out only 35 dollars a week for rent and food. Most of the time, in obedience to medical advice, Roy went home early from the makeshift studio for his afternoon nap, after which he got up and prepared the evening meal for when Walt came home. He was a poor cook, and Walt was always complaining. One night, when Walt yet again pushed his plate to one side in disgust and remarked that he couldn't possibly eat 'this mush', Roy grabbed the plate of stew and poured it over his head. 'That does it,' he cried. 'I'm finished! No more cooking. No more of your goddamned complaints,' and he slammed out of the room.

Next day, Roy Disney sent a telegram to Edna Francis in Kansas City: 'WHAT ARE WE WAITING FOR? WHY DON'T YOU COME OUT HERE AND TIE THE KNOT?'

Edna Francis arrived in Los Angeles with her mother on 7 April 1925, and she and Roy were married on 11 April. The ceremony took place at the home of Uncle Robert Disney at Kingswell Street. Elias and Flora Disney came down from Oregon for the wedding, and Herbert Disney accompanied them. Walt, who had made it up with his brother, was best man. And, at Walt's request, there was one maid of honour: a pretty girl named Lillian Bounds, who had recently come to work for the Disney Studio as an inker at 15 dollars a week.

Chapter 7

RABBIT TRICK

WALT Disney's daughter once described her father as 'a low pressure swain', and it is an accurate assessment of his attitude towards women. Two attractive young women, Margaret Metzinger and Marian Couger, fell in love with him while he was working for the Film Ad Company in Kansas City. Both found him funny, bright, charming and attractive, and made it plain they would have welcomed any amorous approach he might have been inclined to make towards them. They always accepted organized weekend outings (to Swope Park, for instance, a favourite picnic rendezvous for Film Ad Company employees) in the hope that he would be there. He usually was because Walt was a gregarious young man who liked company; but though they repeatedly tried, neither ever succeeded in cutting him off from the others, even temporarily, so that they could make time with him alone. He deftly evaded all their ploys and stayed with 'the gang', and carefully refrained from indicating a preference for one over the other. Even when he went to a charity ball, he usually invited both Margaret and Marian to go as his partners, and though they always accepted, it must have been a frustrating experience for both of them. What they can hardly have failed to realize, in the end, was that his innocent attitude towards them was quite deliberate. That he knew exactly how Margaret Metzinger, for instance, felt about him was shown by the trick he had played on her and Ub Iwerks. It was the reason why she had been so angry and had thrown a pot of ink over him.

No girl who fell for Walt Disney during this period seemed able to swallow the truth about him: that he just wasn't interested in women sexually, and that all he really wanted from the female sex was what he wanted from the male sex too – friendliness and companionship.

In later years, he indicated that the great crush of his life had been Su Pitowski in Chicago in his teens, and that the way she had let him down had practically broken his heart. Actually, it was his pride which had been hurt, but what Su's defection seems to have done was

The house on Tripp Avenue, Chicago, where Walt Disney was born on 5 December 1901. *(© Walt Disney Productions)*

Elias Disney as a young man. *(© Walt Disney Productions)*

Walt's parents, Flora and Elias Disney, photographed in 1913. *(© Walt Disney Productions)*

LEFT: Walt Disney, aged 17, pictured before he left for France with the Red Cross in 1918.

(© *Walt Disney Productions*)

RIGHT: Walt Disney went to France as a Red Cross ambulance driver in the last days of World War I. He had already determined to make his future living as a cartoonist and drew avidly in his spare time. This is one of his illustrated letters home, written in 1919 from Red Cross headquarters at Neufchâteau to former classmates in Chicago.

(© *Walt Disney Productions*)

doing something I very seldom

do "work"... on every once and a while I make

trips with this truck.

Walt Disney sends home a photograph of himself and his truck while serving with the Red Cross in France. *(© Walt Disney Productions)*

Walt Disney, aged 20, in Kansas City. Photo taken before he grew a moustache. *(© Walt Disney Productions)*

A WALT DISNEY COMIC

M.J. WINKLER, DISTRIBUTOR, N.Y.

WINKLER PICTURES

ABOVE: Walt Disney does a sketch for the Alice Comedies after his move to Hollywood in the 1920s. (© *Walt Disney Productions*)

LEFT: Ub Iwerks's poster for one of Walt Disney's original Alice Comedies.

ABOVE RIGHT: In both Kansas City and Hollywood, Walt made a series of short live-action/cartoons with a child actress, Virginia Davis (shown here). But she dropped out and was replaced by Margie Gay. (© *Walt Disney Productions*)

RIGHT: Walt Disney, Margie Gay, and Roy Disney during the shooting of an Alice Comedy live-action/cartoon in Hollywood. (© *Walt Disney Productions*)

FAR RIGHT: Original poster by Hugh Harman and Carmen Maxwell for Oswald, the Lucky Rabbit cartoon.

Roy's wife Edna and Walt's wife Lillian, photographed in the 1920s. They remained close friends and confidantes even when the Disney brothers were quarrelling (usually over money).

(© Walt Disney Productions)

Walt Disney and his wife, Lillian, outside the studio in the 1920s. *(© Walt Disney Productions)*

Roy Disney (left) and Walt pose in an orange grove. *(© Walt Disney Productions)*

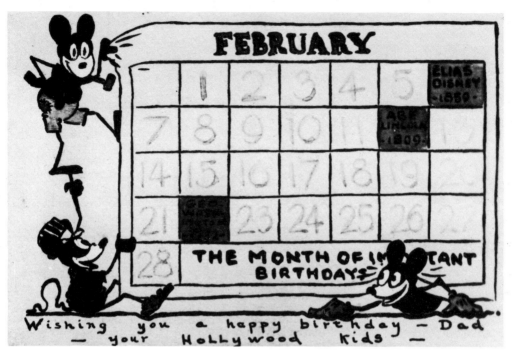

Drawn by Walt, an illustrated birthday greeting for Elias Disney from his two sons in Hollywood. It was sent in the 1920s before they built the new Hyperion studio. *(© Walt Disney Productions)*

In the late twenties and early thirties, Ub Iwerks drew Mickey Mouse with button eyes and 'hosepipe' limbs. Seven years later, Fred Moore gave him a rounded body and eyes that moved.
(© Walt Disney Productions)

Animator Fred Moore, a self-taught artist, first gave Mickey Mouse eyes that moved. He liked to doodle drawings of lightly clad young ladies between studio chores, and the results were widely sought after by his colleagues.
(© Walt Disney Productions)

A sound-syncing session for a new Mickey Mouse short in the 1930s. Walt Disney is second from left. To the right of Mickey is his long-time associate, Ub Iwerks. *(© Walt Disney Productions)*

Leopold Stokowski (with baton) at the Burbank studio during the making of the animated feature *Fantasia* (1940). Walt Disney is next to him, on Stokowski's left. *(© Walt Disney Productions)*

turn him off women because they couldn't be relied on. He proclaimed that a young man was a fool if he married before he was twenty-five years old and only then if he had at least 10,000 dollars in the bank, and it seems likely if Roy had not suddenly decided to wed Edna Francis, he might have happily continued to share bachelor quarters with his brother for many years.

It was not that he hated women. The more beautiful they were the more pleasure he got from admiring them. In California he enjoyed taking a pretty girl to a movie or inviting her back to the apartment he shared with his brother (where, it must be admitted, he and Roy usually inveigled her into cooking the meal), and he was pleased when he was congratulated on the charm and beauty of his female companions. But, he insisted, the female of the species was someone you lived with only when you had achieved financial independence and the wisdom of maturity, and only after your chosen companion knew her place, was willing to cherish and obey you, look after your home, see to your creature comforts, and be a good mother to your children. As far as he was concerned, passion or love did not really come into it.

It is doubtful that he would have considered Lillian Bounds as a potential wife had not Roy's sudden decision to marry acted as a catalyst. Walt was the most undomesticated of young men, he did not cook (not in those days, anyway; he learned later), could not make a bed, and was completely unaware that dust and dirt accumulated in an untended household. He found bachelor life acutely uncomfortable for purely practical reasons, and for a time was seriously tempted to move in with Ub Iwerks. Only the prospect of having to face that moody and lugubrious young man at breakfast every day restrained him. Life with Lillian Bounds, who was pretty, intelligent and cheerful, was certainly preferable.

Lillian Bounds originally came from Lewiston, Idaho. She had arrived in Los Angeles to visit her married sister who lived in Edendale. While there she made the acquaintance of a neighbour, who worked for the Disney Studio as an 'ink girl' – she had the tricky job of copying the animators' drawings with ink and paint on to the actual celluloid of the film.

Lillian, who liked California and wanted to stay, asked her if there were any jobs going and was told to apply to the 'ink' department at Disney, where there was a vacancy. She was taken on at the prevailing wage of 15 dollars a week and quickly learned the painstaking routine of 'inking' the celluloid, a tedious and eye-aching job, since sixteen frames of celluloid had to be inked and painted for every single movement of a cartoon character. But she soon grew to like the work and was beguiled by the atmosphere of the Disney studio, the friendliness of the animators, the willingness of everyone to work hard and stay late, and, particularly, the lack of stiffness and protocol in the attitude of the two Disney brothers.

Her friend had warned her not to try to marry herself off to either of them, since they were confirmed and determined bachelors, but after Roy confounded everyone by his sudden decision to marry Edna, Lillian found herself regarding Walt with new speculation. She found him an immensely attractive and personable young man, even if she thought the moustache he was growing at the time – in an attempt to make himself look older – highly unsuitable, and the stained and shabby clothes he invariably wore hardly respectable attire for the head of a film studio. Except for a friendly wave of the hand, he never seemed to take much notice of the girls in the ink department, but sometimes, on late or rainy nights, he would give her friend and her a lift home in his old Ford jalopy. Once during one of these rides she plucked up the courage to ask him what he looked like in a tie and suit, and he laughed and replied that he didn't have either – what he was wearing were the only clothes he possessed. Shortly after that, he came into the ink department one night when Lillian was the only girl working late and said he would give her a lift home. She became acutely aware that he was hanging around the office staring thoughtfully at her, and presently she felt him coming up behind her. Suddenly he leaned over and kissed her on the back of her neck. She was startled and pretended not to notice, though she remembered she was blushing furiously.

When he left her on her doorstep a little later, he suddenly blurted out: 'If I went out and bought myself a suit, would you invite me inside to meet your sister?'

'You can come in now, if you like,' Lillian said. 'My sister won't mind.'

But he refused and, as if nothing unusual had happened between them, got back in his car, waved his hand, and drove away. Next day, he went to Roy and asked him for 40 dollars out of the money reserves his brother guarded for both of them and for the studio. Roy was always reluctant to part with any of their savings, even now they were beginning to be in the money.

'What do you want 40 dollars for?' he asked, suspiciously.

'I want it to buy a suit,' said Walt.

'A suit! For God's sake, what do you want a suit for?'

Walt took a deep breath. 'To get married in,' he said.

Not that he had even proposed to Lillian yet, though she was, by now, aware he was becoming increasingly attracted to her. Somehow he did not seem to be able to make up his mind about her, even though, now correctly besuited, he frequently went to supper at the home of Lillian's sister.

Lillian thought he looked so smart in his new light-blue outfit that, on one occasion, she commented that now he wore it he made his old Ford car seem even shabbier than when he had driven around in it wearing his old clothes. He was silent for the rest of the outing and seemed preoccupied when he finally kissed her a chaste goodnight.

Next night, he drove her out to a cinema at Riverside, and when they were on their way home, he burst out impulsively: 'You're right about this car, and I know it's time I bought a new one. But I know you're a practical girl, Lilly. So tell me, which would you rather have me buy – a new car for both of us or an engagement ring for you?'

'An engagement ring,' said Lillian, without hesitation.

Lillian told her daughter many years later, 'He seemed quite disappointed I didn't let him buy the car.'

She was more than satisfied, however, with the ring he bought and still cherishes it. It is a three-quarter carat diamond in a basket, surrounded by blue sapphires, and it was Roy Disney who found it. He knew a jeweller in downtown Los Angeles who was reputed to specialize in bargain (stolen?) jewellery and he took Walt to see him.

The jeweller drew the two young men conspiratorially into the back of his shop and brought out of a drawer a ring with a stone in it 'which looked like a locomotive headlight to me', Walt said later. He thought it was 'so fancy' he was attracted to it at once and asked its price. When they learned it was 75 dollars Roy became very interested in a tray of smaller stones for 35 dollars, but to Walt they seemed cheap and mean. He was determined to have the 'locomotive headlight'. Dragging Roy to one side he vehemently whispered that he had to have the ring because it was a bargain, insisting no one would ever be able to buy such a marvellous ring for less. At which point the jeweller told them they could have it for 70 dollars.

'It's a deal!' cried Roy, unable to resist a bargain.

Lillian's brother was fire-chief of Lewiston, Idaho, and it was in his home, in the presence of her widowed mother, that she and Walt were married on 13 July 1925.

They had made arrangements to spend their honeymoon sailing

aboard the coastal steamer, *H. E. Alexander*, from Seattle to Long Beach, California, and their wedding night was spent aboard the Lewiston-Seattle express. It was not quite what Lilly had expected, for Walt was suddenly stricken with a violent toothache and passed the night not with his new bride but helping the Pullman porter to polish the passengers' shoes. He explained to her it helped him forget his pain. The infected tooth was pulled out in Seattle, but he spent the next few days, including a trip to Mount Rainier, with a scarf wrapped round his face, 'looking like a bear and just as grumpy as one', as Lilly said later. But once they were on board ship, the sun and sea breezes seemed to cure everything, and Lillian was soon writing home to her mother that Walt was 'sweet' and she was 'divinely happy'.

Just before leaving for Idaho to marry Lilly, Walt had made what then seemed to him an even bigger decision. He and Roy had withdrawn 400 dollars out of their joint bank account and put it down as part payment on a new studio they planned to build at 2719 Hyperion Avenue, in the Silver Lake district of Los Angeles. Lilly had her eye on a house in the same area the moment they could afford the down payment, but for the moment the newly-wedded couple arranged to rent a one-room apartment with kitchen facilities for 40 dollars a month, and Roy agreed that now that Walt was a married man he should increase his weekly stipend to 40 dollars a week. Out of this modest salary Lilly received ten dollars a week housekeeping allowance, and another 30 dollars a month went on paying instalments on furniture for the apartment – plus a new car, because Lilly, remembering Walt's disappointment, had persuaded her new husband he needed a replacement, after all.

Marriage seemed to make a change in Walt Disney's relations with his brother. From the moment he came back from his honeymoon, he began relying less and less upon Roy's advice and judgement about production matters, though he still left his brother in complete charge of the company's finances.

One evidence of his new-found independence was his decision, once they moved into the new Hyperion Avenue studios, to change the name of the operation from Disney Brothers Studio to the Walt Disney Studio, and he made it plain to everyone, including Roy, that from now on he was in charge of the show.

In his dealings with the distributor, Charles Mintz, the note of subservience disappeared from his correspondence and acerbity crept in. This was principally because of Mintz's increasing dilatoriness in making payments for the Alice films Walt went on delivering. Mintz had altered the method of payment and now had the money delivered personally to the studio by his brother-in-law, George Winkler, whom he had appointed his Hollywood representative. Winkler was almost always late in arriving with the badly-needed cash and sometimes did not turn up at all. At the beginning of October 1925, Walt made his exasperation plain in a letter to Mintz:

It is my intention to live up to my contract and I expect you to do the same. I intend to continue shipping pictures to you as fast as completed, which is about every sixteen days. I will expect you to take them as delivered and remit immediately. Your failure to do so will constitute a breach of contract and will force me to seek other distributors.

Mintz did not take the rebuke lying down: 'Haven't you a single spark of appreciation in your whole soul?' he wrote back. 'You should be whole-heartedly ashamed of yourself.' He went on to criticize the appeal of recent Alice films and claimed their popularity was decreasing with both renters and paying public. Walt was honest enough to realize that he might have a point, even though, for the moment, he believed the improved quality of the animation and production values more than made up for their lack of freshness and humour. But he was aware that the Alice series had suffered a blow from the loss of winsome and attractive Virginia Davis. Virginia's parents, tempted by offers from other Hollywood movie producers, had decided that their daughter had a big future as a child star with the major studios, and had refused to sign a new contract with Disney. Both sides lost from this decision. Virginia's new career quickly petered out. Margie Gay, the simpering little girl Walt enrolled as a substitute, lacked her warm, innocent appeal and forced him more and more to rely upon the cartoon characters with which he surrounded her, particularly an eccentric animal he called Julius the Cat.

The Alice series was flagging, there was no doubt about that. And when the question of a new contract came up, Mintz's offer was considerably below what he had been paying in the past.

'This may seem a little hard on you,' Mintz wrote, 'but before making any definite decision I would advise you to digest this letter thoroughly, talk it over with Roy and your uncle or whomever you wish, and don't make any hasty decisions.' Walt talked it over with no one. He hastily sent back a counter-proposal asking for more money 'in view of increased production values', to which Mintz replied: 'If you think this is a fair offer, you have another think coming.'

Upon receipt of this communication, Walt sent an angry telegram:

MY OFFER IS THE LIMIT I CAN GO. YOUR OFFERS ARE ALL UNACCEPTABLE TO ME. THEREFORE UPON THE DELIVERY OF THE NEXT SUBJECT THE FINAL OF THE 1925 SERIES I WILL CONSIDER ALL MY CONTRACTUAL OBLIGATIONS FULFILLED.

The quarrel was patched up eventually and a new agreement signed, but everyone sensed Alice's appeal was slipping. Even Walt, who remained stubbornly convinced the series had not yet worn out its welcome, was stunned when Mintz's wife (the former Margaret Winkler), who had always been the young man's most sympathetic supporter, secretly wrote to advise him to look for a new subject for a series. She was tactful enough not to make it plain what she thought about the talents of the new Alice, but she did suggest that it was time he began thinking of an all-cartoon film, since the public were growing tired of 'live' actresses 'who have so much less animation than the creatures of your marvelous imagination'.

In the autumn of 1926 Mintz came to Hollywood, bringing his wife with him. A few days later Margaret Mintz turned up at the Hyperion Avenue studio. Walt was delighted to see her and they spent a pleasant afternoon together. He showed her over the new studio, a neat and spacious one-storey complex, and she was amused to find him so boyishly proud of the fact that for the first time in his life he had his very own office space and bathroom facilities. She looked around and said the office was missing only one thing, and that was a desk. To which he replied that he didn't like desks, and pointed to a low table by the window.

'That's what I use,' he said. 'It puts me on the same level with kids when they come in to see me, and adults with a grievance find themselves looking down at me, and it makes them feel better at once. Desks seem to intimidate people and give those who sit behind them a false sense of grandeur.'

He took her into the adjacent building to say hello to Roy Disney and Ub Iwerks and introduced her to his team of animators (who now had a spacious studio to themselves). She then suggested they go back to his office for a talk, and revealed the real purpose of her visit. She told him that she and her husband had spent the morning out at Universal City conferring with Carl Laemmle, the head of Universal Pictures. Laemmle had informed them he was in the market for a new cartoon series which he wanted to distribute through his cinema chain, and had asked the Mintzes for suggestions. When Charlie Mintz mentioned he was thinking about a new series of Alice films from Walt Disney, Laemmle had dismissed them with the savage comment: 'Out of date crap.' The novelty of live actors with cartoon characters had worn off, Laemmle said, and what movie audiences wanted now was some sort of series starring a zany animated animal who got into all kinds of crazy and comic situations.

'What sort of animal?' Margaret Mintz had asked.

'How about a rabbit?' said Laemmle. 'A lovable ball of fluff – but with brains, guile and mischief.'

Margaret Mintz had then persuaded her husband that a cartoon rabbit was just the sort of character Walt Disney would be able to develop. Looking Walt straight in the face, she asked him if he would be prepared to phase out the Alice series and substitute one starring a zany rabbit. Of all the women in the world, Walt considered Margaret Winkler Mintz his friend and felt he could trust her. She was lively, intelligent, and he admired her judgement. For her he was ready to try anything.

In a sudden rush of enthusiasm, he went across to his low table, grabbed some paper and began a series of sketches. A few minutes later he had already roughed out half a dozen drawings of a long-eared, pointy-nosed animal with a twitchy white tail and a saucy, knowing grin, dodging dogs and ferrets, diving down rabbit-warrens, sailing over hedgerows, stealing rides from birds.

Margaret was delighted and bore off the sketches in triumph to her husband, who said he would take them along for Carl Laemmle's inspection the following morning.

'But you can't show him this cute thing without giving him a name,' said Margaret. 'What do we call him?'

Mintz woke up in the early hours of the morning and shook his wife awake. 'I have it,' he said, triumphantly. 'Oswald! Oswald the Lucky Rabbit! He *always* gets out of trouble!'

Next day Carl Laemmle gave his approval of Walt's sketches and offered a contract, backed by a 2,000 dollar advance.

Walt Disney Studio settled down to make its first all-cartoon film. Universal wanted the initial film in the series in a hurry, so Ub Iwerks was called in and told to get working on the sketched outline of a story. He did a masterly job of turning Oswald into a plump, eccentric country-cousin of a rabbit, dressed in ill-fitting trousers held up by braces, with a gormless and innocent look which belied his native shrewdness and cunning. When he saw the outline sketches, Roy Disney expressed the opinion that Ub had created Oswald as a mirror-image of himself.

'It's the way Iwerks sees himself, and I can't say that I think it works,' Roy said.

Universal Pictures didn't like the conception one bit. Walt delivered the first of the Oswald the Lucky Rabbit series, called *Poor Papa*, to Mintz in New York in April 1927, and a showing was arranged for the New York booking agents. They came back with a scathing report in which they listed several problems.

1. Approximately 100 feet of the opening is jerky in action, due to poor animation.
2. There is too much repetition of action. Scenes are dragged out to such an extent that the cartoon is seriously slowed down.
3. The Oswald shown in this picture is far from being a funny character. There are sometimes hints that something is going on underneath, but it is buried too deep to bother about. He's just flat. He has no outstanding trait. Nothing would eventually become characteristic insofar as Oswald is concerned.
4. The picture is merely a succession of unrelated gags, there being not even the thread of a story throughout its length.
5. Why is Oswald so old, sloppy and fat? Audiences like their characters young, trim and smart, and this one is practically decrepit.

For all these reasons, they concluded, they were unprepared to accept *Poor Papa* and could not recommend it for public showing under the Universal banner.

Walt was stunned. Angrily, he leapt to Ub's defence, maintaining that he was 'now without question the most talented animator in the business', but he did admit that the film had been made in a hurry, that they had 'taken short-cuts to meet deadlines', and insisted the purchase of a new automatic camera would correct the 'wobbles'. He went on to reassure the Universal distributors that he was now working with his animators on the task of transforming Oswald into 'a younger character, peppy, alert, saucy and venturesome, keeping him also trim and snappy'.

Then he and Ub got down to the task of recreating Oswald. They smartened him up, took off his old-fashioned overalls and braces, and made him a faster-moving, altogether younger and more virile animal. But there were still grumbles from the New York office, and it was not until Oswald's third adventure, into which Walt poured his best ideas and his most painstaking, and expensive, production values that Mintz and the Universal renters were satisfied.

In truth, the crisis produced by Universal's disapproval could not have come at a more appropriate moment. It forced Walt Disney to face up to his own faults as a cartoon film-maker just when a reassessment of himself was necessary. He had forgotten how, back in Kansas City, he had once criticized his predecessors for their easy gags and sloppy characterizations. He had hardly noticed how, since moving to California and getting himself accepted by the bookers, he had fallen into their lazy habits himself. If he was to save the situation (and the future of Walt Disney Studio) he had to rethink his whole outlook and transform his methods of presentation. He resolved never again to take it easy as a creator, and to make sure his cartoon characters were never mere drawings brought to life only by the gags and situations in which they were involved.

The first Oswald the Lucky Rabbit to be shown publicly, *Trolley Troubles*, was the second made at the Disney Studio, the first having been destroyed by Walt, who informed Universal that it would not count as part of the series. *Trolley Troubles*, with Oswald as conductor of a trolley-car, was hailed by the trade press and public alike. New York was then the centre of the animated cartoon industry, and among the cognoscenti Walt Disney's deft (albeit costly) presentation of the rabbit was noted and admiringly commented upon. *Trolley Troubles* became something of a classic in the trade. The experts were made aware, as they had not been before, that here was a newcomer who was revolutionizing the nature of their craft and would be a force to be reckoned with in the days to come. The film made its impact on audiences too. The public showing of this and others in the Oswald the Lucky Rabbit series led to an interesting development, although no one except Walt and Ub Iwerks grasped its significance at the time.

Letters began to come in to the distributors asking not for Walt's autograph, as had happened in the past, but for Oswald's. As his popularity grew, merchants approached Universal Pictures for the right to use Oswald's name or image on their products. His likeness was printed on boxes of sweets, and schoolchildren could buy Oswald

93

the Rabbit badges (these were the days before logos on T-shirts). If Universal and Mintz received any royalties for these gimmicks (and Carl Laemmle was surely too smart to miss out on any means of making a profit) they did not pass any of them on to Walt Disney, who had to be content with the free publicity. Otherwise, Walt Disney Studio did well with Oswald, and everyone felt the benefit. Even Charlie Mintz started paying on time, and a cheque for 2,000 dollars arrived (still by the hand of George Winkler) within days of the delivery of a new film in the series.

Money began coming in at regular intervals from then on. Walt and Roy were so pleased that they did not question the amounts they were receiving or wonder why they were always the same (the sums were supposed to vary according to their share of the rental fees). Walt was able to raise the salaries of his overworked animators, who were lucky if they were making more than 25 dollars a week, and to bring in more of them from New York. As a result, the work went more easily and the quality of the product improved; it became possible to deliver a new film in the series every ten days or two weeks.

He was also able to eliminate the 'time-savers' about which the Universal bookers had complained. There have always been short-cuts in animation work — so-called 'cycles', for example, which, by using repeat action-sequences, enable the animators to duplicate earlier frames and so eliminate hours of work at the drawing board. But from now on, Walt could afford to ban such tricks in his studio. Each sequence had to be newly and painstakingly drawn.

With money in the bank, Roy persuaded his brother that both of them now had enough to provide decent homes for their wives, and, maybe, he added, for the children both their wives so patently yearned for. They found plots of land side by side on Lyric Avenue, around the corner from the studio, and erected houses for themselves at a cost of 7,000 dollars apiece. Lillian and Edna were delighted.

Walt made one other gesture as a result of his new affluence. He knew Ub Iwerks had been badly bruised by the criticism of his early animation work on Oswald the Lucky Rabbit. Now he raised his salary to 120 dollars a week (a very good wage at the time) and, with Roy Disney's agreement, gave him a block of shares in the studio, thus cutting him into the annual profits, if any.

He could not have chosen a better moment to make the gesture to his touchy associate because a conspiracy against the Disneys was developing, and Ub was involved in it. A few days earlier, Ub had been secretly approached by George Winkler, who was still Mintz's

Hollywood representative, and had received an interesting offer. If he would join a new operation which the Mintz organization was about to set up, Winkler told him, he would be offered a long-term contract at double his present salary. Winkler had blandly assured Ub that the new organization would do absolutely no harm to Walt Disney's operations, and added that the Disney brothers would eventually be invited to join it on such favourable terms that they would undoubtedly accept. (Walt, of course, would have done no such thing.) At the same time, Winkler had emphasized that all this was extremely confidential, but had gone on to reveal to Ub that several of Walt's animators had already accepted offers to transfer to the new operation. Would Ub be interested?

Ub had certainly been tempted, since he was always strapped for money. Besides, harbouring the secret resentments that he did against Walt, he could not help relishing the prospect of seeing him humiliated. He had told George Winkler he would think the matter over and let him know.

Now Walt's generous gesture had intervened and it was so unexpected and sincerely offered that Ub decided to stick with the Disney organization. One of the first things he did after gratefully accepting Walt's offer was to telephone George Winkler and turn him down. But that was far from being the end of it.

In the spring of 1928, Walt's contract with Charles Mintz for the Oswald series was due for renewal, and the success of the sprightly rabbit was such that, at the time, both Walt and Roy were convinced they could win a renewal on much more lucrative terms. So confident was Walt of gaining a more favourable contract that he told everyone he and Lilly would be going to New York, where he would personally conduct the negotiations with Charlie Mintz.

Ub Iwerks heard about the trip and, after much soul-searching, he warned Walt about George Winkler's poaching trips to the studio, without mentioning the offer which he himself had received and rejected. To his astonishment, Walt laughed at him. What, George Winkler trying to steal away his animators? Ridiculous! They were far too loyal, far too dedicated to Walt Disney Studio, and neither Winkler nor Charlie Mintz had a hope in hell of tempting them away. Anyway, why should they want to leave, when things were going so well and he had treated them so fairly?

Ub Iwerks was both appalled and enraged by Disney's naïvety. It had taken a great deal of courage on Ub's part to break his unspoken pledge to George Winkler and snitch on his colleagues, and it was particularly humiliating not to be believed. And what arrogance on Walt Disney's part to be so confident of his employees' loyalty. It irked Ub that Walt should feel so comfortably immune to the normal jealousies, envies and resentments of the people around him. How could he be so sure of himself – and of other people? Ub was very angry, particularly when Walt sent him away feeling like a fool.

Walt and Lillian arrived in New York on 6 February 1928. Charlie Mintz had booked them into a suite at the Astor Hotel, a favourite haunt of film people, and the day after their arrival they lunched with him and his wife, Margaret, in the hotel's restaurant. The meal was a happy occasion, frequently interrupted by film people coming over to say hello. Mintz introduced his guests and always mentioned that Walt Disney was the talented young man from Hollywood who produced the Oswald the Lucky Rabbit series, which did not fail to make a good impression.

Later that afternoon, however, the warmth of that first encounter quickly cooled. Mintz took Walt back to his office off Times Square to begin negotiations over the new contract. Walt and Roy had already mutually decided they would ask for 2,500 dollars per cartoon (instead of 2,250 dollars) plus a percentage of the gross takings. This, they thought, was a modest enough financial demand in view of the success of their recent efforts. But when he presented this proposal to Mintz he was, to his astonishment, turned down flat.

'I'm only prepared to offer 1,800 dollars a film, and no percentage,' Mintz said bluntly.

'But that's less than the films are costing to make,' Walt protested.

Mintz shrugged. 'Take it or leave it,' he said, then added: 'Look, Walt, don't be a fool. I have to remind you that I and Universal own Oswald. We thought him up and he's our rabbit, and we have documents to prove it. You'd better face up to the situation, kid. If we want to carry on production without you, we can do it. I can take your organization away from you just like *that*,' with a flick of his fingers. 'Why, you don't even have a production organization left if I decide otherwise. Don't you know what's been going on in your own studio?'

He picked up the telephone and offered it to Walt. 'Here. Call up your studio and find out what's really taken place out there. Ask your animators who they're really working for. Kid, you don't even have a production staff any more. They belong to me. I have all your animators already signed up.'

Angrily, Walt refused to believe it and stormed out of the office. When he got back to his hotel he called Roy and repeated what Mintz had told him. Roy telephoned back a few hours later to say it was true: all the animators in the studio, with the exception of Ub Iwerks and two others, had contracted to go with the Mintz organization.

'Yes, I know it's terrible,' said Roy. 'But hold on, kid. Don't do anything foolish. Go back to Charlie Mintz and be polite with him. Don't, for God's sake, make any definite break with him. Maybe it's true what he says, and he's working in our own best interests. But meantime, contact the Universal organization in New York and find out what they think about Mintz's position. And find out how they feel about Oswald.' He added: 'And whatever you do, kid, keep calm. Hold on to everything and don't offend *anyone*. Otherwise, we could have a disaster on our hands.'

Meanwhile, Margaret Winkler Mintz had heard what had happened and immediately intervened in the situation. She telephoned the Astor Hotel to offer her advice and sympathy to Walt, and beseeched the young man not to be too hasty but to talk to her husband.

'He really likes your cartoons and wants to go on working with you,' she said. 'He has a plan for avoiding any break between you, and I think you ought to listen to it.'

He had indeed. Mintz offered a new contract under which he and Universal Pictures would, in future, pay all expenses for new films in the Oswald the Lucky Rabbit series, would take over the salaries of the animators in California, put one of their supervisors into Walt Disney Studio, and henceforth work in full partnership with Walt. Universal and he would guarantee all expenditures and would, in return, receive 50 per cent of all profits. In an apparent afterthought, he added that as part of the deal copyright of the Oswald character must be recognized by the Disneys as belonging to the Mintz Agency, which would have full control of all the rabbit's activities, on screen or off.

It was only too obvious to Walt that what both Charlie Mintz and Universal wanted to do was not just take the Oswald series but get their hands on his whole operation. He still believed Mintz was the chief villain behind the whole thing and was convinced Universal would never consent to such an outrageous rip-off. In any case, he refused to accept the claim that Oswald the Rabbit did not legally belong to the Disney organization – although, in fact, Mintz had a good case to prove otherwise – and made an emotional appeal to the heads of Universal's New York office, stressing the work his studio had done on Oswald and beseeching them to recognise his success instead of penalizing it. On 7 March 1928, he wrote to Roy:

Well, we are still hanging around this Hell Hole waiting for something to happen. Before you get this letter, I hope you will have had a wire containing good news. I can't rush things any faster – just have to do the best I can. *But I will fight it out on this line if it takes all summer.* It sure looks like a fight to the finish. Charlie is very determined to get control of everything and will do everything in his power to gain his end. But unknown to him we have a stronger power on our side.

[Disney Archives]

They hadn't.

Universal Pictures soon demonstrated they were fully and completely in cahoots with Charlie Mintz, and were convinced that eventually the Disneys would give way to his demands. They were confident that there was no other way out for the Disneys, and that a promising little studio full of bright young men would soon be falling into their hands.

Outraged by the perfidy and double-dealing of the distributors, heart-broken by the disloyalty of the animators with whom he had worked so hard and for so long, Walt eventually made up his mind. One day towards the end of March 1928, without informing Roy, he marched into Charlie Mintz's office, flung an Oswald the Lucky Rabbit badge on to the renter's desk, and said: 'Here, you can have the little bastard! He's all yours.'

When Mintz started to reason with him, he shouted back: 'Can't you understand what I'm saying? I renounce my rights to Oswald the Lucky Rabbit! I don't want him any more! Just trying to draw him after all this would make me sick to my stomach! You can have him – and good luck to you!'

'But you can't do that!' cried Mintz. 'You still have three Oswald films to go on your contract. Sick or not, you'll have to stay with him.'

'Not me,' said Walt. 'All those animators you stole – they can work out their notices finishing up the lousy series.'

Once more Mintz attempted a soft-spoken approach.

'Come on, kid, be reasonable,' he said. 'You know we need each other. We want to keep Oswald going, and so do you. I know your situation. You need the money. What's going to happen to you if you walk out now? How are you going to get by without Oswald?'

'Don't worry,' said Walt. 'There are plenty more characters where he came from.'

Roy Disney was appalled when he heard the news.

'Don't worry,' said Walt, yet again. 'We'll find new animators and we'll soon get a new series going.'

Roy shook his head. He was close to tears.

'You make it sound so easy,' he said, bitterly. 'It isn't easy. I am the one who has to find the money.'

Then a sudden thought struck him.

'And if we do get new animators and do start a new series, what do we use? What in the hell are we going to choose as a new character? A rabbit? Those bastards have stolen and copyrighted our rabbit. A cat? The public is goddamn sick of cats! Every cartoon film has one. A dog? Always pissing against the wall or a tree to get a cheap laugh? Ugh!'

Walt shook his head, and then clapped his brother comfortingly over the shoulder.

'We won't use a cat,' he said, 'and no dog either. Relax, Roy. We'll think of something.'

In fact, he already had. Two days earlier, as their westbound train was crossing the Mississippi on their melancholy journey back to California, Walt Disney had looked up from his drawing board where he had been doodling since leaving New York, and said to Lillian: 'How about a mouse? Someone like this, for instance.'

And he had passed a rough series of drawings of a big-eared mouse across to her.

'I think I'll call him Mortimer,' he said.

(This was one version of Mickey's creation. Ub Iwerks later maintained he was thought up at an animators' meeting in Hollywood.)

Chapter 8

AND BROUGHT FORTH
A MOUSE

In the last week in March 1928, Walt Disney returned to the Hyperion Avenue studio. It was rather like walking into a morgue. By this time, most of the animators who had signed up with Mintz knew Walt had broken off negotiations with him, and realized their days at the studio were numbered. Besides Ub Iwerks, of the fourteen staff animators, only two, Les Clark and Johnny Cannon, had resisted George Winkler's blandishments and would therefore be staying on. Since the rest were still under contract to the Walt Disney Studio for another four weeks, they were informed by Roy that there would be no question of letting them go early. On the contrary, they should count on being busily engaged for every remaining hour of their time, finishing off the last three of the Oswald series for 'your new boss, Charlie Mintz'.

Clark and Cannon were instructed to oversee the final chores of the departing animators, and Walt instructed them: 'Keep the bastards' noses to the grindstone. I want those Oswalds all finished before it's time for them to quit. Don't even give them time to wipe their noses.'

He had another reason for keeping the disloyal animators busy. He suspected they had been primed by Mintz to find out what he was up to, and he was determined not to have another of his cartoon characters stolen. So, while they slaved sullenly over their drawing boards in the main animators' studio, Walt and Ub Iwerks worked in secret on the new series about a mouse.

Iwerks had been shown Walt's preliminary sketches and his first comment was that the tiny rodent 'looks exactly like you – same nose, same face, same whiskers, same gestures and expressions. All he needs now is your voice.'

Walt admitted he had occasionally used his own face in the mirror as a model, and a lot of the expressions were his, though he swore the character was based on an actual mouse which had once prowled his tiny office in downtown Kansas City. 'I called him Mortimer. Don't you think that's a good name for him? Mortimer the Mouse.'

100

But Lilly thought that Mortimer was a 'sissy' name for a mouse, and she came up with Mickey. *Mickey Mouse*. They liked that much better.

Ub agreed with Walt that Mickey should be a brash, impudent little chap, kind to old ladies but mischievous with those who could look after themselves, and up to all sorts of tricks. Painstakingly, they built up a personality for him. His main trouble was he hated bullies and his gallantry and courage were bigger than his muscles. He was always running into trouble trying to rescue weaker people from oversized villains, and getting beaten for his temerity. But it never stopped him, and his resourcefulness always won out in the end.

The concept was effective enough. But how were they going to introduce Mickey Mouse to the public? They were all aware of the need to give him a really splashy debut.

As it happened, the newspapers at that time were still full of the exploits of Charles Augustus Lindbergh, who had been the first man to fly solo across the Atlantic and was being hailed as a national hero. Both Walt and Ub thought it might be a good idea to exploit the current passion for planes and pilots, and Walt had typed out a rough scenario called 'Plane Crazy', which Ub promptly took and turned into a vehicle for Mickey Mouse.

Ub worked in the back garage of Walt's house on Lyric Avenue away from the curiosity of the sacked animators. He was always a prodigious worker and he excelled himself on the first Mickey Mouse cartoon, knowing how urgently the new series was needed.

For a 500-foot cartoon film, over 14,400 pictures were required, and Ub produced an impressive 600 drawings a day. To keep the secret operation in the family, Lillian Disney was brought back to work and she and one of Herbert's daughters, who had also worked in the studio, went to the garage and spent hours inking and painting Ub's animation on to the 'cels'. Then, when the studio closed for the day and the animators had departed, Walt took the cels back to Hyperion Avenue and spent the night putting them on camera, carefully cleaning up all traces of his work after his nocturnal labours were finished.

Plane Crazy, the first cartoon film in which Mickey Mouse ever appeared, had a sneak preview at a Hollywood cinema in May 1928, and was pleasantly if politely received by the audience. Mickey's impact on the public was, to begin with, negligible, and officials at the big Hollywood studios were not much more enthusiastic. Walt took *Plane Crazy* out to Culver City and showed it to the bookers for MGM, who all seemed to enjoy it. Nevertheless Walt realized what he was up against when one of them leaned back and said: 'Very nice. There's only one problem. Nobody's ever heard of Mickey Mouse.'

It was such a stupid remark that all Walt could think of to reply was: 'They will.'

No booking was forthcoming. Nevertheless, Walt Disney believed in his creation enough to risk putting a second Mickey Mouse film into production, called *Gallopin' Gaucho*.

Since the disloyal animators had by this time departed, there was no longer any reason for secrecy and Ub was able to move back to the studio to draw the master frames for this second film. Moreover, he had the help of several newly hired animators. As usual, Walt sat in on the preparation, and, with uncanny mimicry, acted out every scene in which Mickey appeared. Sometimes, to heighten the effect of the atmosphere he was trying to create, he ad-libbed dialogue for Mickey in a high-pitched voice that sent everyone who watched and heard him into fits of laughter.

'If only we had sound,' said Ub Iwerks, 'you'd bring the house down as the voice of Mickey.'

Sound in films was, in fact, very much in the news. Before Mickey Mouse made his debut, the sensational première of the first talking film, *The Jazz Singer*, had taken place in New York, and the whole nature of the movie business had radically changed. Overnight, exhibitors had begun to clamour for sound films, and every producer in Hollywood was desperately trying to give his latest epic music, sound effects and dialogue.

Meanwhile, there were still no customers for the first two Mickey Mouse films. Although most exhibitors liked the new character, they hesitated over the price and conditions. Each Mickey was costing the studio 2,500 dollars to make, so Walt and Roy had decided to ask for 3,000 dollars per film plus an agreement to take a minimum of twenty-four in the series. Walt blamed the lack of takers on the confusion caused by the advent of sound. In view of the revolution that was taking place in the industry, you could hardly fault exhibitors for wondering whether anyone would want to see a silent cartoon film a year from now. They needed to be reassured that Mickey Mouse, too, would be moving with the times.

Walt decided to give them that reassurance. Although the first two productions had put a serious dent in the studio budget, he declared he was going ahead with a third Mickey Mouse film, this one to be called *Steamboat Willie*. Moreover, he announced, this one would have full sound, including music.

In the roughly written and illustrated draft-scenario which he prepared, he inserted two main music sequences, and stressed that the sound effects – the Mississippi steamboat's whistle, the noise of ship's engines, the splash of paddle wheels – must be used in a novel and amusing fashion. He also emphasized that although Mickey would not be talking much in this particular cartoon, every effort must be made to delineate his character, with, where necessary, the aid of sound. When he whistled or sighed, for instance, he would be heard doing so.

The original script of *Steamboat Willie* is still to be found in the archives of the Disney Studio at Burbank, California, and the following extract gives an idea of the effect Walt was trying to achieve in rounding out the character of Mickey Mouse:

Scene no. 32
Dolly-Mickey ... Medium shot ... Mickey looking into open mouth of Captain with a frightened expression on his face ... Little girl at right of scene with surprised expression as she watches them ... doorway to kitchen between girl and captain ...

Mickey draws away from captain and stands with scared look on face ... Captain closes mouth and gives him a mean look ... Mickey tries to appear at ease ... Does a silly forced grin at captain ... this slowly dies away into scared expression ... He puts hands in pocket and whistles a couple of measures of 'Yankee Doodle' ... Looks back to captain with a sickly forced grin ... then does a sickly little laugh ... which gradually dies of[f] as his expression changes to scared look ... turns to camera and gives a deep nervous sigh ... The captain is very sore ... He grabs Mickey by the tail and drags him into kitchen ... girl watches with frightened bewildered expression ...

However, there were problems. For instance, how were the sound effects to be added? And what method of recording were they going to use? For the moment, Walt Disney Studio possessed no sound equipment, and no technicians who knew how to use it, anyway. At this time even the major studios were still trying to work out the best method of sound synchronization, and there was widespread confusion. Certainly, no one had yet given a thought to the peculiar problems of fitting sound to cartoon films, where synchronization was especially tricky.

All Walt Disney knew was that sound film ran through the projector at the rate of twenty-four frames every second, and from this it was easy to work out that if the musical accompaniment to the cartoon was two beats every second, they had to have a beat every twelve frames of the cartoon. But how did you make sure of the precise timing?

Luckily, a young man named Wilfred Jackson had recently come to work for Walt Disney Studio, and he was fascinated to the point of obsession with the art of cartoon films. Eager to become an animator, but completely ignorant of the technique, he had turned up at the studio one day and offered to work for nothing until he had gained experience. Although he had graduated from the Otis Art Institute and was an efficient illustrator, he was put to work at the humblest and messiest job in the studio, washing the ink and paint off the cels so that they could be re-used. But one day, while he was wrestling with his synchronization problems, Walt wandered through the lab where the cel-washing was done and heard the sound of a mouth-organ. The performance was highly professional, and the performer was Jackson.

Walt stopped and asked him if he knew anything about music, and Jackson said: 'A little.'

Walt prided himself on knowing a little about music, too, and he thought that between them, he and Jackson might find a way of solving the synchronization problem.

'Jackson went out and bought a metronome,' he said later, 'and we moved to the studio and began to work things out. I had a pad of bar music-sheets and I started the metronome and asked Jackson to play a tune on his harmonica. While it tick-tocked away, he would play out our frames so we had exactly the right ratio of frames to each bar of music.'

Next Walt went on a shopping spree, buying up gadgets and noise-makers like cow bells and tin-cans. 'I bought a couple of plumber's friends [rubber suckers for cleaning out blocked drains – when in action, they make a squishy sound] and some slide whistles and ocarinas,' he said later. 'We played around with these for a while to work out the sound effects. When I say we I mean Ub Iwerks, young Jackson and myself. A few nights later, we asked our wives to come over and see something new. We had no projection room, and our sheet hung on a garage doorway. It was a warm night, so we put our wives in chairs facing the open garage doorway with the sheet hanging over it. Then Roy turned on the projector and began to run *Steamboat Willie*. Iwerks, I and Jackson got into the garage behind the sheet, where we could watch the picture from the rear and make our various noises.

'Jackson tootled music on his mouth-organ,' he said. 'The rest of us hit cow bells, ocarinas and whistles, and scrubbed away at the washboard. Iwerks had rigged up a microphone to an old radio speaker, so our wives would be able to hear the sound-effects clearly.'

Walt had scored the cartoon so that sound came out of everything Mickey looked at or touched. The steamboat whistle tootled a tune, cows, pigs and kettles mooed, squealed, fizzed and plinked to music.

'We beat our brains out synchronizing that cartoon,' Walt recalled, 'and when we were through we ran around the sheet, and Roy came running up from the projector, and we looked at our wives expectantly and said: "How was it?" All they said was "Nice," and went on gossiping, as they had done, Roy said bitterly afterwards, all through the screening.'

'What did they expect?' said Lilly, later. 'We had absolutely no idea what was going on. And in any case, it sounded terrible.' But the effort was not completely wasted. The al fresco performance had enabled Walt, Ub and Jackson to mark off the film in exactly the right places for synchronization.

There was only one place to get it professionally recorded: New York, where all the latest developments in sound recording were being perfected. With the cans of *Steamboat Willie* under his arm, Walt set off for Manhattan, stopping off en route in Kansas City to persuade his old organist friend Carl Stalling to compose him a score for the film exactly timed to the beats they had marked out. The score included two big musical numbers that were incorporated into the film, 'Turkey in the Straw' and 'Steamboat Bill', and it was a complicated job. But Stalling did it in seventy-two hours and agreed to be paid later. Walt never forgot his debt to Stalling – who had already, it will be remembered, come up with a loan of 275 dollars when the Disneys badly needed it – and he made sure the organist was richly rewarded for his efforts when the Disneys were finally in the money.

Walt described New York in a letter to Lilly which he wrote on 9 September 1928, as 'a madhouse'. People were scrambling to get their hands on recording equipment, and bootleg models of Radio Corporation of America (RCA) sound recorders were the hottest black-market items along Film Row. So far only a few of the major companies had the right to use the sound-on-film method pioneered by RCA, and they were desperately trying to keep it out of the hands of their rivals. As a result, Walt was advised to use the alternate (and cheaper) method. This meant putting his score on phonograph discs, as many companies were already doing. He went to see a movie using this system, and walked out in disgust, determined to have no part of it. During one reel, the projectionist put the needle in the wrong groove of the disc with the result that all the dialogue and sound effects were suddenly out of synch. He realized that if something like that happened to *Steamboat Willie* it would ruin Mickey Mouse's debut. In any case, the idea of having cans of *Steamboat Willie* going around the country with separate sound discs accompanying them, and the danger of their being mislaid or damaged, was too awful to contemplate.

No matter what the experts said — and they were still arguing — Walt was convinced that only the sound-on-film system would do for *Steamboat Willie*, and therefore only RCA could synchronize the film.

He queued up at RCA and showed *Steamboat Willie* to the chief sound technician, who was extremely blasé about the film ('He didn't crack a smile once during the run-through,' Walt said later) but said he could certainly add sound effects to it. But he warned that it might be expensive, and that they would want cash on delivery. Did he have sufficient money for a deposit — say 500 dollars?

Walt swallowed hard, said he was sure he could find what it cost to do a good job, and went back to telephone Roy. Roy said if Walt was sure RCA could produce the goods he would find the money somehow, but begged his brother to drive a hard bargain and watch every penny he spent from now on.

'They sound awful expensive to me,' Roy said. 'Are they gonna throw in a booking for the film too?'

Unfortunately, there was no chance of that. Not only did Walt agree that they did sound expensive, he might have added — but for the moment did not — that they also seemed excessively complacent and superior about their technical abilities. Initially, he had been overawed by the RCA engineer's patronizing manner, but gradually he became increasingly suspicious of the whole set-up, and grew apprehensive about what terrible things they might be planning to do to his masterpiece.

By this time he had grown very attached to *Steamboat Willie*. Convinced it was the best cartoon film he had ever made, he had a strong premonition that his future and those of his associates would stand or fall on what happened to it.

To find out how they operated, he asked RCA to demonstrate something they had already worked on, and they gave him a run-through of a Movietone cartoon of an Aesop fable. Walt was astonished and alarmed. So far as sound effects were concerned, all they seemed to have added were music and trap-drum rolls to emphasize action. To him it looked and sounded just like a silent film, except it now had canned instead of live accompaniment, and, in his view, had been ruined in the process.

After the demonstration was over he swung round to the expectant engineer.

'Is that *all* you can do?' he asked.

'What more do you want?' asked the engineer.

'I expected *real* sound effects,' said Walt.

He pulled out the marked score Carl Stalling had written for *Steamboat Willie* and indicated the beat marks on the film's frames.

'This is the method we have worked out for my film. See, every word and every sound effect has been meticulously timed, and these marks show you exactly when and how to get them right on the beat.'

The engineer glanced casually at the score and scornfully threw it back at him. 'Why, to do it that way would cost you a fortune,' he said. 'You'd have to hire an orchestra, pay royalties to a publisher, plus music tax and all the trimmings, not to mention our fee.' He did some quick figuring with a pencil and paper. 'Cost you around 3,500 dollars at the very least. Have you got that kind of money?'

'No,' said Walt, 'but if you can do the job exactly the way I want it done, and if you can get the sound effects exactly right, I'll find the money somehow. The question is, are you capable of doing it – properly, I mean?'

'Here, what are you trying to do, teach us our job?' the engineer asked, suddenly angry. 'Look, sonny, we know all about this sound business, and we've worked out how to do it cheaply and effectively. We have our own methods and our own music. You just give us your film and leave it to us. We'll put in the sound.' His tone changed and he added: 'You know the best thing for you to do, son? The best thing for you to do is go away and relax. Forget about your precious film, and put it in our hands. We know what's best for it. Come back in a couple of days, and we'll have it all blended in. Nice music, nice sound effects, and nobody'll notice whether it's synchronized or not.'

'I'll notice,' said Walt, firmly.

Clutching the cans of *Steamboat Willie* under his arm, he walked out of the office. He was finished with RCA.

But where was he to go now? Surely, somewhere in New York, there was someone who could understand why *Steamboat Willie* was special, and why it was so vital to give it the authentic sound effects

Mickey Mouse needed in order to turn him into a star?

There was indeed someone. His name was Pat Powers. He had access to all the new sound equipment and knew just what Walt's production required. Unfortunately, there was one thing wrong with Powers. He was a crook.

Patrick A. Powers was one of those professional Irishmen whose brogue makes them sound as if they are just off the boat. But he was, in fact, a second-generation American from upstate New York whose easy smile and charm concealed a heart of stone. In a milieu never exactly notable for its honesty of purpose, most veterans of Film Row regarded him as one of the most unscrupulous and untrustworthy of their brethren, and were full of tales of his genial rapacity.

Pat Powers had been in the movie business from the early days when fur-salesmen like Adolph Zukor came out of the Bowery and began making films. His capabilities as a con-man can be measured by the fact that he even talked Carl Laemmle into making him a partner in Universal Pictures, and then proceeded to rob that shrewd and hard-headed character blind. When the truth finally dawned on Laemmle that he had been well and truly cheated, he challenged Powers to produce the financial records of Universal's transactions – records that Laemmle had foolishly allowed him to keep, and manipulate. Passionately protesting his purity as a God-fearing son of the Auld Sod, Powers angrily rejected what he termed Laemmle's outrageous impugning of his honesty, and melodramatically flung the records out of the window of Universal's New York office at 1600 Broadway. What he did not tell Laemmle was that he had an accomplice waiting on the pavement below ready to catch the manipulated records and make sure the police and Universal's watchdogs never saw them again.

In 1928 he was still at his old tricks. The advent of sound in the movies was just the sort of gimmick he needed in order to make yet another fortune. Aware that RCA and Movietone had secured a monopoly of the sound-on-film system and that they were now worth their weight in gold, he had bribed and corrupted company engineers into providing him with the technical details, and then persuaded them to build him a bootleg system, slightly modified, which he called Cinephone. All he needed now was a movie to which he could add music and sound effects and launch it as the first Cinephone talking film; then he would be in business and all those Hollywood companies which had been locked out of RCA would come flocking to his door.

So when Walt Disney walked into his office one morning in the autumn of 1928 with the cans of *Steamboat Willie* under his arm, Pat Powers listened to his story, put an affectionate arm around the young man's shoulders, and drew him, an unwitting fly, into his parlour.

Chapter 9

UNSEEMLY POWERS

Walt Disney was twenty-six years old in 1928, but in many ways he was still a naïve kid from the sticks longing for someone to hold his hand in the big city. New York and its glib citizens, especially the fast-talking smoothies along Film Row, scared him and sapped his courage. 'This DAMN TOWN is enough to give anybody the HEEBIE JEEBIES,' he wrote home in a letter to Ub Iwerks, after his bruising experiences with RCA.

For the moment he had lost his self-confidence. There were moments when he even began to have doubts about *Steamboat Willie*. Was it worth all this struggle and expense to get it properly wired for sound?

Indicative of his mood just before his meeting with Pat Powers was a letter (now in the Disney Archives, Burbank) he wrote to Ub in which he did not bother to conceal his feelings:

Personally I am sick of this picture, Steamboat Willie. Every time I see it the lousy print spoils everything. Maybe it will be different looking at the picture with sound. I sure hope so. I am very nervous and upset and I guess that has a lot to do with my attitude in the matter . . . I sure wish I was home. I sure wouldn't make a good traveling salesman. I can't mix with strangers and enjoy myself like some people. This is not affecting my attitude toward the matter I came here for. That is the only thing that is on my mind. But I have so much time to kill at nights that I almost go nuts.

In this mood, he was an easy mark for Pat Powers's hospitable charm and persuasive manner. Powers did not just enthuse about the qualities of *Steamboat Willie* but also promised that, once it had been fitted with 'the magical sound effects it truly deserves', he would see to it that it was adequately publicized and sold to the biggest chain of cinemas in the nation.

Walt was so taken with his powerful connections ('he seems to know everybody who is anybody in the film world and talks to them all the time on the telephone – uses their first names too – it's all Adolph, Louie and Myron') that he agreed to pay Powers 1,000 dollars plus a percentage of the fees for handling the film and arranging the recording session. He wired Roy to make sure they had enough cash in the bank to cover the down payment he handed over. Powers also produced a distinguished musician named Carl Edouarde, who ran the pit orchestra at the Strand Theater on Broadway, and said he was the one to conduct the players needed for the dubbing sessions. Walt spent some worrying hours with Edouarde going over Stalling's score for *Steamboat Willie*. He carefully pointed out the guide-posts which had been inserted into the film to make sure every bar of music and every sound-effect would be on the right beat.

'We had drawn a mark on our film every twelve frames in India ink,' said Walt later, 'and when projected it made a white flash on the screen. If you watched for the flash, it was a substitute for the tick-tock of an old-fashioned metronome. Just by watching it, the conductor could stay on the beat and know just when to allow for a sound effect.'

Unfortunately, Edouarde was sublimely contemptuous of such unmusical aids and kept interrupting Walt's lecture with a comment he had already heard only too often during his pilgrimage along Film Row: 'Why don't you just leave it to me?'

When Walt confided his doubts to Pat Powers, his new protector responded soothingly: 'Don't be impatient. Do like he says. Eddie's a good musician. If you have any doubts, just sit in on his sessions and make sure he gets in all your sound effects. But let Eddie handle the musical side. He knows what's what. In any case, if it doesn't work out right, don't worry. We'll do the recording over again – and it won't cost you a nickel. I'll stand the expense.'

Walt needed such reassurances because the spectre of a money-shortage was beginning to hover before his eyes again. Roy communicated regularly to warn him their resources were draining away, and began to suspect his hick brother was being taken for a ride.

By now Walt seemed to have put his complete trust and confidence in the ability of Pat Powers to lead them to fame and fortune, so much so that he had telegraphed Ub Iwerks to put yet another Mickey Mouse film in the works. Though it would be the fourth in the series, not a single one had so far secured a booking or made any money. The new one, to be called *The Barn Dance*, would cost yet another 2,500 dollars, more money than they now had in the studio kitty.

Meanwhile, Maestro Edouarde, who had originally calculated that all he would need for the recording sessions on *Steamboat Willie* was a five-piece combination plus drummers, turned out, on the appointed day, to have called in a seventeen-member orchestra plus no less than three trap-drummers and sound-effects men.

It was the first dubbing session that Walt Disney had ever attended and everything went wrong. At seven o'clock on a cool September morning in 1928 he arrived at the downtown recording studio. The first musician to make an appearance was a double-bass player who had come, pale, haggard and unshaven, straight from an all-night recording session for Victor Records at their studio in Camden, New Jersey.

'The first thing he did,' remembered Walt later, 'was open his double-bass case and take a swig from a bottle.'

When the full orchestra was at last assembled, Maestro Edouarde proceeded to put them through a full rehearsal of the main musical numbers in the score, including 'Turkey in the Straw', 'Yankee Doodle' and 'Steamboat Bill'. Since it was costing him seven dollars an hour for the players plus ten dollars an hour for the sound-effects men and 20 dollars an hour for Edouarde, Walt felt a full rehearsal was hardly called for, especially as it was setting him back 270 dollars before the dubbing had even begun.

And once it began, there was a succession of disasters.

'Every time the bull-fiddler sawed into his instrument and went *zoom*,' he said later, 'the volume was such that he blew out a bulb in the recording mechanism. The first time it happened, the sound men moved the bass player further back. But it made no difference and he promptly blew another bulb. Even when they moved him to a far corner of the studio he still went on blowing bulbs each time he dug into his fiddle. Finally, he was told to go play outside the studio door, where even we couldn't hear him. At seven dollars an hour!'

Maestro Edouarde's arrogant self-confidence was beginning to seep away, too, as he began to realize that sound-recording was not as simple as he had assumed. Time and again, when *Steamboat Willie* had finished, he found himself with pages of sound effects left over. He kept reassuring Walt by saying: 'Never mind, we'll get them all in next time.'

Only they didn't.

By the end of the morning, everyone realized the recording session had gone catastrophically wrong. Walt, anxious to conceal from his brother just how disastrous it had really been, sent him a telegram:

ALL CONCERNED DESIRE BEST RESULTS OBTAINABLE THEREFORE ARE
REMAKING IT USING DIFFERENT EFFECTS MEN. I AM VERY OPTIMISTIC
ABOUT RESULTS AND OUR FUTURE LOOKS BRIGHT. GAVE POWERS
CHECK $1,000. BE SURE IT IS OK.

In fact, the future looked anything but bright. After Edouarde had
sent his musicians off to lunch, he said thoughtfully to Walt: 'Next
time, I think I'll try that idea you were telling me about – you know,
using those flashes as a visual metronome. It'll mean a whole new
session.'

'You mean, a complete re-recording?' asked Walt, thinking of the
extra cost that would involve.

'Oh yes,' said Edouarde.

Walt went to see Pat Powers and reminded him that if a re-
recording became necessary, Powers had promised he would pay for
it.

'That's right,' said Powers. 'I said I'd pay for any re-recording, and I
will.'

'What about the orchestra?' asked Walt. 'It's costing 270 dollars an
hour.'

'I didn't say anything about the orchestra,' said Powers.

With some trepidation, Walt telephoned Roy and said they would
need another 1,200 dollars, since he had run into some unexpected
charges. Roy immediately went to see Lillian and told her Walt's new
car would have to be sold to meet the fresh expenses.

'It's either the automobile or Mickey Mouse,' he said. 'From now
on, we can't afford both.'

Walt was stunned when he heard the news. In some ways, that
beautiful new, open Moon four-seater had been his most treasured
and pampered possession. Its loss galvanized him into demanding
drastic economies at the recording sessions, demanding that the size of
the orchestra be cut to sixteen and the sacking of two sound-effects
men. This time he stayed close to the conductor's podium to make
sure Maestro Edouarde followed the flashes on the screen. The result
was that this time the orchestra finished up simultaneously with the
fadeout, and all the vital sound effects were right on the beat. Late
that night, at the end of a nerve-frazzling and exhausting session,
Steamboat Willie had been wired for sound at last, and exactly the
way he wanted it.

All Walt's earlier doubts about *Steamboat Willie* as a production and Mickey Mouse as a brand-new star were dissipated when he saw the first run-through of the completed film. It was funny, it was fresh, it was entertaining. With pride and joy, he handed it over to Pat Powers and told him that now was the time to make good on his promise and get out and sell it. He did not tell him how badly he and his associates now needed the money.

Weeks passed and there were no sales.

This was not entirely the fault of Pat Powers. He arranged special showings of *Steamboat Willie* all over town, and the bookers for the big movie chains all turned up to see it. Some of them even laughed in places and told the anxious Walt they thought it might well have a future. But no one booked it.

Walt was so downcast he later confessed, 'I sometimes felt like shooting myself.'

I have certainly learned a lot about this game already [he wrote to Lillian on 20 October 1928]. It is the damndest mixed-up affair I have ever heard of. It sure demands a shrewd and thoroughly trained mind to properly handle it. There are so damned many angles that continually come up that if a person hasn't the experience, etc. it would certainly lick one. They are all a bunch of schemers and full of tricks that would fool a greenhorn.

He still had implicit faith and trust in the benevolent interest of Pat Powers, and he went on:

I am sure glad I got someone to fall back on for advice. I would be like a sheep among a pack of wolves. I have utmost faith and confidence in Powers and believe that if we don't try to rush things too fast that we will get a good deal out of this. We will all just have to have patience and confidence. I am very optimistic about everything and want you all to feel the same way. I really think our big chance is here. [Disney Archives]

One morning, after yet another trade showing of his film, he hung around in the lobby, listening to the comments of the exhibitors as they came out, hoping to hear one of them say he was going to make a booking. He felt a touch on his arm and a man named Harry Reichenbach introduced himself.

'Trying to find out what they think about your little number?' he asked, jerking a contemptuous thumb at the bookers. 'I can tell you what they *think*. They like it. In fact, they like it a lot. But it doesn't mean they're going to book it,' he added. 'That's the trouble with all these guys. They're scared to make a decision. It's the same in Hollywood. It's the disease of the movie business . . . They're waiting for someone to tell them what to do. And do you know who's going to tell them? John Q. Public, that's who. The paying customers themselves.'

'And how in hell are they going to do that?' asked Walt, helplessly, 'when I can't even get a public showing?'

'Well, now, as far as that's concerned, I have an idea,' said Reichenbach. He began leading Walt out of the movie house. 'Look, let's you and me go and grab a bite to eat. I have a proposition I want to put to you.'

Although Walt Disney didn't know it at the time, Harry Reichenbach had once been one of the most successful press agents in New York. He was the man who had been hired to promote the public showing of the famous pre-Raphaelite painting, 'September Morn', and had drummed up a raging scandal over the exhibition of this modest display of female nudity. He had now gone into the movie business and handled the films for Universal Pictures through its Manhattan outlet at the Colony Theater. He thought *Steamboat Willie* was terrific and would wow the general public once it had a chance to see it. His proposition to Walt was that he was ready to put it on at the Colony Theater for a two-week showing with his latest Hollywood feature, *Gang War*, starring Jack Pickford. Would Walt be prepared to let him have it for a rental of 500 dollars a week?

'It's more than anyone has ever paid for a cartoon film before,' Reichenbach informed him, 'but I happen to think it's worth it. This little film is going to cause a sensation. And once it does, all the bookers are going to come knocking at your door. But I'd like to get in first.'

Steamboat Willie opened at the Colony Theater on 18 November 1928, and the press as well as the general public had been invited to what was billed as 'the first animated sound cartoon'.

It was a cold night but the reception could not have been warmer, and next day many of the critics ignored the main movie and stage show to lavish praise on the cartoon film, which *Variety* called 'a peach of a synchronization job all the way'.

It was left to *The New York Times* to register the debut of 'a new cartoon character henceforth to be known as "Mickey Mouse" '; it saluted the production as 'an ingenious piece of work with a good deal of fun', and, in a reference to its sound track, added: 'It growls, squeaks and makes various other sounds that add to its mirthful quality.'

At last. After all the pain and anguish, Walt Disney's work had been recognized.

As if to prove Reichenbach's cynical point, almost at once the bookers came beating a path to Walt Disney's room at the Algonquin Hotel. Almost without exception, every big cinema chain in the United States sent round its representatives – the same ones who had earlier held back – with offers of bankrolls and contracts. There was one unexpected touch to all this excitement. Reichenbach gave a celebratory luncheon at the Waldorf Hotel after the press showing of *Steamboat Willie* and, by happenstance or design, Margaret Winkler Mintz was one of the guests. In the few minutes which was all they managed to snatch alone, she asked Walt once more to listen to a proposition her husband was planning to make to him.

Two days later, at a meeting in the boardroom of Universal Pictures at 1600 Broadway, at which Harry Reichenbach and Pat Powers were both present, Charlie Mintz said he was speaking on behalf of the Universal board of directors and offered Walt Disney and his partners a tempting deal to make future Mickey Mouse pictures for them.

It was an ironic occasion, in more ways than one. For instance, Carl Laemmle, the Universal chief, had once sworn that his arch-enemy Pat Powers would never contaminate his offices again with his thieving presence after the crimes he had committed against the company. And yet here he was once more, gazing fondly and proprietorially around the familiar Universal boardroom as if he were back in his ancestral home. Then, too, for Walt, there was the monstrous irony of staring into the smiling faces of Charlie Mintz and the Universal directors, the same men who had stolen Oswald the Rabbit and his artists from him, who were now benevolently regarding him as if he were their long-lost son.

'Join us,' urged Charlie Mintz. 'We'll give you studio space, all the finance you need, and a generous share of the profits if you'll only bring your superlative new cartoon character, Mickey Mouse, over to Universal.'

He even had the nerve to add, with a roguish twinkle: 'Furthermore, we can provide you with your own animators, if you still want them. They've been waiting all this time to get back to work with you.'

Walt could not help replying: 'I wouldn't have them back if they came crawling on their knees.'

In spite of the hypocrisy, the Universal offer was tempting because it would make him and his associates rich from now on. But there was, of course, a catch: in return for the long-term contract they were offering – plus all the money – Universal wanted control of, and the copyright on, Mickey Mouse.

Walt said no. Mickey was his creation, and no one was going to get his hands on him. Ever.

After the meeting, when they were back on Broadway again and strolling towards the Algonquin Hotel, Pat Powers said: 'Nice going, Walt. I'm glad you turned them down. Show you're independent. It's the only way to treat those bastards.'

In the bar of the Algonquin, he took a long pull at his tumbler of Bushmill's and said: 'Now I've got a proposition for you.' He saw the expression on Walt's face, and hastily added: 'Now, don't get me wrong. You know me. I'm on your side. Besides, I'm not really interested in that crazy mouse of yours. All I'm interested in is the future of my sound apparatus, Cinephone. So here's what I'm going to do . . .'

Chapter 10

THE REVENGE OF UB

IF only Pat Powers had been trustworthy, there would have been absolutely nothing wrong with his proposition. On the face of it, the deal he offered Walt Disney was an attractive one.

In 1928-9, if a producer made a film and could not or would not sign a distribution contract with one of the major Hollywood studios (who controlled their own chains of cinemas at the time) he could sell the 'states rights' of his film to the so-called 'independents'. These were the owners of movie houses – sometimes quite large chains – who operated in different states in competition with the cinemas controlled by the Hollywood companies. They booked their own films. They made their own deals with the producers whose movies they rented and had exclusive rights to show them in the particular areas which they controlled. And all depending on the part of the country in which they operated, they paid a percentage of what would have been a national rental for each film. So, for example, New York State rights were calculated at 12 per cent of the agreed national rental, New England at eight per cent, California territory (which then included Arizona, Nevada and Hawaii) paid six per cent.

Powers offered to advance the Walt Disney Studio the money to pay for future films in the Mickey Mouse series. At his own expense he would pay the salaries of the salesmen who would be sent out to sell the films to the independents. All he would ask in return was a modest ten per cent of the gross receipts. For their part, Walt Disney Studio would retain complete control of Mickey Mouse and their only obligation would be an agreement to rent and use Powers's Cinephone sound equipment for all their animated films in future. As a pledge of his benign intentions, Powers pressed a cheque for 3,000 dollars into Walt's hand – a gesture which was warmly and gratefully appreciated.

He signed the contract Powers offered him without a moment's hesitation and, reading it through later in the privacy of his hotel room, had absolutely no qualms about its conditions. He now had only one more chore left to perform before he went back in triumph

118

to Hyperion Avenue to show it to Roy. Ub Iwerks had done a marvellous job of animating the new Mickey Mouse cartoon, *The Barn Dance*, and delivering it on time, and now he called Carl Stalling and asked him to come to New York and write a score for it. He also asked him to do the same for the earlier Mickeys, *Plane Crazy* and *Gallopin' Gaucho*, to which sound would now be added. This time it was Stalling who sat in on the recording sessions with Maestro Edouarde, and they went without a hitch. By the time the films were dubbed and ready, Pat Powers's salesmen had no less than four Mickey Mouse films to offer to the independent renters. On his last night in New York, Walt went down to the Colony Theater to say goodbye to Harry Reichenbach and to watch the final performance of the local run of *Steamboat Willie*. As the ripples of happy laughter spread through the cinema, Walt was so relieved he felt tears rolling down his cheeks.

His experiences in New York had, indeed, been shaking. He had met some real cheats in his dealings along Film Row. But he comforted himself with the thought that two men had proved to be real friends in need and he would never forget what they had done for him. One was Harry Reichenbach. The other was Pat Powers. His feelings towards them at that moment were such that he would willingly have trusted them with his life.

Not even Roy Disney's scepticism rocked his faith in Pat Powers. Roy went through the contract his brother had signed and strongly objected to some of its terms. What particularly irked him was a clause under which Walt Disney Studio agreed to pay 26,000 dollars a year for ten years for the use of Cinephone sound equipment. He considered that a real rip-off. Were the rumours he had heard correct? Did Cinephone really belong to Powers or were they likely to be involved in a lawsuit over patent infringements? Walt brushed his doubts aside. He grew particularly incensed when Roy mentioned Hollywood gossip that Powers was a con-man and not to be trusted. He refused to listen to a word against him, and once the Mickey Mouse films began their meteoric rise, he insisted they change the agreement with Powers and begin paying him a regular distributor's fee of 35 per cent of the gross receipts.

'He's earned it,' Walt declared. 'He's made Mickey Mouse into a household name.'

There was no doubt at all of Powers's success in building up the fame of the Disney cartoons. In less than a year, Mickey Mouse had made it as a national character – and an international one, too. Movie houses were even beginning to put his name and the title of his films on the marquee alongside the big feature, which had never happened before. He drew big crowds. Magazines published articles about him. Newspaper cartoonists picked him up and used him as a feisty symbol in their work. Each new Mickey Mouse film was an immediate hit and feature writers flocked to Hyperion Avenue demanding interviews with the creator of what they now began calling the Mighty Mouse.

There was only one problem. Walt and Roy should have been rich by now, as well as famous. True, more animators had been hired, and budgets for the cartoons had increased, but *Variety* calculated that the Disneys were making 40,000 dollars in receipts from each cartoon, and the profits should have been rolling in. Only they weren't. Pat Powers was proving a little dilatory in his payments.

To excuse him, Walt insisted to his brother that film people were always like that – they just couldn't maintain an efficient accounting system – but as the weeks went by without any cheques, the time came when Roy announced he was leaving for New York himself and was going to get some money out of Powers 'even if I have to squeeze the s.o.b. like a lemon'.

He came back a week later completely frustrated. Powers had smothered him in Hibernian charm but had skilfully avoided showing him the accounts, meanwhile maintaining that the expense of launching Mickey Mouse and the Disneys meant the series hadn't yet earned a dime. All the profits had been swallowed up in the cost of publicity. Moreover, Powers had taken the wind out of Roy's sails by launching into a more-in-sorrow-than-in-anger attack on Walt Disney himself, accusing him of abandoning Mickey Mouse just when he was about to become a money-spinner for all of them.

'He wants to kill off the Mighty Mouse,' Powers had announced, sententiously, 'and begorra, he's going to kill all of us off in the process.'

It was a wild exaggeration but contained at least a grain of truth. Walt Disney, who was, by this time, in an extremely nervous and exhausted state, had begun to grow tired of sketching out plots for more and more Mickey Mouse films. Furthermore, his relations with Ub Iwerks, who still took Walt's creations and turned them into actual cartoon films, had grown increasingly strained. Nowadays, Walt didn't just tease the timid Ub; he barked at him and criticized his work. Seemingly oblivious of the fact that Ub was wearing himself out trying to keep up with the public's demands for more Mickey Mouse shorts, he would sometimes come into the studio late at night, lean over the desk where Ub was working overtime, and tear his sketches off the drawing board. Flinging them across the room, he would angrily complain that this wasn't what he wanted, that Ub was turning Mickey into a silly, simpering clown.

As usual, Ub never complained. Sometimes, Lilly Disney came to the studio with Walt and, as time passed, would curl up on a couch and go to sleep while Walt mooned around the office, checking on the day's work. But then she would be awakened by the abrasive sound of her husband barking at the crushed and silent Ub.

'Really, Walt,' she was often moved to remark, 'you shouldn't be so rough on that poor little man. The way you treat him! The things you say to him! Sometimes you're so rough on him, he looks as if he could kill you.'

'Nonsense,' said Walt. 'Ub doesn't mind criticism from me. He knows me too well to get mad with me. He's the most understanding character in the world. He'd do anything for me.'

Walt, in fact, was sick and tired of Mickey Mouse and would have been critical no matter how Ub animated him. He was longing to create something new – and he had an idea. It is a measure of how much he still trusted Ub's judgement and understanding that it was to him that he first expounded it. He described how Carl Stalling had played him a piano extract one night from Saint-Saëns's *Danse Macabre*.

'It's all about skeletons coming out of their graves at midnight and doing an eerie dance,' Stalling had said. 'It would make a riveting cartoon.'

Walt asked Ub what he thought of the idea, and his associate was enthusiastic. He went off to the library and came back in triumph with some reproductions of skeleton dances from the walls of ancient Etruscan tombs, and of a graphic series of drawings of skeleton dances by Rowlandson, the English cartoonist. Together he and Walt got down to work. Walt, as usual, did the original drawings. Iwerks did the rough conception and handed it on to the animators. Between them they sat in and superintended the result.

In a couple of weeks they had sent a finished cartoon to New York for dubbing. Stalling and Edouarde between them dubbed it to the music of Grieg's 'In the Hall of the Mountain King' from *Peer Gynt* and the main theme from Saint-Saëns's eerie and macabre piece.

Walt thought he and Ub had created a startlingly effective cartoon, both novel and amusing, and he told Lilly he was convinced 'it will be a real hit when it is shown'. At first he called it 'The Spook Dance', but then changed the name to *The Skeleton Dance*. He planned to send it out as the first of a series which, he said, would probably be known as the Silly Symphonies.

Pat Powers saw *The Skeleton Dance* just about the time when Roy came to see him in New York, and he hated it. So did all the exhibitors to whom he showed it.

'What's he trying to do, ruin us?' Pat asked Roy. 'You go back and tell that brother of yours the renters don't want this gruesome crap. And as for calling a whole series of them Silly Symphonies, what sort of a crazy idea is that? Why, the name alone will keep the public away in droves. What they want is more Mickey Mouse. You go back and tell Walt. MORE MICE, tell him, MORE MICE!'

He made such a fuss about *The Skeleton Dance* that Roy never got around to persuading him to show him the Mickey Mouse accounts. It was only when he returned to California that he realized he had been conned.

'That man's a crook,' Roy said to Walt when he got back. 'I'm sure of it now. He's cheating us out of our money.'

Still Walt Disney had faith. Not even Powers's devastating criticism of *The Skeleton Dance* could shake his trust in him. Anyway, he could be right. Maybe the new cartoon was too gruesome and Silly Symphonies was a ridiculous name for a new series. For the first time in his life, he began to have doubts about his own work. He kept calling in Ub Iwerks and over and over again they would sit in the tiny projection room running *The Skeleton Dance*.

'Tell me, Ub,' Walt would ask desperately, 'is it any good or not?'

Ub stared at him in astonishment.

'Don't you really know?' he asked.

Ub did not believe his self-confident boss had suddenly developed doubts. He was convinced Walt was having him on, that he was indulging in a new form of teasing. So he said nothing, refusing to play Walt's game. And it widened the gulf between the two men.

Walt's uncertainty about his new cartoon was hardly helped by the hesitation he encountered when he tried to hawk it around the bookers in Los Angeles. One of them shivered after he had seen it and said it would give his customers goose-bumps. Then, after some desperate manoeuvring, he persuaded Fred Miller, owner of the Carthay Circle Theater, to have a look at it. Miller liked it so much that he put it alongside an upcoming feature film and announced its arrival on his marquee: 'A Walt Disney Silly Symphony: The Skeleton Dance.'

Not only was *The Skeleton Dance* a hit with the public but all the critics praised it too. Miller held it over for a couple of weeks and, when he heard of its failure to find a New York booker, alerted his friend, Sam Rothafel, who ran the big Roxy Theater in Manhattan. By the time Walt had shipped the Los Angeles notices to Pat Powers, Rothafel had already been on the telephone demanding a viewing of *The Skeleton Dance*. The new cartoon went into the Roxy programme a few days later and was such a success that Rothafel held it over an extra week. Then bookings began to come in from all over the country.

At the end of a few months, *The Skeleton Dance* was a smash hit and launched the Silly Symphony series on a successful career. Pat Powers, of course, hastened to claim all the credit: he insisted he had known all along that it was a potential winner. It had needed extra-careful nurturing, that was all.

'If you believe that, you'll believe anything,' said Roy scornfully to his brother.

And for the first time, the seeds of doubt about Pat Powers's honesty and good will were planted in Walt's mind.

Pat Powers was, in fact, on the horns of a dilemma. To begin with he had quite genuinely taken on *Steamboat Willie* as a vehicle for selling his bootleg Cinephone sound system, and the success of the Mickey Mouse series had surprised him. Suddenly, the money had come pouring in, and the temptation to hold on to most of it had been too strong to resist, especially since Walt Disney was so trusting and naïve. But now he realized the bonanza might well be coming to an end. So negative a feeling had he had about Mickey Mouse to begin with that he had signed up to act as Disney distributor only for a year – just long enough, he had thought, to give the public a chance to listen to Cinephone in action. Only it was Mickey Mouse who had made the impact on them. And at any moment now, his participation in the success of the cartoons would be over. The year was almost up. How could he persuade the Disneys to renew the contract, for a really long period this time? The Disney boys were growing up, and it was now going to take more than Irish charm to persuade them to renew.

By the spring of 1929, when contracts for the future needed to be made, Pat Powers was prepared to use any method – blackmail, strong-arm methods or guile – to hold on to the gold mine that Mickey Mouse, the Silly Symphonies and the Disneys were proving to be.

Meanwhile, Roy Disney had heard rumours Pat Powers was planning something. He still did not respond to Roy's repeated demands for an exact accounting of the Mickey Mouse rentals, but money did begin to arrive – not nearly as much as the Disneys calculated they should be receiving, but they began to get cheques from Powers for 3,000 dollars and once even for 5,000 dollars. It was not enough to pay the studio bills but it was sufficient to whet Roy's appetite for what he was now convinced they were due. He decided the time had come to consult a lawyer.

It so happened that a legal adviser had recently arrived in Los Angeles with some publicity fanfare. His name was Gunther Lessing and he had represented, of all people, the Mexican revolutionary leader, Pancho Villa, who had fought a war along the US-Mexican border in 1916 against the American Army under General Pershing. Gunther Lessing had managed to sue successfully on behalf of Pancho Villa's widow and heirs. Roy Disney figured that if an attorney could get away with that, he could probably handle Pat Powers. Walt had already arranged to go to New York and have a showdown with Powers, and Roy persuaded him to take Lessing with him. Lillian Disney went along for the ride.

The first meeting took place on a cold January day in 1930 at Powers's office, and, at Walt's insistence, he went alone. Powers received him as usual with fond affection and was full of flowery compliments about the wonderful entertainment value of Mickey Mouse. Once more he insisted that all he was interested in was pushing the success of Cinephone, and that the only reason he had acted as a distributor for Disney and the cartoons was out of the kindness of his heart. When the question of a contract renewal was eventually broached, Walt immediately said, as Roy had instructed him, that he was not going to sign any further agreement with Powers until he had seen the accounts and found out what monies were owed to the Disney organization.

Powers looked as if he had been struck by his own son.

'After all I've done for you!' he said. 'Are you suggesting I've been cheating on you and your brother? After all the sleepless nights I've spent worrying about how I can make you some money, is this the way you repay me?'

Walt retorted mildly that all they wanted was what was due to them.

'And how much *is* due to you?' asked Powers, a wicked gleam in his eyes. 'Don't you think I know who is the real reason for your success?

Who made the Mickey Mouse cartoons? Who was responsible for *The Skeleton Dance* and the Silly Symphonies? Well, you may have kept it a secret from everyone else, but I know who it is. His name is Ub Iwerks, and you can't do without him!'

Walt Disney, startled at the sudden introduction of Ub's name, managed to stammer out that Iwerks was certainly a valuable associate of the Walt Disney Studio, but what did Powers mean by saying he couldn't do without him?

'Exactly that,' said Powers. 'If you lost Ub Iwerks, you'd lose everything. Your studio would come to a halt. Who's done all your animation? Who's made sure you've met all your deadlines? Ub Iwerks, that's who. I know he's indispensable to you, that losing him would be a disaster for your operation. And let me just make this clear to you, Walt. If you don't renew your contract with me, losing Ub Iwerks is just what you're going to do. Because I've got him – signed, sealed and delivered!'

'I don't believe it,' said Walt. 'Ub would never do this to me.'

'Read this,' said Powers. He passed over a telegram from his representative on the West Coast. It confirmed that Ub Iwerks had signed a five-year personal contract with Powers the previous day. He would soon be heading a new animation operation and creating a new cartoon series – for a salary of 300 dollars a week.

'I still don't believe it,' said Walt.

Powers suggested he call Roy and find out exactly what was going on. When Walt demurred (he didn't want to talk to his brother with Powers listening in), Powers changed tack and became the charming Irishman again.

'Listen, Walt,' he said. 'Don't be upset over Ub. You haven't really lost him. Not if you sign up with me. Look, I've been going over our association, and although my primary interest is Cinephone, I don't want to run out on you. I like you. Truly, I have the best interests of you and your brother at heart. And I'd like to make you a wonderful proposition. I know you and Roy need money, and I hate to see you worrying about it. Now I know how to handle these things. So let me take over your operation. I'll look after all the expenses in future, and you'll never have to fret about bills ever again. What's more, I'll pay you and your brother 1,500 dollars a week. Just think of it! Not only that, I'll give you back Ub Iwerks to work for you as long as you need him.'

Walt said bitterly: 'If Ub's done what you say he's done, I wouldn't ever want him to work with me again.'

'Don't be like that,' said Powers. 'Just go back and talk to your brother.'

Later that night, Roy Disney confirmed that Ub Iwerks had been in to see him. Without mentioning the fact that he had signed up with Powers, he had said he had decided to quit the Disney Studio. When asked the reason, he had cited increasing tensions between himself and Walt and said he couldn't stand the quarrels any longer. He wanted to leave at once and asked Roy to arrange for his interest in Walt Disney Studio to be liquidated. His contract was later terminated legally, and Iwerks's 20 per cent interest in the company was bought out for less than 3,000 dollars. Though it was all the Disneys could afford at the time, it was calculated that Ub's interest in Disney would have been worth millions of dollars had he not insisted on an immediate buy-out.

Walt was so shocked over Ub's action that he could hardly bear to continue his discussions with Powers. He mentioned to Roy that he was seeing him the following day and taking the lawyer with him. This time, he added grimly, there would be a showdown.

'Don't break with him completely until you've got some money out of him,' said Roy. 'Our situation is desperate. We need cash and we need it badly.'

The following day, Walt changed his mind and saw Powers alone again. He found him surprisingly conciliatory. When the question of a new contract came up, Walt said he had been told not to discuss it until he had some money. At which Powers pulled a cheque book out of his desk and wrote out a cheque for 5,000 dollars.

'Will this be enough?' he asked.

Walt rushed the cheque back to Roy and as soon as it had cleared the bank, sent in Gunther Lessing to deal with Powers. Lessing later confessed that handling the affairs of Pancho Villa had been much easier. Pat Powers was used to dealing with lawyers and was not one whit abashed by Lessing's demands that he open his accounts to him. Of course he was willing to show the lawyer his books, he said. All Walt and Roy had to do was sign a new contract appointing him the sole representative of the Walt Disney Studio and he would be glad to open his records to any inspection the lawyer wished to make.

'We'll get a court order,' said Lessing.

'You do that,' said Powers. 'And see how much time and money it will cost you.'

By clandestine means, Roy had discovered Powers owed him and his brother a minimum of 150,000 dollars in receipts from the Disney films. He was also unpleasantly aware that they would have to spend much more than that if they hoped to get a dime of it back through the courts. After much discussion, they decided to take their losses and walk away. But who would they sign up with now to distribute their films?

MGM suddenly showed an interest but then shied away when Pat Powers sent them a writ and threatened to sue if they attempted to handle Disney's productions. Powers was no longer the charming stage Irishman. He was good and mad, and he let it be known along Film Row he would in future take to court anyone who associated himself with the Disneys. Though it now seems hard to believe, because it was all bluff and he knew he didn't have a leg to stand on, he succeeded in scaring off the distribution companies. Suddenly no one would handle Mickey Mouse and the Silly Symphonies. There was one exception. In Hollywood at that time there was an up-and-coming young director named Frank Capra, who subsequently made some classic movies, and he happened to be a Walt Disney fan. Every time he felt low or out of ideas, he slipped into a movie house and watched Mickey Mouse or a Silly Symphony and came out enlivened and refreshed.

Capra was working for Columbia Pictures at that time, and when he heard what had happened to the Disneys – and that it might mean no more cartoons from Walt – he stormed into the office of his boss Harry Cohn, and told him he had to take over the distribution rights of Disney's cartoons.

Harry Cohn had the reputation of being one of the most ruthless and unsavoury producers in Hollywood, but he knew a good movie proposition when it was put to him. Moreover, he had one virtue. No one could scare him – not even Pat Powers. He told his legal department to fight any attempt by Powers to stop Columbia from handling Disney productions in the future. Meanwhile, he offered the Disneys a contract under which Columbia would finance their future productions and pay them 65 per cent of the gross receipts received, with books open to inspection by their legal representatives.

Cohn turned down only one request the Disneys made of him. He refused to have anything to do with the Mickey Mouse films and the first of the Silly Symphonies, *The Skeleton Dance*, which Pat Powers had previously handled. It would get them involved in too much legal wrangling, he said. Why not let Powers keep them and put someone in to keep an eye on his accounts? But Walt, who would never forgive Powers for his perfidy, could not bear the thought of continuing an association with him in any shape or form. He was determined to get him out of his life. He instructed Gunther Lessing to arrange a settlement with Powers under any sort of conditions that would sever his connection with the Disneys once and for all. It ended with Walt Disney Studio paying Powers 50,000 dollars (which they borrowed from Columbia) to return the rights of all the cartoon films he had previously handled. And though it was Powers who should have been compensating them, for he still owed them 150,000 dollars, Walt made no complaint. He felt every penny was worth it just to be rid of him.

On 7 February 1930, he telegraphed Roy from New York:

HAVE DEFINITELY BROKE[N] WITH POWERS. WILL DELIVER NO MORE PICTURES. PLAN TO TEMPORARILY SUSPEND PRODUCTION OF MICKEYS AND CONCENTRATE ON SYMPHONIES WHICH WE WILL DELIVER TO COLUMBIA.

The trauma was over.

Or was it? A few months later, Lillian went into their bedroom and found her husband breathing stertorously and apparently in a coma. She called the family doctor, whose first instinct was to rush in a medical team and pump out the contents of his stomach. Eventually they managed to bring him back to consciousness without resorting to such drastic measures, but Lilly confirmed to the doctor that Walt had been taking sleeping pills.

When he had recovered sufficiently, the doctor went to talk to Walt and afterwards admitted to Lilly that he was deeply worried about her husband's state of mind. He said he believed Walt was on the verge of what was known in those days as a nervous breakdown. From the way he looked and talked, in fact, there seemed a strong possibility that he was in a severe emotional depression, and heaven knows what might happen next unless some drastic action was taken. He was badly in need of some kind of remedial therapy, the doctor said. Otherwise, he could not answer for the consequences.

Among the many telegrams that flooded in when news hit Hollywood of Walt Disney's illness was one that he kept and never destroyed. It came from Ub Iwerks. 'PLEASE GET WELL' was all it said.

'That bastard,' said Roy, when he heard about it. 'I'm glad he's out of your life.'

'He isn't,' said Walt. 'He'll be back.'

Chapter 11
APOTHEOSIS

LOOKING back, Walt attributed his bouts of suicidal depression in 1931 to worry about the future of the Disney Studio. Ub Iwerks's 'betrayal', as he called it at the time, was seldom mentioned again after his recovery. Disney finances were certainly giving the brothers cause for concern. Even under the terms of their new distribution contract with Columbia, they were still not making enough money to meet their commitments. New animators had had to be brought in from New York (in part to take the place of Ub Iwerks who had always done the work of at least three men), and as they were highly qualified, they were paid more than the usual rate.

It was as well they were, because Walt had become a highly critical and demanding employer. In the period between Ub's departure and his own breakdown, Walt's manner and attitude towards his staff changed radically. So did his temper. No longer was he the smiling, easy-going boss who joshed around with the animators and the inkers and then walked out of the room with a wave of his hand, telling them to 'take it easy'. The phrase now became taboo around the studios. He had once taken short-cuts himself with cartoons to save time and money, but now he became angry with anyone who took an easy way out with a drawing or tried to cut corners with a cartoon sequence. He was constantly setting his artistic sights higher and demanding more from his animators. And it showed in the quality of the new productions. Disney cartoons noticeably improved during this period, even if studio morale deteriorated.

As the quality of the product went up, so did the cost of each new film. Certainly the cartoons were more popular than ever and Walt Disney's name was now, as one studio publicist put it at the time, 'better known than Confucius in China, Shakespeare in England, the Blarney Stone in Ireland, Voltaire in France and Tarzan of the Apes in Tanganyika. Walt Disney – a household name from Tel Aviv to Timbuktu!' On the other hand, profits were not coming in quickly enough to meet the studio's bills, in particular the money the Disneys had borrowed and still owed to their distributors, Columbia Pictures.

'Each [cartoon] we finished just about paid off for the next one,' Walt said later. 'I kept adding people to the staff but in spite of that I had to work overtime. I'd either go to a restaurant or I'd drive home for an early dinner, and then I'd say, "If you don't mind, I'll go back and do a little work." Lilly would go with me. I had a davenport in my office and Lilly would lie down and go to sleep.' Sometimes he would continue at his drawing board until dawn.

'I guess I was working too hard and worrying too much,' he said later. 'In 1931 I had a nervous breakdown. Each picture we made cost more than we figured it would earn. First we began to panic. Then I cracked up. I couldn't sleep. I reached the point when I couldn't even talk over the telephone without crying. I was in a highly emotional state.'

However, the financial state of the studios was not the root cause of his breakdown. Walt left money matters to Roy, and it was Roy who did the worrying over them. Walt was uncaring, even a spendthrift, about money. True, he never lavished it on himself or on Lilly, because any money he could lay his hands on he spent on his cartoons. The more money they made, the more he would pour into his productions, to improve their quality, to reshoot, to try out new ideas and techniques, and to introduce new characters. And if the profits weren't there, he went on spending anyway – until Roy called a halt. No, the real cause of Walt Disney's emotional breakdown in 1931 was much more complicated than that. He was thirty years old in 1931, and his trouble was that he had suddenly lost faith in himself not as an artist, not as a cartoonist and film-maker, but as a man.

Walt Disney was a product of his time and his background. Like most white American males of his day, he had been brought up in a male-dominated society in which women were indulged, cherished and protected – and even worshipped when they became mothers of strong sons and healthy daughters. But it was with other men that a man made his friendships, men whom he respected and whose advice he took, men with whom he usually spent his moments of leisure. Women were very much the second, and inferior, sex, regarded by their menfolk as adorable but fallible creatures whose intentions might be good but who were likely to be unreliable. Your pals never let you down, if you picked the right men in whom to put your trust, that is.

It was because these ideas were so deeply ingrained that his disillusionment with Pat Powers had been so profound. He had counted Powers as a friend, and the fact that he had so shabbily deceived him had shaken both his self-confidence and his belief in his ability to judge the worth of his fellow-men. Coming on top of Pat Powers's deceitfulness, the defection of Ub had hurt him even more, for he had always considered Ub Iwerks to be his closest and most reliable friend. What kind of a world was he living in where two men he had so implicitly relied upon could betray him? It shattered his faith not only in them but in his own judgement, and he blamed himself for not having seen through them, for having been so naïve and vulnerable.

Roy, too, had unwittingly dealt him another blow, and this one was even more painful to bear. Roy had become the father of a son: Edna had given birth to Roy Edward Disney Jr in January 1930. And nothing had brought home more poignantly to Walt Disney the sense of his own inadequacy. He saw himself not only as a poor judge of men, a sucker for cheats, tricksters and traitors, but as a weakling who couldn't even match up to the ordinary American male and produce a child of his own. He and Lilly had tried hard enough. Ever since their marriage six years before, they had been longing for a child. They had consulted doctors and were told to go on trying. But it hadn't happened. And since their consultant had broadly hinted that it wasn't Lilly's fault, it had hardly helped the marriage to run smoothly. Each time Walt produced a new cartoon character – Julius the Cat, Oswald the Lucky Rabbit, Mickey Mouse – it began to seem like a form of sublimation, and there were times during their quarrels when Lilly hinted as much.

It was this gap in his family life, plus his bitterness over the defection of his friends, which brought Walt Disney low in 1931. He went to the christening party for Roy Edward Disney Jr and found it hard to share Roy's pride in being a father. He felt hypocritical when congratulating his brother and his wife and he knew he would never be able to love his nephew – though he could not guess what trouble his attitude would stir up in the future. He went home with Lilly after the christening party and felt so disgusted with himself that there came a point when he seriously contemplated killing himself. What good was he to anyone?

Walt Disney had never really forgotten a dream he had shared with his Red Cross buddy, Russell Maas, of travelling down the Mississippi on a raft with their two dogs. The trip had never taken place but that boyhood dream of adventure had stayed in Walt's mind, and now, as he convalesced from his breakdown, he had a sudden urge to do something about it. His doctor had advised him to take his wife on a trip. He told Lilly to pack their bags and they boarded an eastbound train for St Louis. From there he knew what they were going to do. They would take the next best thing to a raft, a paddle steamer, down the Mississippi to New Orleans, and perhaps sail on – who knows where? Lilly, as always, was willing to go along with his impulses. Unfortunately, reality rarely measures up to boyhood dreams, and it turned out that passenger boats had for the time being ceased making the trip between St Louis and New Orleans. The disappointment did nothing to improve Walt Disney's pessimistic mood.

Lilly, who loved travelling, was determined to enjoy herself and immediately proposed they go on a sightseeing tour of Washington, DC, instead. Her ebullience was catching and after three days Walt's spirits began to lift. She had been quietly patient, sympathetic and understanding all through her husband's crisis, and now she felt the turning point had come.

Walt's fame as the creator of Mickey Mouse had preceded him to the nation's capital, and the publicity man at the Mayflower Hotel, where they were staying, put himself at the service of the Disneys, offering to open any doors for them. Walt, who had once chauffeured General John Pershing's son in France, asked if a meeting with the general could be arranged. Pershing had commanded the US armies on the Western Front in World War I, and was one of Walt's boyhood heroes. Crestfallen, the press agent came back and confessed that Pershing was too busy to see him but, to Walt and Lilly's amazement, offered instead a private audience with President Hoover at the White House.

'It sure restores your sense of American values,' Walt laughed.

The trip lasted nearly two months, took them via Key West to Cuba and back through the Panama Canal to California, and by the time they returned Walt Disney was his old resilient, optimistic self. It made all the difference to the marriage. In the summer of 1932, some months after their return, Lilly happily told him she was pregnant. As it happened, it turned out to be a false alarm, but at least it was an indication of the change in the nature of their relationship.

Just before Walt had left on his recuperative vacation, Roy had informed his brother that he was breaking their connection with Columbia and seeking a tie-up with a new studio. The burden of paying off the 50,000-dollar debt to Columbia had proved to be impossible so long as Harry Cohn would advance only 7,500 dollars for the cost of each new cartoon. When Roy had asked Cohn to increase his subvention to 15,000 dollars a cartoon, he had turned him down flat. So Roy had searched for a new studio which would prove to be more financially generous, and had found one at United Artists. Walt was pleased when he heard, since UA was the home of his favourite comedian, Charlie Chaplin, who was known to be a Mickey Mouse fan. United Artists had agreed to finance future Disney cartoons at 15,000 dollars each, and signed up for a series of twelve Silly Symphonies, but they wanted quick delivery and exhibition of their first brand-new Disney cartoon.

Roy had asked Walt to put a new Silly Symphony into production before he and Lilly left for their holiday. It was a moment when Walt was in the depths of his depression and no flash of inspiration had come as he sweated over the drawing board. In the end he had concocted a rough draft which he called 'Flowers and Trees' and left it to the animators to flesh it out with sequences of daisies dancing, oak trees swaying in the wind, and birds twittering through the forest glades. In truth, he didn't give a damn how it turned out. By the time he came back with Lilly, *Flowers and Trees* was finished and ready to be delivered to the new distributors. And when he saw it, even in his new and buoyant mood, he thought it was terrible. It lacked all those qualities that had made the earlier Silly Symphonies so special. His impulse was to start all over again – a prospect which appalled the budget-conscious Roy.

When Lilly told him she was pregnant, he was so happy he got a better (if even more expensive) idea. Nathalie Kalmus, the head of Technicolor, had recently given him a private view of his lab's new three-colour process, which he was preparing to launch on the Hollywood film world. Walt was entranced by the revelation of what the addition of colour could do to a movie, and he came back full of enthusiasm, convinced his future cartoon films must, whenever possible, be made using this spectacular new process. He would make it all over again, despite Roy's qualms, and he would add colour. He would be celebrating not only the birth of his first child, but a new kind of Disney cartoon such as no one had ever seen before.

Roy Disney sourly pointed out that remaking *Flowers and Trees* in Technicolor would add two-thirds to the budget of the film. He added they had already settled the price with UA for the twelve-film series and it was now too late to go back on the agreement. If they added colour, the increased costs would ruin them. When Walt took no notice of his warnings, Roy went back to his office to study his figures and brood. Then he heard some news that galvanized him into making one more effort to curb Walt's extravagant ideas.

After Ub Iwerks had quit the Disneys, he had started a new Hollywood operation on his own (financed in part by Pat Powers) and the rumour was that the first of the productions from the Ub Iwerks Studio would soon be appearing, and that it would be a Silly Symphony-type cartoon film. Moreover, the story was that Ub had been to Technicolor, too, and had let it be known his first venture would also be in colour. Roy hoped the news would goad his brother into halting his own plans with Technicolor. In fact, it had the opposite effect.

Walt went to Kalmus and put Disney's prestige on the line. If Technicolor desired to exploit the Disney name as one of their customers, there had to be a quid pro quo. Kalmus immediately understood what Walt was suggesting. Technicolor gave the Walt Disney Studio a two-year exclusive right to use their new system in cartoon films, and Ub Iwerks – along with all other cartoon film-makers – was turned away. Ub went back to black-and-white cartoons with a character called Flip the Frog.

By that time, Lilly had discovered it was a phantom pregnancy and she was not going to have a baby after all. *Flowers and Trees* was well into its new production and Walt did not tell her that it had been intended as a special tribute to her. But halfway through the remake, he brought her to the studio to see the rough-cut. She told him she thought it was wonderful.

'I'm glad you think so,' he said. 'I made it for you, and,' with a sigh, patting her empty stomach, 'for him.'

'Don't worry,' she added. 'There's always a next time.'

On the strength of Lilly's reaction to *Flowers and Trees*, Walt showed the rough-cut to Sidney Grauman, who ran the famous Chinese Theater on Hollywood Boulevard. Grauman was so sure it was going to be a winner that he booked it into the Chinese for his next world première, which would be a Hollywood version of Eugene O'Neill's *Strange Interlude*, with Norma Shearer and Clark Gable. As it happened, *Flowers and Trees* got a much more enthusiastic welcome from the critics than did the main feature.

Roy was not as euphoric as Walt. 'They'll never be satisfied with black and white again,' he grumbled. 'And just think of how much extra that's going to cost us!'

He was quite right, of course. The difference in the impact between this and the earlier Silly Symphonies was so striking that it was obvious they would all have to be made in colour in future, greatly

134

inflating Roy's budget. But, in fact, Walt Disney Studio gained rather than lost because of the transformation. So entranced were audiences by the dramatic effects of colour that the Symphonies were held over in the cinemas, sometimes for more than a month. The rentals doubled, trebled and quadrupled in consequence, and the extra profits more than compensated for the added cost.

Flowers and Trees was also boosted by becoming not only the first Disney cartoon to win Walt an Oscar, in November 1932, but also the first cartoon ever to win the award. Later that same evening his contemporaries added a special award for his creation of Mickey Mouse. Among the thousands of congratulatory notes he received next day was one that surprised him – from Ub Iwerks. Walt threw all the others away, but this one he kept.

Early in 1933, Lilly informed Walt she was pregnant again, and assured him that this time it was no false alarm. She had seen her doctor, had been through all the tests and her condition was confirmed. Walt celebrated by moving his wife into a new house he had built in the Los Feliz area of Los Angeles, and, since the money was now beginning to flow in, he encouraged Lilly to furnish it in any way she wished and damn the expense. It was a much more spacious and handsome home than either had ever had before, with a large swimming pool, and it had a spectacular view over the southern Californian hills. Lilly loved it.

But that, he decided, was not enough; he just had to make a film for her, as he had intended to do with *Flowers and Trees*. Talking it over with his friend, Carl Stalling, he was reminded of Richard Wagner, who had celebrated the birth of his son by giving his wife, Cosima, the first performance of the Siegfried Idyll. Ironically enough, Walt did not particularly like Wagner's music, which he found a little too rich and solemn for his taste, but he liked the nature of the gesture. What could he produce for Lilly that would move her to laughter instead of Wagnerian tears?

Pigs!

Pigs made Lilly laugh. He remembered telling her about how as a boy he had herded hogs on the farm in Marceline, and the way she had laughed over his story of riding the big sow home each evening and being tipped into the duck pond. The story of *The Three Little Pigs* had been on his desk for a long time as a possible subject for a cartoon, and he and Ub Iwerks had played around with the idea before Ub's abrupt departure. But somehow, it hadn't worked out. As a black-and-white cartoon, the confrontation between the hungry wolf and the innocent pigs had seemed too grim. Both of them had felt audiences would be turned off by the sinister aspects of the story. But would the addition of colour lighten it?

Walt did a colour sketch from memory of Porker, the old sow from Marceline, and circulated it through the studio along with an outline script, and asked for ideas and conceptions. The response surpassed all his hopes and expectations.

One of the newly-arrived animators from New York, Norm Ferguson, came into Walt's office shortly afterwards and produced a series of brilliant drawings of the Big Bad Wolf. The wolf had slavering fangs and an evil look, but with extraordinary humour, adroitness and dexterity, Ferguson had somehow turned him into a kind of raffish stage villain more likely to move audiences to chuckles than to send shivers down their spines. It was the youngest member of the Walt Disney staff, an eighteen-year-old named Fred Moore, who did the drawings of the three little pigs. Moore was a self-taught artist who liked doodling around on a drawing board; the only art classes he had ever attended had been in high school. His favourite doodles were saucy pictures of sexy girls; and, as it turned out, he also had a deft line with pigs. He had grasped what Walt Disney was seeking and had humanized the pigs, so that an audience could laugh with them, share fear, joy and panic with them, and identify with them too. Shrewdly, he had kept his boss's original sketch of Porker but added a mannish and roguish look.

'Know who he is?' he asked Walt.

'*She* used to be an old sow I knew in Missouri,' said Walt, 'but you've changed her sex. Now – well, let's see.' He studied Moore's drawing more closely. 'Yes, I know! This is the Foolish Pig character, isn't he? Couldn't be anyone else.'

Fred Moore nodded and grinned. He knew his boss was already sold on his drawings.

By this time they had a scenario which Ted Sears had fleshed out from Walt's outline. Ferguson and Moore, on the strength of their sketches, were assigned the film and had a feeling from the start that they were on to a winner. When someone suggested that they give it music and songs, Walt enthusiastically agreed. Agents were alerted to approach famous composers like Gershwin, Rodgers and Hammerstein and Irving Berlin to come up with tunes and themes. Then someone mentioned the name of Frank Churchill. Churchill was a humble piano-player in the Disney music department who helped put soundtracks on the cartoons. He had read Walt Disney's memo and inquired whether there would be any songs in the film. When told that there would be, he turned up with a sheaf of catchy jingles. To one batch Ted Sears added words, and played and sang them for the animators. Norm Ferguson and Fred Moore were both delighted and rushed over to tell Walt. He didn't have much faith in his own musical judgement, but the enthusiasm of Norm and Fred was such that they won him over. With a warning that they still might have to fall back on Gershwin or Berlin, he told them to go ahead. One of the ideas they came up with a few days later was a song for the little pigs to sing. It became a world hit under the title: 'Who's Afraid of the Big Bad Wolf?'

The Three Little Pigs opened at Radio City Music Hall in New York in May 1933 and, much to Walt Disney's disappointment, was received at first with only lukewarm enthusiasm. He had hoped to take Lilly along for the first performance, since it was 'her' film, but she was not in a fit condition to travel. It was just as well. Roy Disney went to the New York opening instead, and believing as he did that this was the best thing Walt Disney Studio had ever done, he fumed with frustration at the wooden public response and the lacklustre reception from the New York critics.

Maybe it was the sheer size of the Music Hall and the vastness of the screen which inhibited audience reaction to *The Three Little Pigs*. At any rate, the moment it moved out of the gigantic showplace to upper East Side movie houses in New York, the film seemed to catch fire as it did later at the Music Hall. Queues began to form and radio stations around town suddenly all began clamouring for permission to play 'Who's Afraid of the Big Bad Wolf?' Since the United States was still in the depths of a depression, the Big Bad Wolf became a symbol of hard times and the survival of the little pigs a message of hope.

So unexpected was the impact of *The Three Little Pigs* and its music that the Disney organization hadn't even issued sheet copies of 'Big Bad Wolf' or the other songs, and a familiar sight at the showings from now on was that of arrangers scribbling away by flashlight in the audience, frantically copying down the words and music from the screen so their band-leader bosses – like Paul Whiteman and Guy Lombardo and the Dorsey Brothers – could respond to the hundreds of requests they received to play the increasingly popular song. Publishing houses rushed to buy up the rights, and Roy made a profitable royalty deal with Irving Berlin's own music company.

The Three Little Pigs eventually became one of the most popular and profitable cartoon Disney films of the thirties. It rarely ran for just a week but was held over with different feature films, sometimes for months. It had given three young members of Walt Disney's staff the opportunity of showing what they could do. The two animators became famous inside Hollywood as masters of their craft, though they did not figure in the credits for the film and remained unknown to the public. Norman (Fergy) Ferguson went on to draw Pluto, Disney's imperishable dog star, and the Witch in *Snow White*. Fred Moore became a key animator of Mickey Mouse (doing the first colour Mickey Mouse in 1935). Their success could not have come at a more opportune moment for the future of the studio: Hollywood was still prophesying disaster for Disney after the loss of Ub Iwerks, but Ferguson and Moore proved they could more than fill the gap, and that Walt Disney had lost none of his talent for inspiring and galvanizing them.

On 8 December 1933, Lillian Disney gave birth to a baby daughter. She was christened Diane Marie. A week later, on Christmas Day, Walt rigged up a screen in the nursery of the Los Feliz home and gave Lilly her very own showing of *The Three Little Pigs*.

'It's the best thing you've ever done,' she said, when it was over. And then she went on: 'But you know, I somehow feel I ought to have given you . . .' for a moment it seemed as if she were about to say 'a son', but then she added quickly, with a laughing nod at the screen, 'Triplets!'

'This piglet is good enough for me,' he said, nodding to their new baby daughter in the crib.

Part Three

HEY-DAY

Chapter 12

VOICES

THE sun shone upon the Disneys in 1933. The highly profitable success of *The Three Little Pigs* made any kind of Disney cartoon a necessary item in movie programmes, and the scramble to book the Silly Symphony and Mickey Mouse series was such it was hard for the studios to keep up with the demand. All over the nation (all over the world, in fact) cinema distributors were now echoing Pat Powers and stridently demanding 'More mice!' or 'More pigs!'

Both Walt and Roy Disney sensed the nature of their operation was changing, if not their personal functions. Walt would go on being the brains, the inspiration and the catalyst in the organization, and Roy would always be the money-man. But, of necessity, their day-to-day roles were being transformed and so were the pressures under which they worked. They now had to learn how to cope with the problems of success instead of with the possibility of failure. And, in learning, Walt showed a new side to his nature – and it was a tough one.

As an expanding enterprise, the Walt Disney Studio was already bulging at the seams, despite the fact that an extra administration building had been erected on Hyperion Avenue. The number of personnel now employed by the studio passed the 100 mark early in 1933, and doubled that number in the next twelve months. More animators were desperately sought to keep up with the demand for more Disney cartoons. The studios of rival companies in New York were combed for bright, restive and ambitious illustrators, and scores were tempted with good contracts and brought to the West Coast. But the supply of real talent was limited, and more sources needed to be tapped to cope with Walt's own ideas for improving the nature and quality of his cartoons.

Walt Disney showed his new side in 1933. One morning in the autumn of that year, he called a meeting of his artistic staff and told them he had worked out a revolutionary new policy for future productions, and planned to commit the studio's growing capital to improving the all-round quality of Disney cartoons. By spending large amounts of money on training new talent, implementing new techniques and adopting new processes, he believed he could give his output a kind of 'fluidity' and 'realism' such as had never before been achieved in animated cartoons. Not only would there be no more short-cuts to save production expenses, but there would be no more tricks-of-the-trade on the part of his animators to save themselves time and trouble. To an increasingly apprehensive audience, he announced that much of the expertise they had acquired at the studios over the years was now unnecessary, out of date and would have to be unlearned. There were a lot of veterans around who had come up through the 'stick figure' era and had never really lost their old habits, and were not likely to do so now. He knew how much the Disney Studio owed them for their loyalty and dedication over the years, and since, he joked, he did not expect old dogs to learn new tricks, they must not think that Disney was about to let them go. They could rest assured the studio would find other jobs for them somewhere. But Disney had to move on, and new talent was needed. To fill the gaps in the animation department, recruiters were being sent to art schools all over the country and signing up promising young students to train as animators at the studio.

It was a chilling outline of things to come, and it was a very sober bunch of animators who went back to their desks. No one raised any objections at the meeting, mainly because everyone was suddenly frightened for his or her job. They were jolted and shocked not so much by Walt's action as by the abrupt way in which he had announced it. Is this what success did for a man? Though they kept silent for the moment, they would remember that meeting in the years to come – when they felt stronger.

There was still a depression in the United States, and jobs were scarce. The Walt Disney Studio did not have much trouble in persuading young artists to join the organization, even though the salaries Roy Disney offered were extremely modest. Why should they be paid full salaries, he argued, when they were amateurs learning on the job, when work elsewhere was non-existent, and when there was the additional prestige of being associated with Disney?

Meanwhile, Walt made a deal with Mrs Nelbert Chouinard, of the Chouinard Art Institute of Los Angeles, to teach apprentice Disney animators in her night classes. Because many of them did not have transport, he ferried them there in his own car and paid for their tuition. When the numbers grew too large, he hired one of the Chouinard teachers to give lectures on classical art and biology at the studio.

142

Don Graham, who taught the life classes, ran into criticism and derision from his students. They had all done this kind of work in art school, and they accused him of being too rigid about the living forms he asked his classes to reproduce. What possible connection could this have with new ideas in animated cartooning? Walt was increasingly demanding that his young animators make their cartoon characters 'flow', and how could that be achieved if they were expected to do as Graham demanded, meticulously sketch the models he brought to the studios? It was true that the models changed poses, but the poses were always static. After some sarcastic comments had been scrawled on the studio notice-board by sceptical students, Walt consulted Graham. They changed the routine and now had the models move around the studio during the sketching sessions, doing hand-stands and acrobatics; they never stood still. Then they would slip away and leave the students to sketch all their different poses from memory, in the hope that they would recapture the flow of their movements. It worked so well that even some of the old hands in the animation department started attending the sessions.

At the same time, Walt started a small private zoo at the studio and filled it with deer, rats and mice, rabbits, parrots, cougars and ostriches, whose movements the students were expected to study and sketch. In addition, to induce his animators to get more liquidity into the movement of their characters and more drama into their backgrounds, he established a laboratory where water dripping from a height was filmed in close-up with macro-cameras. Balls were bounced and shot in slow motion to show in detail how they changed in shape as they hit the ground or a wall or a baseball bat.

The search for new effects worked well. The new recruits proved to be bright, fresh, willing and innovative, and though they were resented and cold-shouldered to begin with, after a time their enthusiasm stimulated their older, professional colleagues.

Connoisseurs of Disney films have noted that the cartoons made at this period show a dramatic improvement, the characters seeming suddenly to become living and breathing and all but three-dimensional images instead of mere animated drawings.

It was a fecund period in another way, too. New characters were being born, some of them spin-offs from the Mickey Mouse and Silly Symphony series. Norm Ferguson, who had created the Big Bad Wolf, had been experimenting and achieved some notable comic effects with a dog, a bloodhound, which had made his first appearance in a cartoon short called *The Chain Gang*. The comic characteristics of the

143

animal were such that he stood out from the others in the cartoon and made audiences remember him.

As Ben Sharpsteen (later head of the animation department) remembered it later: 'Fergy was successful in getting a looseness into the bloodhound that exaggerated its ability to sniff (a wrinkling of the nose) and to think (facial expressions, such as a quizzical look or a sudden smile directed at the audience). Fergy succeeded in getting a feeling of flesh into his animation. No one realized what Fergy had done, however, until after the preview.'

After the preview everybody wanted to see the bloodhound again. Walt Disney called Ferguson into his office and suggested he play around with the bloodhound and develop his potential.

Walt did not tell Fergy to do a different dog. Veteran animators remember that he never at any time suggested in words how the dog should appear – that was not his method. But they also remember that he did act out the character, scratching, sniffing around until everyone was laughing at his comic canine antics.

So far as the bloodhound's development was concerned, the animators remember that Walt called a staff meeting and started reminiscing about an old dog from his boyhood on the farm at Marceline, and he began describing the animal's antics. It became funnier and funnier. He would clown the dog's expressions, lifting one eyebrow and then the other, using those penetrating eyes of his to reinforce his comic expressions. And, all the time, Fergy was watching him.

The first tests of the bloodhound that Fergy showed at the studio were so effective that everyone was enthusiastic, and he was encouraged to do more. He went on to sketch a famous comic sequence in which the bloodhound accidentally sits down on a roll of sticky fly-paper, and his contortions and facial expressions as he attempts to free himself are excruciatingly comic. No one who saw these preliminary sketches had any doubt about the bloodhound's future. He was so delightfully funny in Fergy's conception that he was bound to end up as a star. But what would they call him? Finally, someone said that since this was a hound whose voice came from the depths, why not call him Pluto? The suggestion took Walt Disney's fancy, and Pluto went on to be one of the most durable and likeable of Disney's stars.

Responsibility for Pluto's invention and development was to cause some unhappiness at the Walt Disney Studio in the months to come. Most of Walt's veteran animators had learned early to accept one of the rules of the establishment: the boss took the principal credit for everything achieved in the studio, and their contributions to a film or a sequence or a character were expected to remain anonymous. Most of Disney's employees had loyally accepted this, until the new apprentice animators began arriving and veterans who had been with the studio for years suddenly realized they were expendable. What if they were suddenly thrown out to make way for a talented tyro? Shouldn't they be able to take their credits with them? Shouldn't they be able to boast they had invented Pluto or the Foolish Pig or Donald Duck? One of the animators who had been particularly shocked by the change in Walt Disney's attitude towards his loyal veterans was Norm Ferguson. He now made it plain that he wanted recognition as Pluto's creator and did not like sharing credit for his invention with Walt. He admitted that his boss had partly inspired Pluto and that no one watching the way he had drawn the character could have any doubt about where he had found the model for his creation. The way the bloodhound's eyebrows moved and his excruciating facial contortions could only have been copied from Walt Disney's own facial mannerisms. But did that make Walt responsible – or even partly responsible – for Pluto? Norm Ferguson did not think so. Not all of his fellow animators agreed with him. Two old hands, Frank Thomas and Ollie Johnston, have no doubt that Walt Disney should have equal share of the credit; they seem to chide Fergy for insisting otherwise.

Norman Ferguson certainly did not agree with them. And his dissatisfaction at being given what he considered less than his due over Pluto's creation was to have an unhappy outcome.

Unaware of this gnawing bitterness among his veterans, Walt Disney was worrying about what Pluto would sound like and who would be his voice. Now that the Disney cartoons were wired for sound, Walt appreciated only too well the importance of making his cartoon characters sound authentic or the effect of the image on the screen could be ruined.

It was hardly surprising, and not simply by accident, that Walt had found his own voice ideally suited to become that of Mickey Mouse. The squeaky high-pitched notes which he had used when acting out Mickey's character made the mouse so funny, and yet so believable, that his voice was incorporated on to the sound-track. In any case, everybody around the studio had by this time accepted that Mickey Mouse was really Walt Disney's screen alter ego, resembling him both in appearance and character; he had the same habits, the same outlook, the same mischievous sense of fun, and the same tendency to take foolish risks. The addition of Walt's own voice to the cartoon character logically completed the conception. Having heard Mickey speak for the first time, it was thereafter impossible to imagine anyone else repeating the dialogue – which is why Mickey sounded so strange in French or German or Italian versions, where he was dubbed by native speakers.

As the new characters spilled on to the sketch boards of Disney's animators in the thirties, Walt found himself eagerly seeking to match their appearance and mannerisms with their voices. It was obvious that Pluto should speak with a deep and commanding bass or baritone. He tried out opera singers and the bass voices of the Mormon Tabernacle Choir. Finally for Pluto (and eventually for one of his spin-offs, Goofy) he found the ideal vocal chords right inside the studio. Pinto Colvig worked in the Disney music department and played the clarinet and ocarina. When Frank Churchill, composer of 'Who's Afraid of the Big Bad Wolf?', had been searching for an effective way to end his song, it had been Pinto who had found the ideal envoi in a five-note musical flourish on the ocarina. No one seemed to have noticed that this narrow-framed little man also had a deeply mellifluous baritone voice until one day Walt came into the music studio and found him doing a vocal imitation of Pluto. He was quickly put to work dubbing the dialogue first for Pluto and then for Goofy, and he gave them that extra dimension that brought them to life on the screen.

Other voices were found among the studio staff. An animator named Fred Spencer could talk with a gargle, and sounded like a fish speaking under water for a cartoon called *Three Little Fish*. Ollie Johnston did a marvellous imitation of a talking sheep in a Silly Symphony.

This was the period when yet another of Disney's most memorable characters was in the process of conception. A duck had caused a lot of laughter and attention in a Silly Symphony in 1934 called *The Wise Little Hen*, and he became the egotistic and short-fused bird afterwards known as Donald Duck. But all Donald's peculiarly feisty characteristics remained two-dimensional without the right voice. Then, one day, Walt listened to an amateur radio show and heard a contestant named Clarence Nash doing bird imitations.

'That's Donald Duck!' he cried, as Nash launched into a particularly raucous bird-call.

Clarence Nash, who had been a California schoolteacher until then, joined the Disney staff as the voice of Donald Duck, and was still doing it as abrasively as ever on Donald's fiftieth anniversary in 1984 (he died in February 1985, aged eighty). In Donald Duck's case, Nash did the foreign voices, and as he later said he learned to squawk in French, Spanish, Portuguese, Japanese, Chinese and German.

Now the money positively poured in, so that even Roy sometimes didn't know what to do with it. It is doubtful that the public was conscious of the technical changes Walt was making, but it was certain that Disney cartoons were out-distancing the competition everywhere. Statesmen and politicians mentioned Mickey Mouse in their speeches. It was leaked from the White House that *The Three Little Pigs* was President Roosevelt's favourite screen entertainment. The League of Nations cited Walt Disney for his contribution to the arts. Walt and Roy were now not only celebrated but prosperous as well, and everything connected with them seemed to make them richer and more famous.

The money was so unexpected that the brothers hardly knew what to spend it on. They encouraged their wives to lash out on designer clothes and take up charitable work. They themselves embraced that most expensive sport, polo. Joined by some of their better-paid animators and by the lawyer Gunther Lessing, who had now joined Disney as head of the legal department, they took lessons from a professional in the San Fernando Valley, and then sallied forth to do battle against the film colony's best players. Walt built up his stable to twelve crack ponies. He was a dare-devil if not exactly a skilful horseman and pitted himself against such dedicated and ruthless players as Darryl Zanuck, Big Boy Williams and Will Rogers, at whose hands he took some nasty tumbles. In one such spill, he broke a collar bone and ricked his neck, which caused him a lot of pain later.

Delighted with his baby daughter, Diane, Walt still dreamed of having a son, but conceiving a second baby was the one thing, it seemed, that all this new-found prosperity couldn't buy. This time the doctors blamed Walt's physical condition alone, and decided that though he seemed fit enough to play in the toughest polo matches, he lacked the necessary genes for easy fatherhood. They began pumping his thyroid full of liver extract and other injections. It did no good.

By this time, Walt, who had first taken up cigarettes while still in school, was now consuming at least two packets a day. Curiously enough, none of the doctors suggested that he might lose weight and improve his health and nervous system if he cut down his consumption. He had developed a persistent smoker's cough, and it soon became an alarm signal around the Walt Disney Studio; the animators always knew he was on his way to see them when they heard him hacking his way along the corridors. Walt's sudden prosperity certainly didn't seem to bring him satisfaction or peace of mind. In many ways, he was as racked with self-doubt and angst as he had been in the days before his breakdown.

Roy and Edna worried about him and about the state of his marriage. And when Lilly, too, showed signs of catching Walt's nervous twitches, Roy intervened to suggest that both their families should take a vacation trip to Europe. The excuse was the decision by the League of Nations in 1935 to award Walt a medal for the creation of Mickey Mouse.

The sponsors of the ceremony forgot to inform the brothers the proceedings would be informal, and while the delegates turned up in casual dress, Walt and Roy appeared in formal wear specially tailored for the occasion – the only time in their lives when they dressed in top hats and morning suits. In one passage of his acceptance speech, Walt couldn't resist the temptation and dropped into the famous mouse's high-pitched squeak and said he was 'taking the Mickey' out of himself and Roy for 'getting above themselves'. After the ceremony, they journeyed to Paris. It was the first time Walt had been to France since the end of World War I, and he took his wife, Roy, Edna and the children for a tour of the old battlefields. Afterwards there was a trip to Holland, England and Italy.

Everywhere they went, crowds assembled to greet the creator of Mickey Mouse. In Rome they were given a private audience with the Pope and then had a long interview with the Italian dictator, Benito Mussolini, who said he was a Donald Duck fan.

The trip did them all good, and Walt seemed fully recovered by the time they got back to California. But still Diane remained his only child and Lilly began to think about adoption.

And still the money rolled in, from all over the world, anything connected with Disney could be turned into gold.

One day Walt Disney got a call from someone called Herman (Kay) Kamen. He said he had a scheme for guaranteeing Walt Disney Studio an extra income of 50,000 dollars a year, for which Walt wouldn't have to lift a finger, and could he come out to Hollywood and talk about it? There was something in the approach that Walt couldn't resist, and he told Kamen that if he wanted to make the journey – at his own expense, of course – he would set up a meeting.

In a nation which has produced some remarkable entrepreneurs, Kay Kamen was something special.

'He was a fantastic salesman,' DeWitt Jones, one of the men who worked for him at Disney later, told the present author. 'You meet a certain number of people in your lifetime who make a great impact on you, and Kamen certainly did on me. He was an incredible-looking man. He had a wide nose and wore thick glasses, was six feet tall and very strong physically. And he was proud of the fact that he wasn't exactly pretty. He maintained that his appearance was a great advantage in his profession. Any good salesman will tell you that if you want to be remembered, you're either completely bald, you have flaming red hair, or something else is striking about you. Guys who wear Brooks Brothers suits just get forgotten, but not extraordinary-looking guys like Kay Kamen.'

Kamen was a born salesman. From his sales territory around Chicago and the Middle West, where he represented several big dry-goods factories, he had been watching the progress of Disney's cartoons with particular interest. He was always seeing Disney souvenirs in shop windows and drug stores, Mickey Mouse badges, ties and scarves with the images of Pluto and Goofy and Minnie Mouse imprinted on them. And when he made inquiries about how much the manufacturers were paying the Disneys for these popular images, he was surprised to discover that they paid no royalties – most of them didn't even ask the Disney Studio for permission to use its creations on their products. It was a territory into which Roy Disney had never strayed: he was as ignorant of the potential profits from Walt Disney logos as he had been of the sheet music and reproduction rights to 'Who's Afraid of the Big Bad Wolf?' It was this discovery which had moved Kay Kamen to call up Walt Disney, after which he decided the big moment in his life had arrived and it was time to gamble.

'So Kay got together all the money he possessed in the world,' recalled DeWitt Jones. 'He turned in all his life insurance, and took a mortgage on his house, and it came to about 65,000 dollars. This he changed into 1,000 and 5,000 dollar notes. He sewed them into his coat and then he took the train from Chicago. He had no money for a pullman; and besides, he was so scared because of all that money on him that he didn't dare sleep. He sat up and clutched himself for four whole days, and as soon as he got to California he went straight to see Walt Disney – and what did he do but fall fast asleep right there in his office while Walt was talking to him!'

He offered the Disneys money for no effort on their part. He put 50,000 dollars in cash on Walt's desk as an earnest of his intentions, and said he would guarantee a minimum of another 50,000 dollars a year for the right to handle the use of their name on national merchandise.

'The first 50,000 dollars will be yours,' he said, 'and after that, we will split everything down the middle. I will charge manufacturers 5 per cent of their wholesale price for the use of your name or logo on their product, and from every cent they pay me, 50 per cent will be yours.'

Both Walt and Roy were well aware they could have handled the royalty business themselves, and there was really no reason to pay an outsider for exploiting their name on other people's products. On the other hand, they had no organization for doing it and Roy showed no inclination to set up an appropriate department. Moreover, they were incapable of resisting Kamen's proposal to increase their annual income with absolutely no effort on their part.

As a result, in 1932 Kay Kamen took over the merchandizing of Disney's name on every kind of product from watches to running shoes to ice-cream cones. He was soon paying 2.5 million dollars into Disney's account every year, and, of course, earning a similar amount for himself. It was not until Kamen's untimely death in 1949 – he was killed in an aeroplane accident – that Roy Disney realized they had been making him rich and cheating themselves. And they had barely tapped the potential of the magic Disney name.

Meanwhile, what were they to do with all their money? Roy was all for spending it on improvements to the studios. Realizing that Hyperion Avenue was already cramped and would soon be too small an area to cater for their future needs, he had begun looking around for a place for a new studio, and had his eye on a site in Burbank. Walt had other ideas. The moment he returned from his European trip and settled back at his desk, he felt a surge of euphoria. He was later to say it was one of the most exhilarating moments of his creative life, and he was bursting with ambition. He had loved being hailed in Europe as the pioneer of new discoveries in cartoon films, and he had basked unabashedly in the praise the statesmen had heaped upon him. Now he came back to find that the critics were acclaiming the first Mickey Mouse cartoon in colour, *Band Concert*.

It was his young animator Fred Moore who had given the new and magic vitality to Mickey in this film. As Ward Kimball, one of his colleagues, said later in *Disney Animation*:

Yes, Fred Moore was just right for the time. He was the first one to escape from the mold of the rubber hose, round circle school. He began getting counter movements, counter thrusts in the way he drew. He decided to make Mickey's cheeks move with his mouth, which they had never done before because you drew everything inside the circle. He squashed and stretched him more and was right at the time.

But Walt Disney took all the credit for Mickey's new suppleness and realism, as he did for the fresh, uninhibited elasticity and joyful ease of the characters in the latest Silly Symphonies, such as the well-regarded *Goddess of Spring*. But what new challenges could he meet and overcome next?

The trip to Europe had spawned an idea. In Paris the Disneys had discovered a happy exhibitor who was making a handsome profit from showing nothing but Disney cartoon films – not one but six in succession, one after the other. But what if, instead of six short films, Walt Disney provided exhibitors with a single feature-length cartoon? There had never been a full-length cartoon film before, and all the professionals were convinced audiences would never pay at the box-office to see one, not even if it came from Disney. But since when had the professional movie pundits ever been right?

An indication of the way in which his mind was working was given in a memorandum Walt wrote to his animators just about this time:

The animation has made a very definite advance forward which, in my estimation, is close to 100 per cent over what it was a year and a half ago. I know that eventually we are going to attain a degree of perfection never before thought possible. It proves to me that the time we have spent studying, trying to analyse our problems, and systematizing ourselves, is bearing fruit. The hit-and-miss is going.

Could there be a more effective way to show off the enormous strides Disney had made in technique than through a feature film? As Walt pointed out to Roy – scared, as usual, of changing the formula – making a feature-length cartoon would increase profits rather than threaten them.

'If we put ten of these 700 foot shorts together, we've got us a feature – 7,000 feet,' he said. 'Now they won't pay us but 15,000 dollars for a short, but for ten of these, that would be 150,000 dollars, and surely we can get more than this for a feature!'

It was clumsy financial logic, but by this time Walt was convinced that not only would a feature cartoon bring glory to the Disney name, not only would it entertain the multitudes, but it would be a great financial success as well. It would have a hero, a heroine, music, a theme plus a solid story. All he needed now was the story.

No one is quite sure how Walt Disney finally came up with the decision to make *Snow White and the Seven Dwarfs*. The only plausible explanation is that many years earlier, during his boyhood in Kansas City, he had been enraptured by a silent movie called *Snow White*. Snow White now became the heroine of his dreams, a fairytale heroine who would provide him with the perfect opportunity to portray his ideal of young girlhood on the screen – beautiful to look at, shy, kind-hearted, unsophisticated and terribly vulnerable and innocent.

One night in the autumn of 1934, he called a group of his animators together after office hours and told them he had decided to make a cartoon feature called *Snow White and the Seven Dwarfs*. He then proceeded to give them a sixty-minute preview of how he thought the story should work out, and it was evident that he had already roughed out the scenario. He swashbuckled across the stage in the role of Prince Charming, and fell to the floor to simulate the innocent Snow White after she had been put into a trance by the Wicked Witch. As the Witch herself, he cackled and grimaced hideously. Finally, one by one, he demonstrated the different characters of the Seven Dwarfs. It was a virtuoso performance, and he won them over. They found themselves highly excited at the prospect of the new project. But then he suddenly stopped his clowning and told them this was a film that would be made or ruined by the portrayal of Snow White. The heart-aching appeal of her kindness and innocence meant everything to the feature, and he needed inspiration from his artists as never before to capture her qualities on the screen.

As some of his senior animators remembered it later:

Walt was all fired up. The great problem, he said, would be finding the right Snow White. She wouldn't just need to have talent but also be able to inject sincere moments, tender moments – and these would need to be an integral part of the motivation of the film. He pointed out that it would be a great challenge for the artists, because they would be called upon not just to provide cartoon gags and comic tricks but give the impression of fantasy combined with a real world full of real people doing believable things. Walt stressed that this time they would not just be making a cartoon film but making drama, theatre – with characters coming alive on the screen as never seen before in an animated film.

But if the animators were galvanized by the possibilities of their boss's latest idea, his brother certainly was not. Walt said he had already drawn up a preliminary budget: the production would cost around 500,000 dollars (it would, in fact, eventually cost very much more). But Roy was distressed even by that figure.

'Half a million dollars?' he cried in dismay. 'You're going to ruin us. Half a million dollars for a single film! Why can't we just stay with Mickey Mouse?'

Shooting began on *Snow White and the Seven Dwarfs* in the summer of 1935.

Chapter 13

SNOW BALL

BY late 1934 Walt Disney had worked out the scenario of *Snow White* and knew roughly in his own mind what kind of a cartoon feature he was proposing to make. Roy, however, was still convinced that Walt was heading for disaster. He looked around for allies who might bring his brother to his senses, and found one in Walt's wife, Lillian.

By this time, Lilly was one of the most comfortably established and prosperous of the Hollywood wives, and Roy played on that to convince her that her husband was about to embark on an extremely questionable venture. Couldn't she persuade Walt to think again? Just when both she and Edna had started families, was this the time to risk Disney's reputation and standing on an expensive, and very self-centred, gamble that was almost certain to lose them all their money?

Lilly made her apprehensions clear to Walt in one of the sharpest quarrels of their marriage. She did not persuade him to change his mind, but she did give him some sleepless nights and made him realize he could not afford to fail. Consequently, he began to regard *Snow White* as the most testing ordeal of his career whose failure could not only cost him his fortune but his marital happiness as well.

He spent his nights at his drawing board and his days exhorting his animators to give of their best, and at first he was by no means satisfied with their efforts.

Fred Moore, who had a flair for conveying the zest and vivaciousness of young womanhood, had already done some sketches of the heroine, but the results were unsatisfactory. In the end he became the directing animator for the dwarfs. Meanwhile, Walt decided to search for a real girl who might act as both the heroine's voice and the physical inspiration for the animators. There would be songs for Snow White, of course, and for most of the principal characters. He had already alerted Frank Churchill to work on a compelling theme song, and the first chords of what would subsequently become the popular hit of the movie, 'Whistle While You Work', were already beginning to be heard around the music department.

For Snow White's own voice he sought a special quality of vitality, a bell-like musical clarity and vibrant youthfulness, and when an agent turned up one day with a young Canadian singer named Deanna Durbin, he was enchanted. But when he heard her voice on record, he decided, despite her refreshingly girlish appearance, her voice sounded too mature and professional. He turned her down and Miss Durbin, who was only thirteen at the time, went on to become a famous singing film star in her own right. Instead, he picked an untrained twenty-year-old amateur named Adriana Caselotti to dub the singing voice of Snow White, feeling her thin soprano had the requisite childish timbre. He also hired a slim Los Angeles dancer named Margie Belcher to walk, pirouette and dance before Fred Moore so he could inculcate the rhythm of her movements into his Snow White sketches. She too went on to more lasting fame and later became the female half of a famous dancing team, Marge and Gower Champion.

At this stage, four of the most talented and experienced animators were working full-time on *Snow White and the Seven Dwarfs* (although, of course, hundreds of other artists and inkers would be needed to complete the more than two million drawings required for a ninety-minute feature film). Norm Ferguson was put in charge of setting the scenes and coordinating the action, and he was also doing the preliminary sketches for what would later be hailed as one of the most effective (and frightening) characters in the movie, the Wicked Witch. Hamilton (Ham) Luske was concentrating on sketching out the character and idiosyncrasies of Snow White, and Vladimir (T-bone) Tytla was thinking up situations which the dwarfs would become involved in as the plot unfolded. And overall was Walt Disney, testy, wary and watchful, fully conscious now that his reputation and the studio's future were at stake and doggedly determined that none of his animators would stray a hair's breadth from his conception of his characters. He constantly reminded them – particularly the rebellious Norm Ferguson – that this was his film and nobody else's, and that it would stand or fall by the way he saw it. He became extremely short-tempered and rough-tongued with them when he felt things were going wrong, and only dedicated artists, with complete loyalty to him and absolute faith in the quality of his inspiration, could have swallowed the harsh insults he sometimes hurled at them. (And not all of them did, as will be seen.)

Walt's rough outline script for *Snow White* is in the Disney Archives at Burbank. He set out the ambience and mood for every scene. He had, for instance, no doubt that one of the big moments of the movie would be the first encounter between the innocent Snow White and the jealous and malevolent Queen in her disguise as the Wicked Witch:

At the time the menace comes in [he wrote], Snow White should be doing something that shows she is happy and that she is trying to do something nice for these little men [the Seven Dwarfs]. That's the time the menace should strike. It's most powerful when people are most happy. She's taken aback when she first sees the Queen. She doesn't suspect the Queen, but there's a lunatic around somewhere and he approaches you. You have that funny feeling. It's nothing you can put your finger on. You wouldn't have the police come, but you'd be on your guard.

He urged his animators to bring out the instinctive apprehension of the animals of the forest at the menacing aura of the Queen as she passes by them. 'They are dumb but they have a certain sense,' he wrote, 'like a dog who knows that somebody is not a friend. When the birds see that old witch they know that everything is not right and they're alarmed and back out of the way.'

The top pay of the four chief animators of *Snow White and the Seven Dwarfs* was 100 dollars a week, which, even in those days, seemed a meagre reward for such talented labour. It is true they also earned bonuses for doing the extra drawings to link up sequences and give guides to their assistants and the inkers, and these sometimes doubled their weekly take-home pay, but none of these artists – and they were the best in the world in their field – was getting rich on his Disney salary. Walt and Roy, who were now paying themselves 250 dollars a week and managing quite well on it, did not feel any guilt about the wages their employees were receiving. It did not occur to them. They felt the work was so inspirational and the studio conditions so congenial that no one could possibly feel discontented, either with their pay or their jobs. After all, where else in Hollywood could they find such fascinating work in such challenging surroundings? Despite the fact that an assistant animator had often to get by on 35 dollars a week and an inker, whose work was meticulous, highly skilled and could be a tremendous strain, was lucky if he (or usually she) made more than 20 dollars, both Walt and Roy would have been shocked if it had been suggested that they were underpaying their employees. Roy would have pointed out that for all the modest salaries the Disney staff received, producing animated cartoon films was an increasingly expensive operation. In his constant search for 'flow' and 'realism', Walt was now insisting that more and more individual drawings had to be made to illustrate every single movement. Instant dismissal was the punishment for any animator who attempted short-cuts or inserted repeats. As a result, the labour force expanded. New technical methods of achieving three-dimensional effects, of heightening the reality of each character and each scene, were constantly being introduced, and they were expensive. To keep ahead of rivals, the Walt Disney Studio had financed, tested and adopted new kinds of cameras and pioneered revolutionary new techniques in animation.

Unknown to the rest of the staff, Walt took on colour technicians who had been experimenting with methods of inking cels in new ways and with the use of lighting and a revolutionary multi-plane camera. The results were jolting and were first seen in a cartoon called *The Old Mill*. Even the veteran animators were impressed by the improvements in colour and impact. Audiences, unaware that techniques were changing, were nevertheless conscious that Disney's cartoons were becoming more vivid and lively than ever before.

Some of the veterans confessed to being bewildered by the changes, but desperately tried to keep up. As one of them said: 'You can say that we had to dedicate ourselves to Walt all over again, so hard did we have to strive to keep up with the changes. We had to. Walt was completely in control – and did not forgive anyone who wasn't.'

But it all cost money.

When Walt had broached the subject of the studio's first feature-length cartoon, he had told his brother it would be budgeted at 500,000 dollars. Even in these halcyon days, it seemed a large sum of money. All over Hollywood, the big studios were filling their quotas of first feature films, sometimes with quite well-known stars, for around 250,000 dollars apiece. Walt and Roy considered themselves prosperous and successful, but the total balance in their company bank account was not quite 450,000 dollars, and to finance their first cartoon feature Roy realized he would have to go to the banks for a loan.

Reaction in financial circles was not good. No one would have hesitated to lend money for a new Mickey Mouse series or for half a dozen Silly Symphonies. But they hesitated for a full-length cartoon feature. Roy was always, when it came to the crunch, a loyal supporter of his brother's projects, but he was dismayed when he found himself – in the absence of help from the banks – dipping into the company's own monetary reserves, and profoundly depressed when Walt's weekly demands inexorably mounted.

Eventually, Joseph Rosenberg, a director of the Bank of America, baled out the Disneys when their own money began to run out. But such was the scepticism over the venture that Rosenberg was called a reckless fool and, as he later confessed, he suffered from sleepless nights for a time.

'I was green in the picture business,' he said later. 'I wondered if my judgement was sound. I called up some Hollywood people and asked their advice, and one of them said: "I wouldn't put a dime in it if I were you." ' When he consulted Louis B. Mayer, Jack Warner and Harry Cohn, they scoffed at the idea that a ninety-minute cartoon film could be expected to draw the same audiences as a movie containing 'real live people', and prophesied disaster.

'Who'd pay to see a drawing of a fairy princess,' hooted Louis Mayer, 'when they can watch Joan Crawford's boobs for the same price at the box-office?'

At the stage at which *Snow White and the Seven Dwarfs* had already cost 1.75 million dollars, which was more money than MGM spent on their big musical hit, *Broadway Melody of 1936* (with Robert Taylor, June Knight and a cast of hundreds), Walt needed another 500,000 dollars to finish the film. The Bank of America was balking at his repeated requests to increase their loans and Joseph Rosenberg was not only being called a sucker by the heads of the Hollywood majors but he was now running into trouble with his superiors, who kept asking him what *Snow White* looked like and would it make a profit. Rosenberg was forced to reply that Walt didn't like showing outsiders his productions until they were finished, and he had so far not had even a glimpse of *Snow White*. His embarrassment was such that in the end Roy pleaded with his brother to give him a showing, 'so he can at least report back to his bosses'. He threatened to stop all work on the film before Walt consented to cobble together a rough-cut of the production and give a private showing to Rosenberg. There were still big gaps in the story-line, and Fred Moore, who was the only animator to be asked to sit in on the showing, later remembered it as one of Walt's most glorious feats of spontaneous ad-libbing. He kept up a running commentary throughout the screening, filling in the dialogue and some of the songs which had not yet been dubbed on to the film. But it was his performance during the gaps in the action which won the laughter and appreciation of Roy and Moore. Neither had ever seen him perform more brilliantly.

'He leaped to his feet and pantomimed the missing action,' Moore said later, 'including all the different antics of the Seven Dwarfs, the palpitating scene where the Wicked Witch tempts Snow White into biting into the poisoned apple, and the penultimate drama of Snow White being awakened in her glass coffin by Prince Charming's kiss. "It's so terribly sad," he cried, "because Snow White looks so beautiful lying there. The birds fly around and drop flowers on her. The dwarfs are sneakily wiping tears from their eyes. The whole forest is in mourning. Then you hear the Prince arriving through the forest. He is singing the theme song. As he approaches the coffin, everyone sort of steps back and lets him through. He finishes the song as he lifts the lid of the coffin, and maybe there's a moment's hesitation as he looks down at his loved one, then he kisses her, kisses that beloved face, those beloved lips, so still, so cold! His heart is breaking. He droops and buries his head in his hands. The dwarfs see it and look sadly down at the ground. Everyone is sad, for everyone loved her and now she is dead! But then!" He pauses dramatically. "Then Snow White, roused by her beloved's kiss, begins to wake up! The music swells and picks up, the birds go crazy, the dwarfs go crazy and hug each other! The Prince picks her up as the music crescendoes and all the forest goes mad with joy as he carries her back to his horse and they ride away together and we fade out . . ."

'It was just too brilliant for words! Walt had never been so good, so eloquent. He played every single role in the movie, and each one was worth an Oscar! Even Roy, who was a tough old nut, had tears running down his cheeks.'

Not Rosenberg, however. Hard-eyed, seemingly unaffected, he said nothing until he had shaken Walt by the hand and allowed Roy to lead him back to his car. Only then did he say: 'It should be quite a film. I'm going to recommend that my board advance you the money to finish it.' And he added, with a hint of a smile: 'Pity we won't be seeing Walt up there on the screen. It's the best performance I've seen since Lillian Gish in *Way Down East*.'

Among the exhibitors who kept a close (and sympathetic) watch on the production woes of *Snow White and the Seven Dwarfs* was a dedicated admirer of Walt Disney named Willy van Schmus, who managed and booked films for the Radio City Music Hall in New York. Schmus had always done well with his showings of Walt's shorts, even with *The Three Little Pigs*, which started badly but eventually became a hit. He not only paid bonuses to the studio when his programmes were successful, but also let the movie world know how well he had done with them by taking out full-page ads in the trade papers. He knew Walt Disney well enough to know it would boost his morale if he publicly demonstrated his support of his controversial artistic endeavour; so he not only telegraphed Walt Disney Studio to say he was booking *Snow White* in advance but also made a public announcement about it in *Variety*. He was the first exhibitor to take an option on *Snow White*, and. soon the whole country followed.

Work went on steadily all through 1936, and often the studios were open seven days a week as the animators and inkers struggled to complete the quotas Walt was now demanding of them. So far there were no female animators in the studio, since Walt did not believe they had the flair or the artistic pretensions for the job, but there were plenty of women in the inking department who struggled uncomplainingly and with touching good humour to meet Walt Disney's increasingly strident demands on their time, meticulousness and expertise. Such was their enthusiasm that absenteeism in the inking department, even on Saturdays and Sundays, dropped dramatically. It became so noticeable that even Roy was persuaded to recognize the tremendous efforts they were making, and he announced that he was giving all the women working on *Snow White* a weekly 10 dollar bonus. Moreover, he said that he and his brother would show their gratitude in an even more spectacular way when *Snow White* was finally finished.

Snow White and the Seven Dwarfs had its world première at the Carthay Circle Theater in Hollywood on 21 December 1937. It would be the Christmas attraction that year at Radio City Music Hall, but Walt wanted his professional colleagues in Hollywood to see it first, especially since they had been so sceptical about its chances. Besides, a Los Angeles opening gave Roy a chance to invite Joseph Rosenberg and the board of directors of the Bank of America to join in the celebration; even if Walt did not realize it, Roy was acutely aware that without their financial support the film could never have been completed. Word had already spread throughout Hollywood that *Snow White* was going to be a hit, and the glittering first-night audience – which included most of the top stars and movie-makers in the film colony – left no doubt about it when they rose to their feet at the end and cheered.

Walt was up on the stage with Lilly to receive their acclamation, and he confessed it was music to his ears.

'I always dreamed that one day I would attend a gala première in Hollywood of one of my cartoons,' he told them. 'Tonight you've made it come true. You make me feel like one of you.'

Until that moment, he said later, Hollywood had seemed to regard cartoon film-makers as people they looked down on, like garbage collectors. Now they were not just welcoming him into their club, they were saluting him.

Snow White became one of the most successful films of all time. It earned over eight million dollars in its first release, and has since made the Walt Disney Studio (so far) a profit of 41 million dollars. Its songs became the most popular radio and record sellers of the day. Kay Kamen rushed out millions of replicas of the Seven Dwarfs, and they were soon to be found on mantelpieces and in nurseries around the world. Royalties on the model of Dopey alone made nearly 100,000 dollars for Disney (and, according to the terms of his contract, for Kamen, too). One day in 1938, after the Bank of America loan was paid off and the profits began to pour in, Roy Disney remembered he had promised to reward the studio staff for its unremitting efforts to finish *Snow White* on time. He went to Walt and told him about his pledge; he suggested that it might be appropriate to give the workers a generous Easter bonus. But to Walt, for whom money would always be unimportant, this seemed a poor way of rewarding the staff for its magnificent efforts. 'Let's give them a real celebration instead, a kind of thank-you party they'll always remember,' he said.

A few days later, he announced to the studio staff that he and his brother were going to throw a monster thank-you party for everyone who worked for them and added that their wives, husbands and children (or a nominated friend or relative) were included in the invitation. All of them would be welcome to spend the weekend at a desert lake resort near Palm Springs as the guests of Walt and Roy, and he went on to emphasize that charges for everything, accommodation, food, drink, whatever they might wish to order, would be taken care of by the Disneys.

In a period when many of Hollywood's major studios were notorious for the uninhibited and unbuttoned behaviour of some of their stars – and tycoons like Louis B. Mayer, Darryl Zanuck and Harry Cohn were legendary for the wear and tear they were said to inflict on their casting-office couches — the Walt Disney Studio had acquired a very different reputation. It was sometimes known among cynics as Mickey Mouse's Monastery, and players given a contract to work there, usually dubbing voices for the cartoons, knew that anything less than circumspect behaviour while appearing on the lot would result in instant dismissal. You did not carouse, raise your voice off the set, look lecherously at a member of the opposite sex, or, in fact, indulge in any kind of hanky-panky at Disney. It was a rock-ribbed island of rectitude and middle-American morality in a southern California sea of Bohemian shamelessness. In the thirties, it even had a dress code for its employees. Men came to work in jackets and ties though, like Walt himself, they were allowed to take them off when they settled down to their drawing boards. Trousers for female employees were taboo, and sober-coloured skirts and blouses were a kind of accepted uniform for the demure army of inkers.

Ward Kimball, who later became one of Disney's most distinguished animators, remembers that in those early days he used to change into shorts during the lunchtime break and play volley-ball with his fellow-artists on the chalk-marked court behind the old Hyperion Avenue sound-stage.

'These shorts were not very secure,' he said later. 'They kept precariously dropping down with all that jumping around. A pretty blonde girl who worked in the studio paint department named Betty Lawyer [later, Mrs Kimball] and her friend Dorothy Disney [Walt's niece, daughter of his brother Herbert] used to come and watch the games and giggle a lot over the errant tendencies of my shorts, which many times I had to hold up with one hand while trying to spike the volley-ball with the other. I guess the news of the girls' hilarity about the falling shorts situation finally reached Walt's office, because someone soon hinted that maybe I had better buy myself some better-fitting athletic equipment or give up the lunch-time game. (There was the Disney 'image' to uphold.) After Betty and I were married she answered the often-asked question of how she first met me by usually replying: "When I first met Ward, his pants were falling down." '

Only once had a real scandal been connected with the Disney Studio, and that had been quickly hushed up. One of the animators who had thrown away his glasses as a result of a new therapy involving eye exercises began approaching girls in the studio who wore spectacles. By the use of almost hypnotic powers of persuasion, he enticed a number of the girls to do the eye exercises with him and explained that a prerequisite of the routine was that they must first relax by taking off their clothes. Quite a few of them did so and gained experience in certain male behaviour if not a restoration of 20/20 vision.

But then one girl panicked when asked to disrobe and rushed home to tell her parents; they demanded the immediate arrest of the shameless pervert who had tried to seduce their daughter. Walt was shocked and angry when he heard about it. Gunther Lessing, the studio lawyer, was called in and, on Walt's instructions, compensated the girl for her embarrassment and the parents for their righteous indignation. As for the animator, he was summarily dismissed and told never to darken the gates of the Mickey Mouse Monastery again. Few people ever heard about this unfortunate incident. Walt told Lessing to keep it a secret, pointing out that the wives of his animators and the parents of his inkers – not to mention the staff, decent, respectable people all of them – would be stunned and shocked to learn that the Disney Studio could be just like the rest of Hollywood, with lechers and libertines lurking on the lots. But after that there were no more incidents. Walt walked the corridors and looked over his male and female staff with approval, knowing that in a movieland full of vice and permissiveness, his moral, well-behaved and decent young people were safe from temptation. That, at least, is what he thought – until the weekend of the thank-you party.

What Walt Disney did not seem to realize was something several of his employees could have told him had they dared – that it had been a tense two years at the Disney Studio and most of his staff had been working under a terrible strain.

'When I arrived at the studio [in 1934], I was the youngest person there. I was twenty,' Ward Kimball said later. 'Of course, there were some middle-aged guys there, but most of the artists, including the girls, were in their twenties. Walt was thirty. And he was our father figure and the boss.'

Everyone looked up to Walt and admired him, but they were afraid of him too. If they saw him as a father-figure, he also seemed a very stern father-figure to most of them. For one thing, he had such a terrible temper, and he was so demanding and unforgiving. Though he did not always appreciate it, he had the most dedicated staff in the history of the movies – mostly because they were so proud to be working for such a remarkable man. One of Walt Disney's quirks was that he never praised anyone to his or her face. A worker who had sweated blood to do a good job only learned that his or her efforts had succeeded through other people, to whom Walt might casually mention it. He almost never said thank-you, and took efforts beyond the call of duty for granted. On the other hand, he had no hesitation in criticizing his employees in front of others, and he could be rough. His language was abrasive and the dressing-downs he often gave to those whom he felt had failed him were frequently in public and could be bruising, brutal and humiliating.

By the time *Snow White* was finished, the atmosphere round Hyperion Avenue was stretched to breaking point. It could only have been relaxed by a mass meeting at which Walt expressed his heartfelt gratitude to his staff for the superhuman work they had performed for him. And he did not do it. So when he did eventually get round to inviting them to a thank-you weekend, it was almost an anti-climax.

Nerves were still taut as the young staff and their friends climbed into the buses and set off for Lake Narco one weekend in the late spring of 1938, and no one seemed able or willing – with the exception of some of the wives and children and boyfriends – to relax and enjoy themselves.

But when they arrived at the Narconian Hotel suddenly everything was wonderful. Very few of the animators and their families, and certainly none of the young female inkers, had ever seen or experienced such luxury as now confronted them. No expense had been spared to give the staff everything they could possibly wish. There were pools to swim in, a lake to sail on, tennis courts, putting greens, music, a crèche for the children, a smiling and willing staff – and loads of food and champagne. It started slowly at first. Then the first 'Whoopee!' was heard from around the pool, followed by a female scream, laughter and a splash.

'And,' said one of the animators who was there, 'by the end of the first evening, something snapped. All the animators and assistant animators and inkers, who had always been so staid and contained at the studio, suddenly let go. Nobody worried here whether your shorts fitted or not, because everybody's were suddenly slipping. Playsuits flew out of the windows. There were naked swim parties in the pool. Inhibitions, respectability and tensions vanished with each new bottle of champagne, and all those circumspect characters who had damped down their lecherous instincts around the studio for years were suddenly reaching out and grabbing someone. Everybody got drunk. It developed into what was practically an orgy, with animators reeling around tipsily and staggering off to sleep with whomsoever took their fancy, which was more likely to be that demure little inker from desk number 17 rather than the mother of their children. You'd be surprised who woke up with whom next morning.'

Walt, who had come down with Lilly to share in the fun, was horrified. He was so shocked, in fact, that he did not stay for the rest of the weekend but drove his wife home the following morning. Nor did he ever refer to the party again. As for the Disney staff, they did not talk about it much either. They turned up at the studio on Monday and looked sheepishly at each other, inkers dimpling and animators glancing hastily the other way when they passed in the corridors. It was years before anyone dared make any reference to what subsequently became known as the 'Snow White Orgy'. Even if Walt Disney never really forgave his staff for demonstrating that they could be so weak and fallible it certainly cleared the air around the studio. It had been a most therapeutic weekend, and it gave his staff the relief from tension they needed if they were to face the new challenges with which Walt and his brother were about to confront them.

Chapter 14

THE HOLLOW SOUND
OF MUSIC

In 1936 Lillian Disney asked Walt to co-sign formal papers adopting a little girl as a companion to their five-year-old daughter, Diane. It was only with great reluctance that he agreed. He said he still hoped one day they would have a son. But Lillian realized that by this stage in their marriage he wasn't really interested in producing children – except those of the cartoon kind – and guessed that the only reason he spoke about the possibility of a son was because of his feelings about Roy Edward Disney Jr. She suspected he felt envy, maybe even jealousy, but certainly no real urge to increase the size of his own family.

So Sharon Mae Disney came to join the family. She was nearly Diane's age and had been chosen as a playmate for her so, originally, neither Walt nor Lilly bothered to conceal the fact she had been adopted. But soon Lilly let it be assumed Sharon was her own flesh and blood, and was upset if she was treated any differently from Diane. After Walt's death, when Bob Thomas was writing his semi-official biography (*The Walt Disney Biography*, 1977), Lilly asked him not to reveal in his narrative that Sharon is not Diane's natural sister, and there are no indications in the book that she was adopted. Friends have suggested that Lilly came to favour her adopted daughter over her own, and these hints were revived in 1984 when she backed Sharon's election to the board of Walt Disney Productions at a critical moment – after her son-in-law, Ron Miller, Diane's husband, was summarily dismissed as president of the company. When the official announcement was about to be made of Sharon's election, Lilly requested that she be referred to as 'Walt Disney's daughter', with no hint she was an adopted child.

If she brought a warm light into Lilly's life, Sharon's arrival in his household made little or no impact on Walt, who, in any case, saw little of her. She was still asleep when he left for the studio in the morning, and had gone to bed by the time he got home. He sometimes saw her on Sunday mornings when he accompanied his family to church, but often, whether deliberately or not, professed not to recognize her or remember her name. 'Who's that?' he once loudly asked Lilly during the service, indicating Sharon singing hymns in the middle pew.

The Disney blood relations were coming back into the family circle, 'like bees to the honeypot', as Roy once cynically put it. Raymond, the unmarried brother, moved from Kansas City to California where he opened a new branch of his insurance company. The oldest brother, Herbert, still working for the post office and sharing a house with the Disney parents, Elias and Flora, in Portland, Oregon, got himself and his family transferred to Los Angeles, where he announced he proposed to live permanently when he retired. Meanwhile, he asked Roy to find a job at the studio for his daughter, Dorothy, and she was hired as an inker.

Walt and Roy began to have pangs of conscience about their parents, left stranded in Oregon. Roy went to see them and reported that Elias was doing odd jobs as a carpenter but finding the work an increasing strain, especially as he was now suffering from a bad rupture. Flora looked frail and he suspected she was sick and in pain, though she refused to talk about it.

When he returned he discussed the situation with Walt and they decided they would try to persuade the old folks to move down to Los Angeles, where they could keep an eye on them. They bought a house for them for 8,000 dollars in north Hollywood, just round the corner from Roy, and planned to move them into it in the autumn of 1938. In the meantime, the Disneys came south to stay with Roy and his family, and it was in their home that they celebrated their golden wedding anniversary. It proved to be a somewhat lugubrious occasion.

Flora Disney was now sixty-nine but looked much older than her husband, Elias, who was nearly eighty. Fifty years of marriage to this God-fearing man, who continued to lecture her daily about the virtues of piety, puritanism and socialism, seemed to have squeezed her dry. She had lost her sense of humour and her interest in life. She never even visited the site of the new studio Walt and Roy were building on Buena Vista Street, and though she was sometimes taken to see new Mickey Mouse or Donald Duck cartoons, did not seem to find them entertaining. Walt was unhappy about Flora. He sensed she was hugging some private sorrow to herself, that she not only hated Los Angeles but seemed to have grown weary of life itself and could not wait for death to arrive. He had always loved, admired and respected his mother, and he was distressed by her mental and physical condition. He found himself hoping that she would not have to endure for too long a life she so obviously found so trying – and then felt guilty with himself for wishing her dead.

About a month after the Disney parents had moved into their new home, Roy Edward Disney Jr, who had grown fond of Flora, went to see his grandmother after school and was told she had been found inert on the kitchen floor. He learned later that she was dead – from inhaling the fumes from a defective boiler.

Walt was deeply upset by his mother's death, but took comfort by persuading himself she probably found it a profound relief.

Even before he had started production of *Snow White*, Walt Disney had mentally begun to phase out cartoon shorts from the Disney menu of films, and was sometimes tempted to abandon them altogether. With the exception of Mickey Mouse, he had grown bored with them. He didn't like Donald Duck. He had only a mild affection for Pluto and Goofy and *The Three Little Pigs*. In particular he regretted he had 'wasted' the characters of the three little pigs and the Big Bad Wolf on a short when they could have been put into a real story and won him acclaim – and vast profits – as stars of a full-length feature. Even Roy Disney was now antipathetic to the short-film programme. He had changed his mind about full-length features once he had seen *Snow White* and decided (even before its première) that it would be a money-maker. Soon afterwards he began pointing out to his brother that their short cartoons were no longer economically worth while. In the old days they had made enough money to pay the rent, but they didn't even do that any more. The Donald Ducks and Goofys and the like were sold in batches for not much more than their basic costs, and though the public loved them, the profits were disappointing. As for Mickey Mouse: 'He's passé,' said Roy. 'Nobody cares about Mickey any more. There are whole batches of Mickeys we just can't give away. I think we should phase him out.'

The idea of killing off Mickey Mouse was painful to Walt. Only Roy could have mentioned it so casually, and the callousness of his remark wounded him. Had Roy forgotten what Mickey Mouse meant to both of them, and to the success of their enterprise? He obviously had. But Walt would never forget how he had conjured him up in his mind after the débâcle over Oswald the Lucky Rabbit, and how Mickey had saved them from ruin at a critical moment in their lives. Mickey Mouse was his talisman and always would be. He had a feeling in his bones that when Mickey died Disney would die too. For that reason, whatever happened to his other cartoon stars, he was determined to keep Mickey alive. At the same time, he knew it was true that the public was growing tired of Mickey. Why? Could it be, as his mother had once suggested, that Mickey Mouse's voice was turning them off?

In the summer of 1937, in between cutting *Snow White* and planning the production of *Pinocchio* (which would be his second full-length cartoon-feature) Walt Disney went back to his drawing board and began working on a programme to resuscitate Mickey Mouse. Taking Flora Disney's comment seriously, he planned to make a cartoon in which music would be substituted for the mouse's (or rather, Walt's) falsetto tones. It was Carl Stalling, his old organist-friend from Kansas City, who had originally given him the idea. Stalling had suggested the music from Saint-Saëns's *Danse Macabre* for the first Walt Disney Silly Symphony, *The Skeleton Dance*, and he had gone on to recommend Paul Dukas's *The Sorcerer's Apprentice* for a follow-up. Somehow, Walt had never got around to it, but now he revived the idea, not as a Silly Symphony but as a comic vehicle for a Mickey Mouse comeback, with Mickey playing the part of the magician's over-ambitious assistant.

When he put the idea to the story department first reactions were mixed. Ben Sharpsteen, the studio manager, pointed out that *The Sorcerer's Apprentice* was highbrow music and above the public's head, and suggested that only by using Dopey out of *Snow White* could the project be popularized. But Jim Algar, who had made several Mickey Mouse cartoons, had already dug out an Arturo Toscanini recording of the Dukas piece and declared he could see Mickey's persona in every musical phrase. He was told by Walt to start developing a script and was given the job of directing it. It was at this point that Leopold Stokowski came into the picture. Stokowski was already well-known to movie audiences, having recently had a big success conducting his orchestra in Paramount's *100 Men and a Girl*, starring Deanna Durbin. Walt saw him dining in the Beverly Hills Hotel one night and asked whether he could join him.

'He began to tell me he was interested in Dukas's *The Sorcerer's Apprentice* as a possible short,' Stokowski recalled later, 'and did I like the music? I said I liked it very much and would be happy to cooperate with him.'

He was invited to the studio to discuss the project with the Disney animators. Since Stokowski loved seeing his name in the newspapers and knew a good publicity stunt when one was handed to him on a platter, he turned up at the studio the very next day, before Walt Disney could change his mind. Jim Algar remembers racing around hiding all traces of the Toscanini recordings before inviting him into the music department.

On 15 November 1937, a confidential memorandum was sent to all members of the Disney story department:

We are preparing a special short subject in collaboration with Leopold Stokowski, who will conduct his renowned [Philadelphia] symphony orchestra, 100 men strong, in his own interpretation of the world-famous descriptive score of *The Sorcerer's Apprentice*. *The Sorcerer's Apprentice* will be released as a 'special', so we are naturally hopeful of a special response to the attached outline. It offers a challenge to the best imaginations on the lot. Please *give*.

Almost immediately the ideas came flowing in. Everyone agreed that casting Mickey Mouse as the cocky, over-confident sorcerer's apprentice was an inspiration on Walt's part, and two of the staff artists, Dick Huemer and Joe Grant, came up with some vivid sequences to match it. They were immediately assigned to work on the film. Shortly afterwards, they were joined by, among others, Fred Moore, who was given the task of redrawing Mickey Mouse and designing the broomstick which would play a vital role in the action. Moore's first action was to add pupils to Mickey's eyes to increase the range of his expression, 'because he will really be acting in this one'.

Roy Disney was appalled when he heard the news. All he knew about music was that Stokowski was paid 1,000 dollars a night as a guest conductor and his musicians made 50 dollars an hour. He told his staff to work out a provisional budget, and it was worse than he feared. He figured *The Sorcerer's Apprentice*, as his brother visualized it, would cost three or four times as much as a normal Silly Symphony, and, at the rate paid by renters for cartoon shorts in those days, could not possibly make money.

'I know that,' said Walt. 'How can we merchandize it so it *will* make money?'

'No way,' said Roy. 'What with those overpaid fiddlers and the way audiences feel about Mickey these days, it's going to be a financial disaster.' He added: 'Look, Walt, why don't we abandon the whole Mickey idea and do it with Goofy? That means we can forget the music and send that show-off Stokowski and his long-haired musicians back to Philadelphia.'

'Not a chance,' said Walt. 'This cartoon is going to be made my way. If we don't use Mickey, we're not going to make it at all.'

Ironically enough, Roy Disney might have found an ally in Stokowski in his opposition to Mickey Mouse. Though he would never have said so out loud, Stokowski by no means shared Walt's sentimental enthusiasm for the mouse. In fact, during the first stages of the collaboration, he had suggested abandoning Mickey altogether.

On 29 November 1937, he wrote to Walt Disney from New York, tentatively suggesting the creation of an entirely new character to replace Mickey Mouse as star of the film. He proposed 'a personality that could represent *you and me*,' someone, in other words, who would embody the characteristics of both of them and possibly be built up as a character for future films – which Stokowski was already envisioning. He wanted Walt to create an entirely new personality representing 'every one of us,' and added that he 'might be a valuable factor in the years to come and enlarge the scope' of Disney's films.

He counselled Walt to discard his suggestion immediately if it didn't interest him. In fact, Walt was furious with the conductor and strongly tempted to tell him so. But mindful of Stokowski's reputation, he never answered the letter. To abandon Mickey Mouse at this stage of his preparations would have been tantamount to abandoning himself. For Walt, overseeing the daily work on *The Sorcerer's Apprentice*, rehearsing Mickey's step-by-step actions in the role, the mouse had suddenly come back to life and taken over all his waking thoughts, even his dreams. He was not Mickey Mouse just when he acted out scenes before his animators at the daily story-board conferences; his staff noticed that he looked and moved like Mickey when he walked around the studio, rolled his eyes like Mickey, grinned like Mickey, ate like Mickey. Once, when he walked past a group of animators, they noticed that Walt suddenly glanced behind him as he scampered out of the way of a passing truck.

'What's with the boss?' someone asked.

'Don't you get it?' said Dick Huemer. 'He's looking to see if that truck has run over his tail.'

As one observer, John Culhane, wrote about this stage of his life in *Walt Disney's Fantasia*:

Walt Disney's identity was entwined with Mickey's . . . [in *The Sorcerer's Apprentice*] he dreamed Mickey's dream of being given 'complete control of the earth and the elements' – a dream that [later] resulted in Disneyland, Walt Disney World and Epcot Center. And he built those parks and made his pictures on the dream that he and Mickey Mouse shared with his beloved Tom Sawyer and Huckleberry Finn: the dream of 'having a spectacular lot of fun without being malicious'.

In the end, of course, the Mickey Mouse project never did make it into the cinemas as a separate short. *The Sorcerer's Apprentice* became one segment of the full-length cartoon, *Fantasia*. Stokowski gave Walt Disney credit for deciding to abandon his plan for a Mickey Mouse 'special' and to slip him, instead, into a full-length musical film, but in truth it was he who put the idea into Walt's head. He confessed to the present author many years later that having no wish to be remembered as the conductor of a Mickey Mouse cartoon, he persuaded Walt to add other pieces from the classical repertoire which he would conduct and the Disney staff would illustrate.

The film was given the provisional title of *The Concert Feature*, and only later became known as *Fantasia*. Suddenly Walt Disney, whose interest in music had hitherto been minimal, spent his time listening to concert recordings of the great masters and gravely discussing the tonal phraseology and decibel content of Bach and Mozart with his sound experts. The Disney Studio swarmed with stars from the musical world brought in by Stokowski and the publicity department. Deems Taylor was hired as a commentator. Stravinsky arrived to hear the play-back of his *Sacre du Printemps* and see a preview of its cartoon accompaniment. Stokowski posed happily for publicity pictures with the composer and the great Swedish soprano, Kirsten Flagstad, who was disappointed when she was told *Fantasia* would not include any Wagner.

Stokowski was in his element. He even began to relax about the linking of his name with Mickey Mouse and finally consented to a shot of Mickey shaking his hand at the conclusion of a musical number. But only in silhouette. 'A fabulous little fellow,' he was quoted as saying about Mickey later. But he was glad the mouse had been squeezed out of the limelight, in favour of Stravinsky, Bach, Beethoven, Tchaikovsky, Moussorgsky, Ponchielli – and, of course, himself.

Roy Disney was shaken when the bills from *Fantasia* began to come in. By the time the film was finished, it had cost 2.28 million dollars, Disney's most expensive production so far. Expenses for recording and playing the music alone had come to 500,000 dollars, of which Stokowski received 80,000 dollars plus royalties. Since he would only have been paid 5,000 dollars had the project stayed as a Mickey

Mouse cartoon, he was well content. And, to be truthful, so was Walt. He was enthusiastic about the finished cartoon, convinced that he had discovered a formula for popularizing classical music. For a time, there was a danger that Walt would become a music bore. He began to sound like an echo of Stokowski and the more erudite musical critics. He would buttonhole animators around the studio, many of whom had been enjoying Bach and Beethoven for most of their lives, and talk about them as if they had just been discovered, expatiating learnedly on the special significance of the pizzicato arpeggios in the harp quartets, which they suspected he had never even listened to. Ward Kimball used to upset him deliberately by listening intently to his disquisitions and then remarking: 'Personally, I hate that pretentious crap. Prefer Gershwin myself.'

Walt confined his remarks to Roy about *Fantasia* to its box-office potential. He assured him it was the most brilliant film he had ever made and that it would top *Snow White* (receipts for which were now beginning to roll in) and more than double their fortune. Roy agreed with him. He was impressed with *Fantasia* and thought the public would 'lap it up'.

'People are saying that anyone who can make a box-office smash out of a long-haired musical has to be a miracle worker,' he told his brother after the triumphant première of *Fantasia* in New York. He said he was particularly pleased with *The Sorcerer's Apprentice* segment. 'You've even put that dumb bastard Mickey Mouse – and dumb is right! – back on the map! I take back all I said about this project, Walt.' He couldn't help adding: 'Though I still think we didn't need to spend half a million on that crappy music, and I'll never understand why we couldn't have sneaked a little Tommy Dorsey in there.' He grinned and slapped Walt's back. 'Never mind, all we need to do now is sit back and wait for the money.'

They had to wait a long time. *Fantasia* turned out to be the first of three major Disney box-office flops, the other two being *Pinocchio* and *Bambi*. By 1939, not only had all the profits from *Snow White* been dissipated but the Walt Disney Studio was in debt to the banks for nearly five million dollars. This was not because the studio had made poor or unentertaining films; in the opinion of most critics, *Pinocchio*, for instance, was the most brilliantly executed, as well as the most watchable, cartoon Walt had made so far in his career. But it was struck by disaster.

No one is quite sure nowadays who first suggested *Pinocchio* as a major Disney animated feature. Some years before he died, Norm

Ferguson told the present author it was he who first gave Walt a copy of Carlo Collodi's nineteenth-century classic to read, suggesting it might make a good full-length cartoon. Others, including Walt himself, claimed it was they who first discovered the book. Whoever deserves the credit, it was Walt in 1937 who called a studio conference of his principal animators, Fred Moore, Vladimir Tytla, Milt Kahl, Norm Ferguson and Ham Luske, and told them he had found a marvellous subject, and they were about to help him make the most remarkable animated feature of his (or their) career. This would be a breakthrough film for all of them, he said, in which all the lessons and new techniques they had learned from *Snow White* would be implemented and perfected and all the mistakes they had made in earlier films would be rectified.

'What I will be looking for in this production will be colour and dimension and wonderful effects of a kind that have never been seen in animated movies before,' he said. 'It will be the costliest cartoon film ever made, but we've got money in the bank — and damn the expense. Because *Pinocchio* is going to be the biggest challenge in the history of animation. You've all been sent a copy of the outline, so you know the story. We start off with the puppet Pinocchio — and what will that mean? Even when we bring him to life, folks are going to say: "Who cares about this little freak? He's still just nothing but string and sticks," and what we have to persuade them is that though he still looks and moves like a puppet, now if you prick him he'll bleed, if he falls over he'll hurt himself, if his nose starts to grow or his ears sprout it's because they're growing from inside and not because someone's pinned a new schnozzle or earflaps on the kid. And if something really awful happens to him you'll weep for him. Because he's no longer a puppet. He's real. And that is our challenge. It means we're going to have to surround him with characters who look so alive and treat him so much like one of themselves, that their genuineness rubs off on the kid. And because of that we're gonna have to do a special job on all the surrounding characters in the story. They've gotta look rounder, softer, *realer* than any we've ever put into a cartoon before. So real audiences will imagine at any moment they might walk right out of the screen and sit down beside them.'

He paused and then went on: 'As for backgrounds, they have to come specially alive too. Mountains have gotta look as if you could climb 'em, houses as if you could walk through the front door and find something cooking on the stove in the kitchen, and when we get to the whale sequence, the seas must look real wet and cold and deep and salty. As for backgrounds, they've gotta jolt the audience as never before. It's essential they look and feel genuine. Like this.'

He turned to the studio wall behind him, over which a curtain had been drawn, and dramatically ripped it aside. On the wall, from which roughly drawn story-boards usually hung for a conference like this, they saw displayed a series of huge canvases painted in bold and startling colours – mostly dramatically back-lighted undersea scenes of wrecks lying on the ocean bed, one with a particularly menacing octopus swimming through Stygian, purple depths, and the terrified figure of Pinocchio cringing in the wreck below, away from the probing tentacles. Even the jaded professional animators were impressed by the boldness of the concept. These were meant to be scenes from the sequence in which Pinocchio gets swallowed by a whale, and the paintings had been done by a talented newcomer to the studio, Gustaf Tenggren. One by one the little group listening to him realized they were being exhorted to pioneer an entirely new kind of animated cartoon, and they would be using shock tactics all the way through. Not all of them approved, but they responded to the challenge. In the next few months the animators added a new panache to their usually painstaking craft and with great mastery brought to life the colourful characters in the story. By the middle of 1938 the film had taken on life and shape. The new colour techniques and the skilled brushwork of the women in the ink department brought a remarkable glow to the figures in Collodi's story.

All the animators understood that this time, more than ever, Walt knew exactly what he wanted. He had continual conferences with his colour-model advisers to make sure they would develop the latest techniques – so that, for instance, flat areas would seem to have been changed into solid, rounded forms.

They pioneered a startling effect that softened the harsh areas of colour on the screen. The twenty women working in the airbrush department invented a method of blending colour so that when it was rubbed on the cels and then touched-up with dry brush and airbrush, it gave the animated characters a magical, soft, furry look. It was particularly effective, for example, with the figure of Figaro, the cuddly kitten.

Everything, as Walt had hoped, looked 'realer' than it had ever done before in his cartoons. But though most people who saw them thought the scenes fairly pulsated with life, Walt Disney was not satisfied. For him, a vital element was missing from the action. What else did he need? It took him some time to realize that Pinocchio needed another side to his character to complete his personality and transform him from a wooden, if mobile, puppet into a living being about whom you could laugh or cry.

One day Ham Luske came into the studio and looked over the story-boards on the wall showing a sequence in which Pinocchio is teasing Figaro, the kitten. Figaro is howling with fear and desperately trying to get away. Walt Disney, watching Luske closely, noticed that he grinned at the drawings and then winced a little.

'You know,' Luske said, 'I think he goes a little too far in this one, and the audience ain't gonna like him for it. Oh, I know it's in the script and it's right in character. But the trouble is, he just doesn't seem to know it's cruel to put the fear of God in a tiny creature like that kitten. He just doesn't know what he's doing. Nobody's ever told him – told Pinocchio the difference between right and wrong. That's what's the matter with this script. We've made him into an unfeeling little monster instead of a human being. Walt, what this kid needs is a conscience.'

That was it! Walt was suddenly inspired. Why hadn't he thought of it? Instead of fleshing out Pinocchio, what he had to do was find him an alter ego, a side-kick who would act as his voice of conscience whenever he was troubled by what was right and what was wrong. He was so sure Luske had found the fault in the film that he called a temporary – and very expensive – break in production while he went back to Collodi and read the book through again and again. There was one character in the story who impressed him, though his appearance was so brief they hadn't even used him in the script. This was a grasshopper who admonishes Pinocchio for his waywardness but is casually crushed to death under the puppet's foot. How about the grasshopper as Pinocchio's voice of conscience? Walt got out his scratch-pad in the middle of the night and began to put his idea down on paper. He would resurrect the unfortunate grasshopper and make him a running character in his film. It was at this moment that memories of his dearly beloved Uncle Elf began to swim back into his mind.

At the next story conference he outlined his idea and got an enthusiastic response. Someone produced a name for him.

'After all,' said Tytla, 'what else do we call a grasshopper but a cicada or a cricket. How about Mr Cricket?'

'Too formal,' said Fred Moore. 'What about Jimmy Cricket?'

'What about a first name that's a little more eccentric,' suggested Ham Luske. 'How about Elbert – or Jiminy – yes, that's it! Does that grab you – Jiminy Cricket?'

Walt had his story-men write him up as Pinocchio's sage and salty conscience, always on hand when needed, and a new quality came into the cartoon. But not all Walt's troubles were over. To his intense frustration, no one else saw Jiminy as he did. In his imagination, this perky little grasshopper had to be a personification of his long-regretted Uncle Elf. But try as he might, he could not seem to draw him. Typically, he never mentioned Uncle Elf when he spoke of his conception, so repeated attempts by his top animators to create a believable, memorable and comically endearing Jiminy Cricket failed – to Walt's sentimental eye, anyway.

It was Ham Luske once more who solved the problem for him. He suggested that they solicit the help of his young assistant animator, Ward Kimball, a bright kid brimming with ideas and the talent to draw them. Luske knew that Kimball was in a rebellious mood and was about to quit Disney, and he felt it would be damaging both to Kimball and the Disney organization if he departed. Kimball was disgusted because he had been encouraged to draw several sequences for *Snow White*, and although at least one of them – a bed-making scene in the home of the Seven Dwarfs – had turned out to be brilliantly funny, it had, like his other drawings, ended up on the cutting-room floor. Never one to underestimate the worth of his own work, Kimball felt his drawings had deserved a better fate, and was prepared to try some other studio where his talents might be more appreciated.

Encouraged by Luske, Kimball marched into Walt Disney's office to express his disgust and hand in his notice. But Walt, primed by Luske, and equally appreciative of Kimball's potential, put on one of his best and most charming performances. He did not even give Kimball a chance to air his grievances; instead, he began to talk about the wonderful possibilities of *Pinocchio*, his hopes and dreams of creating a revolutionary new cartoon, and the reasons why he had stopped work on it. He showed Kimball the sketches his animators had done of Jiminy Cricket and rambled on about the kind of character he was looking for. Then suddenly it all came out. As Kimball listened, Walt began to talk about Uncle Elf down on the farm, and how this Peter Pan of a man had changed his boyhood.

'How about letting me see what I can do about getting him right?' Kimball finally asked.

Simulating reluctance, Walt sent him off to try his hand. The young man, fired by his boss's enthusiasm, forgot all about resigning and went back to labour at making Jiminy Cricket into a 'character' as well as a conscience.

He more than succeeded. A few hours later he came back with four sketches which, to judge from Walt's reaction, might have been plucked right out of his mind.

'I saw tears come into his eyes as he studied my sketches,' said Kimball later.

Walt was so taken by the character Kimball had brought to life that he ordered the script to be completely rewritten to bring in all the lines and scenes he needed to make Jiminy a star of the film. Shortly afterwards his story-men suggested he add a couple of sequences in which the chirpy cricket sings, and he agreed. 'When You Wish Upon a Star' and 'Give a Little Whistle' by Leigh Harline and Ned Washington, sung on the sound-track by Cliff Edwards, became the hits of the movie.

Work resumed on *Pinocchio* with new verve and enthusiasm, and it was finished and ready to be shown by 1939. Everyone was vastly pleased and impressed with it, and Walt knew it was the best animated feature he had made so far. There was only one problem. All the delays had driven up the cost, and when the studio accountants came to review it, the figure came to nearly three million dollars, which was a daunting sum in those days, even for an epic with a cast of thousands. Added to the sums expended on *Fantasia* it more than wiped out the studio's surplus and put Disney heavily in debt to the banks. Not that Walt, who never cared about money, worried too much about that. Nor did Roy. Not at first, anyway. Roy was convinced that the studio would get it all back once *Pinocchio* began its world-wide distribution, along with *Fantasia* and *Bambi*. The Disney organization had always relied for much of its success on box-office receipts from overseas, particularly Germany, France, Britain and the Low Countries, and Roy was convinced this latest trio of productions would recoup all their extraordinary expenditures and make them a profit too.

But then something happened to the international box-office that not even the Disney sales office could control. World War II started in 1939, just when the three new features were about to open in London, Paris and Berlin. The European market was destroyed overnight.

To make matters worse, the new films – undoubtedly the finest Walt Disney ever made – proved to be ahead of their time as far as American audiences were concerned. American critics, who still considered Walt Disney an entertainer for children, found them somewhat pretentious. The public, willing to queue up in their millions to see Mickey, Donald and Pluto, were disconcerted when they got illustrated classical music in *Fantasia*, graphic reality and subtleties they did not appreciate in *Pinocchio*, and sentimentalities over a deer in *Bambi*. *Pinocchio* had a modest success and its two Jiminy Cricket songs made all the charts, but the public decided the latest Disney films – particularly *Fantasia* – lacked the simple humour and slapstick they had come to prefer in Walt's cartoons, and receipts were disappointing. But it was the drying up of profits from overseas that hurt them most. Suddenly heavy debts and the horrid prospect of bankruptcy plagued Roy Disney again. He came to Walt with dire prophecies of disaster.

Hollywood blamed Walt for the studio's misfortunes in 1939 and said it was because he had 'gone highbrow', trying to foist classical music and a wooden puppet on an unwilling public. But that was unfair. The films were brilliant, if somewhat ahead of their time. Walt was certainly not to blame for the outbreak of war in Europe, and in subsequent showings, under peacetime conditions, both films have made the Disney studios a handsome profit. In the United States they have proved enduring box-office hits appreciated for their superb effects and production values, as well as for the inspirational quality of their characters. Indeed, a revival of *Pinocchio* in the spring of 1985 was again highly profitable for Disney.

Moreover, three million dollars of the money now owed to the banks had not been lost by the failure of Walt's films but by Roy's over-optimism. He had borrowed that huge sum to pay for the new Walt Disney Studio on Buena Vista Street in Burbank. Roy had been confident profits from the three new features would soon cover the loans. Though Walt didn't worry over money, he agonized when it wasn't around to be spent. When he realized the grimness of the situation, he was in despair. Lillian was concerned about him all over again and thought he might be going to have another breakdown.

She was right to be worried because that was only the start of his troubles. Suddenly, *everything* seemed to go wrong at the studio. For the first time in his life he came up against labour troubles – workers at Disney suddenly went out on strike. It proved to be a strike that changed his outlook and nature.

Chapter 15

REBELLION

In labour relations, Hollywood had been the scene of bitter battles between studio workers and their bosses all through the turbulent thirties. But somehow, Walt Disney Studio escaped the turmoil.

The election of Franklin D. Roosevelt to the presidency in 1933 and the implementation of the New Deal had given union agents the opportunity they had been seeking to organize employees in the big studios, most of whom were restless, insecure, unhappy, and did not belong to unions. The result was a series of bitter strikes as writers and technicians clashed with the studio heads, the majority of whom were not just ignorant and fearful men but ruthless, too. The great depression was still sweeping the United States, and they had used the pervasive fear of unemployment to scare their employees into accepting longer hours and lower wage scales. Those who dared protest were told to accept the new conditions – or else. But then some of the studio bosses went too far and imposed such pressure that even the most craven workers were provoked into rebellion. When the studio chiefs were informed that their workers were listening to the recruiters and queuing to join the unions, it was decided to tighten the screw. Such industry leaders as Louis B. Mayer of MGM, Jack Warner of Warner Brothers, and Harry Cohn of Columbia equated union membership with communism and reached for every weapon at their disposal – from instant dismissal to boycott – to keep their employees in line and 'these Commie agitators out of our industry'. The result was a series of bitterly painful work stoppages.

Though no member of the staff of Walt Disney Studio belonged to a union at the time, these wounding disturbances somehow left the company unscathed and the work force uninvolved. If there were pro-union sympathizers among the Disney staff none was motivated strongly enough to appear on the picket lines with striking colleagues. Work went on normally even when the remainder of Hollywood's studios were closed down. This was not necessarily because Disney workers were better paid or because the conditions under which they worked were more enlightened. When Ward Kimball first arrived at the studio in 1934, he had been offered a job as an assistant animator at 15 dollars a week, the first two weeks' pay to be withheld in case he should prove unsatisfactory. He discovered there were other eager young men around the studio, cleaning, carrying messages, inking cels, who had been hired under the same conditions and were let go at the end of their probationary period, simply to save Disney two weeks' wages. Nor did Disney stay unscathed because it was an oasis of liberal benevolence in the right-wing Hollywood desert.

'When I first went to work for Disney in the spring of 1934,' Ward Kimball said, 'California was in the middle of a hot political race for governor. The Republican candidate, Merriam, was running against the socialist author, Upton Sinclair, representing the Democratic ticket. As a teenager, I had read all of Sinclair's books, and he was one of my literary heroes. We were in the depths of the great depression, and on weekends, even though I was too young to vote, I went door-to-door handing out literature, extolling Sinclair's EPIC plan ('End Poverty in California'). While at work during the week, I would park my 1929 Chevy in the Disney lot with my large Sinclair window-sticker for all to see. This was sheer heresy. I was told by my friends it was a gesture sure to get my ass kicked out of the studio.'

Gunther Lessing was by this time firmly established at Disney as its political adviser, and with Walt's blessing he had taken it upon himself to be the arbiter of the studio's politics.

'You would have thought he would be a liberal-minded guy, having once worked for Pancho Villa,' Kimball said. 'Not Lessing! He called the whole studio to a meeting on the Hyperion Avenue sound-stage and proceeded to give us a fatherly lecture on the danger of a Commie revolution rolling through California if Sinclair got elected. He warned us that if we did not vote for Merriam, the state would turn into an Okie dust bowl, that Sinclair was a radical Marxist, that he would bring in a flood of alcoholics, layabouts, and bomb-throwers from the East who would ruin the film industry, doing us all out of our jobs. Punctuating his tirade against Sinclair, he would quote generously from the *Los Angeles Times* editorial page (it was ultra-right-wing in those days) that dire things would happen to each of us if we did not vote for Merriam.'

After Lessing's harangue was finished, he asked for questions. There was a stony silence.

'Even though many of us were politically mature enough to see how corny Lessing's doomsday rantings were,' Kimball said, 'there were those who were genuinely frightened by his implied threat that if we did not see things his way we would not have our job at Disney. I guess I was naïve about the political situation at the studio. Ham Luske, who was one of the "older" animators, took me aside to counsel me that I had a promising future at the studio, and he thought it would be advisable for me to remove the Sinclair sticker from my car before Gunther Lessing saw it. But I had heard that Lessing had already seen the sticker and was reported to have complained about my heresy to Walt. Nothing happened though. Sinclair lost the election, and I removed the sticker. Many years later, Walt laughingly recalled this episode and revealed that he had brushed aside Lessing's objections by pointing out that Kimball really meant no harm. "And besides, he's too young to vote." '

But Kimball had learned a lesson.

'During the many presidential elections that followed, my politics took an outwardly conservative appearance, and I would prominently display on my car an old "Keep Cool with Coolidge" sign.'

Walt had seen Kimball's specimen drawings and decided he had too much talent not to be encouraged and kept on the staff.

'When I started work doing in-between drawings, my salary was 15 dollars a week,' Kimball said later. 'After a few months it went up to 18 dollars a week. By the end of the year, I was making 22.50 dollars a week, and I had a chance to be an apprentice-assistant to one of Walt's highly respected animators, Ham Luske. Walt's top animators during the thirties were getting around 100 dollars a week, which was a lot of money, especially in those depression days. Disney artists were paid bonuses to finish their sequences under the allotted time at so much a foot. I helped Ham make generous bonuses because he gave me the responsibility of making all of his time-consuming animation corrections, and this allowed me to learn much faster. My only reward was a set of golf clubs that Ham once gave me, but I didn't mind a bit. It was a great learning experience, and in little less than a year I was animating on my own, full time, making 45 dollars a week and saving money at that.'

Kimball recalls that his routine was to animate a group of scenes in pencil and then send his drawings to the camera department where a negative loop of film would be made of his work. This he would view on the moviola.

'After making any corrections needed, the drawings were rephotographed,' he said, 'and the looped scenes cut into the main picture reel for Walt's viewing. In what we called a "Sweat-Box" (a noventilation projection room), we animators would sit behind Walt and the director of the picture, nervously waiting for Walt's critique. Walt was very harsh and direct if he did not like what he saw. He knew what he wanted and we respected his judgement. But we did not like his habit of bawling us out in front of our co-workers. On the other hand, if our efforts pleased him, he merely said, "OK, let's go ahead with it," and walked out of the room. He never complimented us to our face. If he liked our efforts, we would usually hear about it second hand from someone else.'

Walt seemed to need a 'whipping boy', someone to take his abuse when he was in a bad mood. It was usually a director or someone he obviously did not respect.

'Ben Sharpsteen had to be Walt's favourite target,' Kimball recalled. 'Ben was an older guy who started out as an animator and later became supervisor of the studio animation department. Finally, he had the title of producer, but it was in name only. If Walt thought things were going wrong on a picture, he would give Ben Sharpsteen hell. Ben would then turn around and bawl out the directors under him, who in turn would pass on the abuse to the animators. They kept the chain of harassment going by giving their assistants a rough going over. We figured that the assistants, or in-betweeners, would then take it out on their wives — if they could afford one, that is, on 18 dollars a week!'

By 1940, in fact, Walt Disney's staff was the most brilliant and the most overworked and underpaid in Hollywood. Yet unlike the other studios, they stayed out of strikes and remained un-unionized. That was almost wholly due to Walt Disney's influence.

'Walt was our father figure,' Kimball said. 'We both respected and feared him. He ran the studio as a sort of benevolent and paternal dictatorship. He was the total boss. You learned early on never to argue with him or to cross him. Walt might be harsh or egocentric, but we all knew he was a genius whose tough demeanour seemed to stimulate and bring out the best in all of us. Even though he was prone to badger and bully us at one time or another, we knew that Walt had revolutionized the animated cartoon, and we were inwardly proud to be part of this process.'

But they did have their grievances. Perhaps even more than the meagre wages he paid them, what many of the animators objected to was Walt Disney's attitude to credits. Like most Hollywood studio technicians, they wanted professional recognition, in particular the prestige of seeing their names in the credits on the screen. But Walt

Disney insisted on complete anonymity except for himself. No matter how modest his own contribution had been to a film, it was mandatory that his name, and his name only, should appear on it. Time and again, members of his staff came up with new characters which won international fame – Donald Duck, Pluto, the Big Bad Wolf, the Wicked Witch, Jiminy Cricket, Dopey the Dwarf – but he aggressively refused to allow them to take credit for their inventions. Nor would he share it with them. *Everything* was the work of Walt Disney.

One of his youngest and brightest animators, Ken Anderson, remembers that when he first joined the studio, Walt was so struck by his brilliance he did something most unusual for him, and sought out the newcomer to tell him he liked his work. But then, according to Anderson, he added: 'You're new here, and I want you to understand just one thing. What we're selling here is the name WALT DISNEY. If you can swallow that and always remember it, you'll be happy here. But if you've got any ideas about seeing the name KEN ANDERSON up there, it's best for you to leave right away.'

It was rough going, sometimes, but the staff put up with it.

'They thought it magnificent the way he had changed the nature of animated cartoons and given them the chance to be part of the revolution,' Kimball said. 'Some of them were so devoted to his regime that rather than leave they would have worked for nothing, so long as he was around to badger and bully – and stimulate them, too.'

They had stayed particularly loyal during the fraught but exciting early years. Their instinct then had been to say: OK, so he underpays us. How can he do otherwise without going bankrupt? He'll make it up to us when he gets rich. And yes, it's selfish the way he wants to hog all the credit for everything. But why not? Isn't he the catalyst? Hasn't he earned the right to sole recognition?

But then the profits from the showing of *Snow White* began to come in, and they were larger than anyone had anticipated. In 1939 there was even a moment when Walt and Roy Disney, after paying off all their debts, found they had one and a half million dollars in their joint bank account. In those days it was an enormous sum, and neither brother could think of anything but how to spend it. Strangely enough, it did not occur to either of them that the time had come to share the rewards with those who had helped earn them – and in a more substantial way than the occasional bonus or a splashy desert weekend. Roy, ever the practical manager, completed the plans he had already made to move the company to a brand-new studio on Buena

Vista Street in Burbank. The expanding staff of animators, inkers and clerical workers now numbered more than a thousand, and the studios on Hyperion Avenue were bursting at the seams. The move, he knew, would cost much more than their reserves, but he was confident that because of their new financial prestige the banks would lend him all the money he needed.

Meanwhile, Walt plunged into the production of three new feature-length cartoons which, though they would each cost more than *Snow White*, would have no trouble getting finance from the banks, since they seemed bound to be even more successful. It was just a question of sitting back and waiting for the money to come in.

By the time they moved into the new studios on Buena Vista in late 1939, there was an atmosphere of expectancy among the employees. Every animator and inker on the staff believed that now, at long last, the lean days were over. Walt was about to reward them with higher wages and professional recognition for all they had done for him during the time of struggle.

Kimball remembers how, shortly after they moved into their new quarters, a rumour spread like wildfire among the staff that the Disney policy on screen credits was about to change. The film of *Snow White* had actually credited not just Walt Disney but also the many artists, animators, composers and 'voices' who had worked on the production. This innovation had produced startling results. Suddenly, from all over Hollywood, telegrams began to arrive at the studio congratulating Fred Moore, Ham Luske and Frank Churchill, among others, for the parts they had played in the success of *Snow White*. For years they had been unknown workers in the Disney vineyard, and no one had been able to assess accurately what talents they possessed. Now, thanks to *Snow White*'s screen credits, their fellow-craftsmen had a yardstick by which their work could be measured. They were suddenly acclaimed – and it made all the difference to their pride and reputation.

When the rumours reached the new executive offices at Disney, George Drake, the studio manager, was deputed to address a meeting of the animators. He explained that because of the vast number of technicians involved in *Snow White*, Walt had felt it necessary to share some credits. Manifestly, he could hardly have done a whole feature film himself. The studio would continue to follow a similar policy with future feature-length cartoons, but where ordinary cartoon shorts were concerned, there would be absolutely no change in the rules: Walt would continue to get sole credit.

One of the animators spoke up. His name was Arthur (Art) Babbitt. Among the memorable cartoon characters he had invented was the foolish, feckless hound dog, Goofy, and he had also been responsible for the oriental dance of the mushrooms in the Nutcracker Suite segment of *Fantasia*. Now Babbitt asked why Walt himself had not come to explain his attitude to the animators. Since they had moved into the new studio they hardly ever saw him. Everything was done through go-betweens like Drake or Sharpsteen or (grimace) Gunther Lessing. Was Walt avoiding them?

'No way,' said Drake. 'He's too busy. He's got more important things on his mind.'

'Such as?' asked Babbitt.

'Money,' said Drake. He hesitated, and then added: 'We may be in trouble. And it's serious this time.'

Roy Disney had borrowed heavily from the banks to complete the move to the new studios on Buena Vista, hoping profits from the three new features would take care of it. But now the repayments were due and, because of the outbreak of war, there was no money to meet them. He told Walt that the one and a half million dollars in their joint bank account was already spoken for, and they were four and a half million dollars in debt to their creditors. Walt had once thought the world was coming to an end a few years earlier when the studio was in hock for a mere 20,000 dollars. Now he was really in despair. They couldn't possibly find such a massive sum and the spectre of bankruptcy stared them in the face.

If he hadn't felt so desperate, he might have noticed his brother seemed much more cheerful about the situation than he did. In fact, from Roy Disney's point of view the situation had its advantages – as well as its solutions. Over the years he had been trying to persuade his brother to turn Walt Disney Productions into a public company, and offer shares on the open market. Walt had always turned him down because he maintained the change would allow outsiders to have a say in future decisions, a privilege he had always reserved for himself. Now Roy told Walt that the only way out was to go public.

In fact, Roy had already talked over the situation with Gunther Lessing, who prophesied hard times ahead for Disney as the war situation worsened in Europe. Lessing was all for cutting back on staff and production, and for an immediate reduction in the wages of the staff who were retained. But Roy knew it wasn't going to be as easy as that. Walt, as the paternal head of the studio concerned for the welfare of his staff, would never stand for wholesale firing and salary cuts. Not so long as he was in charge. But could he continue to object once Walt Disney Productions was a public company, responsible to its shareholders for its balance sheet? Especially if, once the public company was established, the staff could be persuaded that Disney was in a much worse financial situation than was actually the case – and that wholesale sackings and wage-reductions were the only way out?

Walt was reluctantly persuaded to accept what seemed the only solution to their financial problems, and Walt Disney Productions offered 755,000 units of common stock and preferred shares to the public in April 1940, at prices ranging from 5 dollars to 25 dollars a share. Walt, Roy, Lilly and Edna retained large blocks of shares for themselves and they were quickly sold out, enabling Walt Disney Productions to pay off its outstanding loans of four and a half million dollars and build up a working capital of three and a half million.

The studio was saved. Once more they had credit at the bank. It was obvious that, though they would have to be careful in future, there was now no need for savage reductions in staff and wages. But did Walt realize this? This is where the upholders of Walt Disney's image have introduced an element of conspiracy into the affair: they suggest that Roy Disney deliberately encouraged Walt to believe that the public launching of the company had by no means solved the studio's financial problems, that wholesale staff dismissals and wage cuts would still be necessary. Knowing that Walt would accept widespread firing only to save the studio, Roy (according to these stories) concealed the real facts of the situation both from his brother and from the studio employees. He encouraged rumours of disaster and provoked panic among those who feared for their jobs. It was necessary to prepare them for the worst, Roy decided. They would go more willingly that way.

If Roy believed that, it was a gross misjudgement. Instead of inducing a mood of fatalism around the studio, the rumours sounded a clarion call to the unions. Hitherto they had regarded the Walt Disney Studio as impregnable, mainly because of the work force's faith in the integrity of Walt Disney himself. If things were really as bad as studio rumours had it, one thing was certain: the employees would stand by Walt and accept any cuts he decided to make, no matter how draconian. But then someone inside the office leaked the truth about Disney's financial status to the union leaders. The company wasn't broke at all and Walt Disney, the trusted boss, was pulling a fast one on his work-force, deliberately deceiving them as an excuse for slashing jobs and wages.

Word quickly spread through the Buena Vista headquarters that Walt had tricked them and that if personnel wanted to save their jobs, they had better sign up with the union right away. A sense of betrayal enveloped many Disney workers, made worse by the sneers of the union organizers and their fellow-workers at other studios.

At the beginning of 1941, Walt and Roy Disney were presented with an ultimatum by Herbert Sorrell, the tough-talking head of the Screen Cartoonists' Guild, which was part of the Painters and Paperhangers' Union, a powerful Hollywood affiliate of the American Federation of Labor (AFL). (A rival union, the Federation of Screen Cartoonists, was industry-sponsored and lacked both independence and muscle.) Sorrell said he had signed up enough Disney employees to turn the studio into a union shop, and needed the signed agreement of Walt and Roy Disney. Otherwise, he would black the outfit and declare an immediate strike.

Walt refused to believe Sorrell had signed up the majority of his employees. He called a meeting of the whole studio personnel and pleaded with them not to strike.

'He put on his more-in-sorrow-than-in-anger act as the benevolent and understanding father of them all and he talked to them like wayward sons,' said David Swift, a young animator who was there. 'To his astonishment, a large section of his audience booed him, and he took that very badly. He had never been booed before.'

Next day, when he saw Sorrell again, Walt insisted the question of union membership should be decided by a secret studio vote.

'Don't talk to me about secret votes,' retorted Sorrell, nettled. 'It's taken me two years to get this place lined up. It's about time your workers learned what kind of a boss you really are. Now get this straight, Walt. If you don't do a deal with me now, I'm going to strike you.'

'Not till I've called the Labor Relations Board in Washington,' said Walt, 'and asked them to superintend a secret ballot.'

'You just try that and see what happens,' said Sorrell. 'I can make a dust bowl out of your place here, Walt. I can pick up that telephone on your desk and make just one call and you'll be on unfair lists all over the country. I have connections.'

Indeed he had.

There was a picket line round the Buena Vista studios when Walt arrived one morning in May 1941, and he was cat-called as he drove through the gate. Posters and pickets proclaimed that Walt Disney

Studio was 'unfair' and its workers were on strike. In fact, 60 per cent of the studio staff crossed the lines that day, but 40 per cent – some 400 plus workers – obeyed Sorrell's call, and Walt Disney recognized some of his most talented animators among them, including Art Babbitt. Babbitt had a loud-hailer and was organizing the concerted calls of the pickets. One day as he drove through the lines, Walt thought he heard Art Babbitt scream through his loud-hailer: 'There he is – the man who believes in brotherhood for everybody but himself. All together now – boo!'

Walt was annoyed at the raucous cries, and deeply wounded by the charge and by the man who, he believed, screamed it at him. He stopped his car and took off his jacket, intending to beat up the heckler, but was restrained by a studio guard. Still fuming, he got back in his car. But he decided there and then that however the strike came out, he would make certain of one thing: Art Babbitt would never be forgiven, and he would never work for Walt Disney again.

'Yes, it was a deep wound that Walt suffered over the strike,' said Ward Kimball. 'It hurt him because guys he had trusted were letting him down. He always felt like the benign father who was giving us things, looking after us. Because this was the Depression and people didn't have jobs, and he had kept them all working. And he sort of felt that after all he had done, it was plain ingratitude to call a strike – just because he wanted them to vote before joining a union. What he didn't know was what was going on in his own studio, he was shielded from the truth by the executives in between. For instance, he didn't know that there were guys making 18 dollars a week and they couldn't even buy enough food for their families, and then George Drake would go to New York and hire a bunch of guys who'd come back with him – guys who hadn't even learned the cartoon business yet. Drake put them in the big room and ordered the 18 dollar a week guys to show these new guys how it was done. And the new guys were being paid 50 dollars a week. That sort of crap.'

As strikes usually do, this one began with jokes and cheerful give-and-take between the opposing parties, and at first no one was prevented from crossing the picket lines. But Sorrell and Babbitt were effective organizers, and soon they were exerting pressure on Technicolor not to deliver or process film for Disney. There were other boycotts spawning around the country. The insults got louder and nastier. There were scuffles and heated arguments around the picket lines. The strike took an ugly turn when a gang of pro-Disney workers drove up in trucks, carrying baseball bats and cans of petrol.

They sprinkled the petrol in a circle round the pickets and threatened to set it alight if the strikers didn't move on. The strikers moved but came back next day with police protection.

When the negotiators met, Sorrell packed the most militant of the Disney strikers round the table and goaded them into making increasingly strident demands. Walt was so appalled at the tone of hate and resentment in their voices that he came back to Lilly one evening in despair and said he was resolved to pack it all in – he would close the Walt Disney Studio and go into some other occupation.

News of his pessimistic mood soon reached Washington. Since it was no part of the New Deal's intentions to kill off Mickey Mouse and Donald Duck for the sake of humbling the popular Walt Disney, the administration decided it was time to find a face-saver – but for him, not for the union. First came an invitation to Walt Disney to go on a tour of South America as a good-will ambassador of the United States. That solid capitalist, Nelson Rockefeller, Coordinator of Inter-American Affairs, was recruited to persuade Walt to undertake the mission as a patriotic American duty, and to take animators and technicians with him so he could make a cartoon down there with a Latin American theme – as a counter to pro-Nazi and anti-American propaganda in Brazil and other South American states.

'But what about this terrible strike?' Walt asked.

Rockefeller said he had been assured by the President that if Walt would leave it to the administration, they would arrange a settlement agreeable to all concerned.

'You mean the unions will get what they want?' said Walt.

'It's the climate of the times,' agreed Rockefeller. 'This is a battle you can't win.'

Walt finally agreed to go, grimly resigned to what the government conciliation men would achieve during his absence. He was now sure he would be defeated and that relations between him and his technicians would never be the same again. In an open letter which he penned just before taking off for Brazil, he wrote bitterly:

To me, the entire situation is a catastrophe. The spirit that played such an important part in the building of the cartoon medium has been destroyed . . . The Union refused to use the ballot to give people here the right to determine their choice. In turning down the ballot, they said, to use their own words: 'We might lose that way. If we strike, we know we will win.'

. . .The cards were all stacked against me, so for the time being I have capitulated, but, believe me, I'm not licked – I'm incensed. The lies, the twisted half-truths that were placed in the public prints cannot be easily forgotten. I was called a rat, a yellow-dog employer and an exploiter of labor ... My plant and my methods were compared to a sweat-shop, and above all, I was accused of rolling in wealth. That hurt me most, when the fact is that every damned thing I have is tied up in this business.

Then, deliberately or not, he revealed what the strike had done to his political outlook, and how it was going to affect his attitude towards his workers in future:

I am convinced that this entire mess was Communistically inspired and led. The People's World, the League of Women Shoppers, the American Peace Mobilization and every Communistic outfit in the country were the first to put me on their unfair list. The legitimate American Federation of Labor unions were the last and they were reluctant to move.

... I am thoroughly disgusted and would gladly quit and establish myself in another business if it were not for the loyal guys who believe in me – so I guess I'm stuck with it ...

I have a case of the D.D.s – disillusionment and discouragement.

He flew to South America in the summer of 1941 with Lilly and his crew, and his mood was black. While he was still filming in Brazil, a cable arrived to tell him the strike had been settled. As part of the terms, the Walt Disney Studio would not only become an AFL union shop, but wages and the work force could not be cut. Moreover, Walt Disney would no longer have the monopoly of credits on the short cartoons. His animators and artists would also get their due recognition.

'Ironically enough,' said Walt later, 'the union never even bothered to ratify the agreement. But I insisted on swallowing the terms whole. (He didn't, in fact, as will be seen.) I told Roy he must never employ a non-union man in the studio again. I even insisted that the gardeners join the union, and saw it was one that would pay them the top rate. I accepted every single thing they forced on me.'

There was one exception. When Art Babbitt came back to the studio to resume his old job, he was stopped at the gate and told he could not come in. He would have to sue the studio before he was allowed to work there again.

'OK, so we'll sue,' Babbitt said.

Chapter 16

BAD WAR

ONE day in 1940, some months before the traumatic Disney strike, Walt's secretary, Dolores Voght, broke into a busy afternoon to say there was a man to see him.

'His name is Ub Iwerks,' she said. 'And I have an idea he's looking for a job.'

Walt Disney leapt to his feet and opened the door of the outer office. 'Ubbe!' he exclaimed, then grinned, adding: 'My God, I never thought I'd be pleased to see you, you bastard! Come on in.'

Ten years had passed since his former partner had left the Disney company after trying to sell him out to the New York con-man, Pat Powers. Ub had opened his own small cartoon studio as a rival to Walt Disney Productions. Their operations were only a few miles apart, but the two men had rarely encountered each other, and when they did, at Oscar ceremonies and official movie occasions, they had nodded distantly across crowded rooms and pretended lack of interest in each other's preoccupations. But, in fact, each had kept in touch with the other's doings. Ub had sent a telegram of congratulation when Walt had won his first Oscar, and Walt had carefully preserved it. When Ub, by then head of Ub Iwerks Studio, signed up with MGM to distribute his Flip the Frog series, Walt had sneaked into a downtown Los Angeles cinema to see the first showing, but sent no telegram himself. Perhaps that was because he had liked it, but couldn't bear to say so; it will be remembered he never praised anyone's work but his own. In any case, he had no interest in Ub's successes, but did seem to get a kind of sadistic satisfaction out of hearing of his setbacks. According to rumours in the industry, they had been increasing lately, and a story was going around that Ub's whole operation was in trouble. Since Walt always swore he would never forgive his friend for the disloyalty he had shown him, he didn't seem downcast by reports of Ub's difficulties. Though he would never have admitted it, however, he missed Ub, and felt for him in his misfortune. Regret over the breach between the two men was mutual. Ub Iwerks had probably

192

missed Walt the most, for years of estrangement had made him fatalistically aware he was not a full man without Walt. Now they faced each other like two old lovers who had bitterly quarrelled and parted years ago over something they could hardly remember and wondered now why it had been so wounding at the time.

'I suppose you've heard the news,' said Ub. 'It's happened again. I just don't seem to be able to manage on my own. I'm closing down the studio and you were the only one I could think of to come to for help. I have debts to pay off and I have to find a job.'

'How much do you need?' asked Walt, reaching for his cheque book. 'And when can you start? You know we can always find you a job here. I'll fix up an office for you.'

'Thank you, but that won't be necessary,' said Ub. 'But I would like to use your workshops. I have some new ideas about optics and animation that might be helpful, and I'm sure I can improve the quality of present-day cartoons. Maybe even yours,' he added, apologetically.

He neither asked for, nor was he given, the say he had once had in the running of the Walt Disney Studio. He rarely went near the animators' rooms, where once he had been the busiest and best of them all. Roy Disney viewed his return with a mixture of scorn, contempt and dismay. He carefully refrained from reminding his brother that if Ub Iwerks had held on to the block of shares Walt had once given him, he could have sold them in the market now Disney was a public company, and made himself millions in profit. But he made no comment when, out of company funds, Walt paid off Ub's outstanding debts and provided him with a fully equipped workshop where he could experiment with cameras and animation techniques.

Ub moved back into the Disney organization and no word was ever mentioned of the situation which had caused the rift. It was as if it had never happened. He stayed quietly loyal and supportive during the strike, walking casually through the picket lines as if they were not there. During the following years he produced some invaluable technical improvements in lenses and colouring methods for cels and pioneered other ways of making Disney cartoons more life-like and simpler to produce.

As the years passed, he came to be accepted as a popular, good-humoured, gentle, patient but hardly outstanding member of the staff, and his younger associates would have been astonished to learn that he had once been so consumed with jealousy of Walt Disney that he would like to have killed him – and had once nearly broken Walt's heart by trying to destroy him. They would also have found it hard to believe that Ub and Walt had once been such bosom friends, for much of the intimacy had now gone out of their relationship. But so had the tension and animosity. They had become like an old married couple, aware of the weaknesses and faults in each other which had once driven them to distraction, but now willing for the sake of peace to put up with them with comradeship and good humour.

One day, Walt was walking through the grounds with an acquaintance and passed the studio garage where Ub had his head under the hood of his car.

'Look at that guy,' said Walt with mock indignation. 'Working hours yet, and instead of calling in a mechanic, he wastes the company's time tinkering with his auto. That's what you get when you employ Ub Iwerks, the greatest animator in the world!'

At that moment, Ub's head came up for air, and his oil-streaked face broke into a delighted grin as he recognized his boss.

'Hi, Walt!' he called out happily. 'Just tuning up the old jalopy!'

'When you've finished, have a look at mine!' Walt replied. 'It's falling to pieces.'

This was during the embittered years, when Walt Disney was rarely amiable with anyone around the studio. Yet the acquaintance doing the rounds with him said the tone of Walt's voice and the expression on his face as he spoke to Ub Iwerks was one of unalloyed affection.

'He obviously loved that guy,' he said.

One of the cartoons on which Walt was working when the studio went on strike was a sentimental story about a baby elephant named Dumbo. Originally, Walt had planned it as a half-hour long/short, but the two chief animators who laboured on it and drew the original story-line, Norm Ferguson and Ham Luske, filled it with such effective and touching incidents that it eventually came in at sixty-five minutes – at a cost of 800,000 dollars. When they saw it, the RKO salesmen were dismayed, and asked Walt to cut it. He refused. They then took their complaints to Roy. In their view it was too long to sell as a short and not long enough to sell as a feature.

Roy called Walt into his office and gravely reminded him they were in hock to the banks and badly needed every penny they could lay their hands on.

'And here you are,' he complained, 'spending nearly a million dollars on a cartoon no one can sell. I'm talking about *Dumbo*. It may be about a baby elephant, kid, but as far as the box-office is concerned it's neither fish, fowl nor red herring, and it's not going to fly unless you make it a saleable size – when at least we'll get something back.'

'Have you seen it?' asked Walt.

'I don't need to see it,' said Roy. 'I only know the exhibitors won't buy it unless you stretch it to feature length.'

'No way,' said Walt, firmly. 'It's a little gem just as it is. Adding anything more would ruin it.'

'Then cut it, for Christ's sake,' said Roy. 'You know what the renters are like – anything less than eighty minutes is box-office poison. All you can sell it as is a B-film – and how much are we gonna earn from that? We need cash, Walt – every penny we can grab – and fast. I want you to stretch that cartoon or cut it down to a fifteen-minute short – and please hurry!'

'Not until after you've seen it, Roy,' said Walt. 'Let's go and screen it now. I'd like your reaction.'

'OK,' said Roy, reluctantly. Then he added: 'But I'll tell you this. Even if it's the classiest movie you ever made, it's not gonna change my mind. The renters just won't buy a first feature that's less than eighty minutes.'

But they did.

Roy Disney said nothing to his brother after he had seen the run-through of *Dumbo*, but he went straight back to his office and told the RKO salesmen to sell the new cartoon exactly as it was.

'And,' he added, 'I want the same fees for it as you get for a special feature – and to hell with its length.'

Even Roy had to admit that *Dumbo* was special. It had three touching scenes which have since become classics so far as animation films are concerned. There was the so-called 'trunk touching' scene, when Dumbo's mother has been chained up as a mad elephant after trying to protect her flap-eared offspring. Dumbo makes a secret night-visit to his mother and fondles her trunk through the cage. The sequence was drawn by Vladimir Tytla and executed with such tenderness it probably evoked more tears in the cinema than anything since Mary Pickford in *Daddy Longlegs*. Fred Moore drew an ingenious sequence between Dumbo and Timothy Mouse, when the clowns spill liquor into a bath full of water, and Dumbo drinks some and begins to hiccup. Then the mouse falls into the bath. Then there was the Pink Elephant sequence in the film, conceived with a glow of real fantasy by animator Howard Swift.

In 1941, Walt Disney and his party flew back from Panama, the last leg of their South American trip, by way of New York and attended the world première of *Dumbo* there. It was an immediate hit, and became so popular that it subsequently made the Disney Studio a profit of over a million dollars.

When Walt Disney returned to the studios from South America he was a changed man. The strike had soured him and turned him mean. He was rough with nearly everybody around him. He discovered that the girls in the inking department had a preference for Lorna Doone biscuits with their morning coffee, so he ordered the catering department to cut down on the supply. During the mid-morning break, a lot of the animators had been in the habit of playing volleyball. He had the nets taken out. And employees were ordered to sign in and clock out when they came to work, something they had never had to do before. Despite the agreement with the union, he went back on his commitment to freeze wages and staff and instituted a 10 per cent cut in salaries and let many scores of workers go.

The union sued to get Art Babbitt's job back, and Walt assigned Gunther Lessing to fight the case. Lessing felt as malevolent towards the strikers as Walt did. He had not forgiven them for hanging his effigy on a telephone pole outside the studio and setting fire to it. When Art Babbitt's case came up, his shrewder colleagues advised him to read the rules of the National Labor Relations Board, pointing out that under the terms of the settlement the union could insist that every striker, no matter who, be given his job back.

'OK, if they have to have their pound of flesh,' said Lessing, 'then let them spill some blood in getting it.'

It was Walt Disney's blood they spilt. After a messy case in which a slew of young lawyers from Washington ran rings around Lessing, Disney was ordered to reinstate Babbitt. But Walt saw to it that things were never the same for him. His days as a creative cartoonist (at least as far as Disney was concerned) were over, and the other animators, fearful of Walt's wrath, carefully avoided him. It was a lonely time.

Finally, when the war came, Babbitt joined up. His qualifications were sufficient to gain him a promotion, but each time he went before a board considering him for officer status, he was refused a commission. It was not until the war was over that Babbitt found out why. Someone (whether Walt or Lessing he never discovered) had informed the War Department that he was a dangerous Marxist and likely to spread unrest among the troops if he was given any authority. So he stayed in the ranks for the duration of the conflict. When he came home, he applied once more for reinstatement at Disney and was reluctantly given his job back. But conditions had not changed in the slightest and he could feel the waves of unfriendliness all around him.

Out of touch and out of sympathy with the laws of the new regime in Washington, Lessing had long since been demoted, and his only opportunity to show off his former power was to make life impossible for the reinstated rebels.

'It was kind of pitiful,' said Ward Kimball. 'Gunther had become a shadow. He'd come to the office every day with an umbrella, like it was going to rain at any moment. He always wore his hat to conceal the fact he'd lost most of his hair, and when he took it off the timberline separating what hair he had left from the bald part was way down here. He had a fringe but it wasn't long enough to grow over the top, and he was always combing it when he thought you weren't looking, in the vain hope he could cover up the gaping dome. Pathetic. But God, even when he was hairless he could still be just as vindictive!'

Babbitt found his life made so miserable and so involved in unnecessary litigation that, in the end, he left Disney and went to work elsewhere. But the damaging report about his supposed political affiliations dogged him until his retirement. It was almost certainly Lessing who had put the FBI on him and ruined his career, but Babbitt placed the blame squarely on the shoulders of Walt Disney. Like Walt, the strike had soured a hitherto amiable character and warped his sense of judgement. The irony in Babbitt's case was that he even developed a contempt for Walt's achievements as a cartoon-maker – in the creation of which he had once played so important a part – and professed to despise the standards of both the movies and those who flocked to see them. 'Walt Disney had the innate bad taste of the American public,' he liked to say.

If the impact of the strike had left Walt Disney bruised and resentful, what happened once the US became involved in World War II exacerbated his feeling that the administration was singling him out for persecution. On 7 December 1941, a few hours after the announcement of the bombing of Pearl Harbor, a security guard telephoned Walt at home to inform him that units of the US Army had occupied the Buena Vista studios. (His was the only Hollywood studio to be singled out in this way, and it is still not clear why.) Overriding all protests, they had driven straight to the main sound-stage, thrown out the camera and audio equipment, and set up the space as a repair shop for trucks and guns. The carpark became an ammunition dump and other buildings were annexed as dorms for the troops. The explanation given was the need to have a headquarters from which they could protect southern California from a Japanese invasion.

In vain did Walt and Roy protest they were already, to all intents and purposes, working for the government, and therefore deserved some consideration. Walt had paid all the expenses for himself and his crew during the government good-will mission he had led to South America though, it is true, he more than recouped those expenses by exploiting two cartoon films he had made on the trip, *Saludos Amigos!* and *The Three Caballeros*. He had since been producing instruction films for the Lockheed Aircraft Corporation and the Canadian government. And within hours of the Pearl Harbor disaster, the US Navy was on the phone from Washington asking him to make a series of films training personnel in enemy aircraft identification.

The army stayed in full occupation at Buena Vista for nearly a year, and left skeleton units behind when they went. Space was also pre-empted by the government for outside companies working on service contracts. In cramped quarters, hemmed in on one side by troops and the other by Lockheed assembly shops, the animators practically abandoned commercial movie-making for the duration and concentrated on producing instructional and propaganda cartoons. Walt complained, after a trip to Washington, that his efforts were not appreciated by the administration.

'They can't seem to recognize what sacrifices I'm making to help the war effort,' he said. 'I pointed out we have abandoned three major cartoon features [*Peter Pan*, *Alice in Wonderland* and *The Wind in the Willows*] to make propaganda shorts for them, and some snooty secretary had the sauce to say other Americans were making sacrifices too – some with their lives. As if all of us aren't willing to die for our country if they ask us to! Then I showed the cans of film I'd made of Donald Duck persuading citizens to pay their taxes, and that Jew, Henry Morgenthau [Secretary of the Treasury], had the nerve to complain it had run over budget and he didn't think Donald Duck was a typical taxpayer anyway. I had to tell him what it meant to be given Donald's services for free, and what it was going to cost us in ordinary commercial cartoon rentals. I had to tell him Donald Duck was worth more at the box-office than Greta Garbo. Do you think Louis Mayer would have lent him Garbo – for nothing?'

The Donald Duck cartoon was called *The New Spirit*, and it was in so much demand that hundreds of extra copies had to be made by Technicolor, whose charges inflated the original budget. Far from turning off tardy and reluctant taxpayers, the fact that Donald Duck dutifully paid his taxes apparently made millions of potential dodgers reach for their cheque books. At least, there were fewer defaulters that year.

The most costly fun Walt had during the war was producing a cartoon feature called *Victory Through Air Power*, based on Alexander de Seversky's 1942 book of the same name. Seversky was a Russian ex-pilot from World War I who passionately believed the bomber plane was the secret weapon for winning future wars, and Walt Disney became his most fervent disciple. He asked the government in Washington to let him make a cartoon version of Seversky's book (with the administration financing the project), but he was turned down – chiefly because naval officers were irked by Seversky's obvious contempt for the role of the Navy in general and battleships in particular in winning wars. They strenuously lobbied against any government financing for such an anti-navy project. So Walt decided to make it as a private Disney movie. Ward Kimball was called in to animate the flying sequences and later said he 'had a ball animating the early history of flight'.

Victory Through Air Power was put out as a Disney entertainment feature but was never accepted as such by the movie-going public, who were inclined to believe naval publicists' claims that it was 'just air force propaganda'. Winston Churchill, who was given a private showing, thought it was 'a superb film' and boosted it to Roosevelt, but it lost the studio nearly half a million dollars at a time when it could ill afford it. Forced to cancel all plans for feature-length cartoons for the duration, pinned down to pre-war rental rates for commercial cartoon shorts, and out of pocket on most of the government-sponsored propaganda films they had made, the Walt Disney Studio finished World War II close to five million dollars in the red. The rest of Hollywood had made millions pouring out entertainment features – any old trash made money in those days. Only Joseph Rosenberg of the Bank of America saved them from going out of business.

Rosenberg went to his boss, A. P. Giannini and persuaded him to keep the credit flowing. That did not mean there was now enough money available to finance the projects Walt had been forced to abandon during the war. Feature-length cartoons of *Peter Pan* and *Alice in Wonderland*, two of his favourite books, would need a budget of nearly two million dollars each, and even the Bank of America was not prepared to take the risk of advancing that much. *Fantasia*, *Bambi*, *Snow White* and *Pinocchio* were beginning to get showings in Europe, but the big box-office receipts from them – particularly in

Britain – were blocked by postwar regulations forbidding currency exports. There was enough money available to the Disney Studio for only the most modest postwar ventures.

Walt finished the war deflated, downhearted and short-tempered. He was depressed to find himself surrounded in Hollywood by smug film men from other studios who had grown fat and prosperous turning out pap, while he, who had striven so hard to keep up his standards, had emerged from the war on the verge of penury. He was particularly downcast one day when a studio chief whose capabilities he particularly despised called him up and offered him the millions he needed to make *Peter Pan* and *Alice* – but only if he agreed to sell out his operation to him.

'Can you imagine that?' he stormed. 'Letting that fat Jew rescue me from bankruptcy – just because he made all those crooked millions out of the war!'

Disappointment and resentment seemed to bring out his anti-semitism. He was often heard making snide comments about Jews, particularly the Jewish heads of the Hollywood studios whose easy success seemed to infuriate him. When the young animator David Swift, who had returned to work during the strike because he had become disenchanted with some of the labour racketeers behind it, announced he had been offered a better job at Columbia Pictures, Walt was annoyed at his departure but seemingly too proud to offer him rewards for staying on.

'He called me in finally,' said Swift later, 'and putting on a phony Jewish accent he said: "OK, Davy boy, off you go to work with those Jews. It's where you belong, with those Jews." And when I came back to him later after the war, he was still resentful. "Well, Bud," he said, at the first studio meeting I went to, "you can see we didn't come to any harm while you were away with those Jews. We got on quite well without you. We don't need you – and it looks as if those Jews don't need you, either." '

For the moment, the bleak situation over money drained Walt of his dynamism. Misery and worry brought out the worst in him, and he was apt to blame everybody – Jews, blacks, Commies, union workers – for his misfortunes. He was brusque at home and rough with Lilly. He punished his two daughters with painful spankings for dis-obedience. He even began to have violent quarrels (usually over money) with Roy, and though they always made up later, some sediment of bitterness remained. He was surrounded by a good deal of middle-range talent at the studio, since many of his best artists were still in the forces, and after excoriating the worst of his animators for incompetence, he seemed to lose his zest even for wounding criticism, and lapsed into a kind of apathy. He became so apathetic, in fact, that he even gave up on Mickey Mouse. In the modest programme of cartoon shorts which he now agreed to inaugurate, he made one more attempt to revive the appeal of the Mighty Mouse, *Mickey and the Beanstalk*, but he allowed Donald Duck and Goofy to steal the show. He also decided not to dub Mickey's voice himself, as he had always done in the past. He said his smoker's cough had lowered the tone of his voice and made it difficult to achieve Mickey's falsetto, and he turned the dubbing over to Jim Macdonald. It wasn't the same, and Mickey Mouse began to die from that moment on. In 1968, in Paris, the British artist Ronald Searle did a drawing of Mickey Mouse for his fortieth birthday. He drew him with a considerable paunch, a distinct stoop and no teeth. When they saw it many of his old animators said that was how Walt himself regarded Mickey in those grey postwar days.

Among other things troubling Walt were pangs of guilt over Elias who had died at the age of eighty-two while Walt was away on his South American trip. Why hadn't he rushed back to be with the old man in his final hours? It was true he had never loved his father and had always preferred his mother, but his failure to fly back for Elias's death and funeral nagged at him, an affront to his sense of filial propriety.

One of Walt Disney's great ambitions had been to make a sequel to *Fantasia*, but the war in Europe and public apathy at home, resulting in the failure of the first edition at the box-office, had put paid to that, and the disappointment and frustration had seemed to turn him off cartoon films for good. Roy, irritated and alarmed by his brother's lack of energy and enthusiasm, tried to stimulate him into reviving the plan for a *Fantasia* sequel. Unfortunately, having secured his brother's interest, he then spoiled everything by proposing a cut-price series of 'musical' shorts — which was all they could afford at the time. His idea was 'popular' music numbers with singers like Dinah Shore, Nelson Eddy and the Andrews Sisters. As a sop to Walt's musical pretensions, Roy went on to propose the series should include a single cartoon with a 'serious' classical theme. In the early days of the war one of the visitors to Burbank had been the Russian composer, Sergei Prokofiev, who told Walt he had been so impressed with the qualities of *Fantasia* he hoped to see a subsequent edition including a composition of his own. To that end, he said, he had composed a special piece of music and was entrusting it to Walt Disney's care for him to use whenever he came to make his sequel. At which point he had handed over the manuscript of *Peter and the Wolf*, which had never been performed in public at that time. Walt was extremely touched by the gesture, and had taken it to the music department to be played over, something which both stimulated and depressed him. *Peter and the Wolf* was a natural for the cartoon screen, and he was downcast because he already knew there would be no new edition of *Fantasia* in which he could include it. Nevertheless, he promised the composer that he would make it one of these days, and extracted a pledge from Prokofiev that he would come back for the first performance, when they would settle his contract (Prokofiev had refused to discuss it at the time) and pay him handsomely for the privilege of using his music. Now the opportunity had arrived and it was such a temptation that Walt was persuaded to produce the other cartoons, which he rightly suspected would be dull and tasteless, in order to make it. He put Ward Kimball to work on the Prokofiev and Kimball came up with some lively barnyard inventions, in particular a mischievous duck and a feisty and temperamental cat as well as a highly eccentric wolf. But the 'popular' musical items in the series were extremely dreary, lacking all sense of fun or liveliness. In the end they were all combined into a cartoon feature called *Make Mine Music* (later known as the 3Ms Movie – messy, maudlin and miserable) and sent out to the cinemas in 1946, where it had a success that was less than modest. Except for the *Peter and the Wolf* segment, Walt thought it was execrable and was tempted to sack the animators on the spot. One consolation was that Prokofiev failed to turn up for the première of the movie. Nor did he appear (though Walt was present) at the first public performance of *Peter and the Wolf* by Koussevitsky and the Boston Symphony Orchestra. All Disney attempts to communicate with the composer or pay him fees and royalties went unanswered. But after his death, someone – it has never been revealed who – turned up with the necessary authorization and collected the money.

Walt's sentimental feeling for *Peter and the Wolf* did not diminish over the years, and when it was later suggested that he reissue *Fantasia*, he agreed to do so on one condition: that the *Peter and the Wolf* film (which he gladly ripped out of the 3Ms Movie) be added as an extra segment. Unlike the first production, *Fantasia II* was a considerable box-office success; and since then new editions have not only covered the original cost of the film but given Disney a considerable profit.

In 1946, Walt Disney managed to borrow enough money from the banks to make another feature film, and it indicated the way he would soon be going. It was his version of stories from his childhood reading featuring Uncle Remus, which he called *Song of the South*. In it he reverted to his earliest days as a movie-maker and combined cartoon figures with live-action characters. *Song of the South* had a lavish world première in Atlanta, Georgia, and subsequently scored a big success throughout the United States. One of its songs, 'Zip-a-dee-doo-dah', won the Oscar for the best movie song of 1946. But the film had been extremely expensive to make and, despite big box-office returns everywhere it was shown, Roy sourly pointed out profits were modest in the extreme. Still, bored as he was with cartoon films, *Song of the South* had given Walt Disney a renewed taste for films with real people. The trouble was, real-people movies cost a lot of money.

What about real *animals*? You didn't have to pay real animals.

Chapter 17

BROTHERLY BREACH

GROUCHY and mean with his wife and children at home, contemptuous and insulting to his brother Roy, evil-tempered and spiteful with his staff at the office, Walt Disney was in such a state by 1947 that Lilly was convinced he was on the verge of another nervous breakdown. Fearful he might overdose himself with sleeping pills more thoroughly this time, she persuaded him to consult a doctor about his condition. All the doctor could suggest was he try to forget his problems at the studio and go away for a 'change of air'.

Walt decided to take a trip to Alaska where he had already commissioned nature photographers Elma and Alfred Milotte to make a travelogue. It would give him a chance to look over their work. He asked his wife to come with him and bring their daughters along, but in the end Lilly, whose own nerves were becoming frayed from the unhappy atmosphere around the house, arranged to send Diane off to summer camp and dropped out of the trip herself at the last minute, glad to be rid of Walt and his troubles for a time.

He flew north to Nome with Sharon and ran into some hazardous flying conditions, including a heavy landing which bruised his neck and gave Sharon nightmares. But they did see Mount McKinley and some other dramatic scenery, and came back with some interesting photographs he had taken of the Alaskan fauna, particularly the seals. It was his delight with his own seal pictures which made him look with particular interest at the seal sequences included in the enormous footage the Milottes had shot in Alaska. After a series of showings to selected groups in California, he began to describe these sequences, which were both spectacular and diverting, as 'really a true-life adventure'. He was sharp enough to sense that the movie-going public was becoming interested in the world around it, of which it had still seen too little, and knew that if he found a new cinematic angle on nature films and a good selling title for a movie series to go with it, he might well be able to mine a productive seam. He threw away the bulk of the Milottes' footage, retaining only the seal segments which he assembled as a short nature film. Calling it *Seal Island*, he announced it as the first in Walt Disney's True Life Adventure series. For the moment he had no idea what he would follow it with, except that it would have to be longer than *Seal Island* which the RKO salesmen said fitted into no recognized rental category, neither programme short nor special feature.

He was sufficiently encouraged by audience response to begin sending out cameramen to remote spots all over the globe to shoot spectacular nature and animal sequences.

Walt's problem with nature film-makers to begin with, according to his daughter Diane, was that they were all freelances and they were inclined to be stingy with film because they had to pay for it themselves. 'Walt persuaded them to "shoot, shoot and keep on shooting," guaranteeing he would pay their bills for everything.' (Later he equipped Alfred Milotte with a mobile, dustproof studio which he used in Africa.) One of the cameramen came despondently back from Canada with millions of feet of backwoods material but doubted if there was anything interesting there at all. But when Walt ran it through, he found the sequence which eventually became *Beaver Valley*. It showed a beaver trying to get a tree through a hole in the ice. 'He had to chew that tree into small bits, enlarge the hole, put the bits through, until it became larger and larger. When that beaver pushed the last bit down the hole, you felt like cheering,' wrote Diane.

In fact, when *Beaver Valley* came to be shown, audiences did clap and cheer that segment, and the film was a success. Walt eventually followed it with a series of full-length True Life Adventures, including *The Living Desert, The African Lion, The Vanishing Prairie* and *The Secrets of Life*. No one had ever seen such vivid plant and animal photography before, and their popular success would make him enough profit eventually to help pay for producing the two cartoon features which had been hanging around the studio for years, *Peter Pan* and *Alice*. There also appeared to be enough money to finance a third, *Cinderella*. *Peter Pan* eventually made a modest profit and *Cinderella* did well both at the box-office and with the critics, but *Alice* – which was made before but presented after *Cinderella* – was a costly flop.

Despite its failure at the box-office, *Alice in Wonderland* was probably the most ingeniously experimental of all Walt's animated features. But it was probably ahead of its time – a surmise which seems to be confirmed by the huge success it has had with audiences whenever it has been revived in recent years. It had been in Walt's mind ever since his earliest days, when, it will be remembered, he made the Alice comedies, a series of live-action cartoons with Virginia Davis and, later, Margie Gay and cartoon figures. He even considered making a live Alice film when he first came to Hollywood, with Mary Pickford in the title role, but he was pre-empted by another studio. Even so, he registered his intention to make an animated version one day, but it was not until after the war that he had adequate funds to contemplate actually doing it.

The project ran into trouble practically from the start. For one thing, Walt did not grasp the subtle Englishness of the book and the fact that it was not one of those stories to which he could add his brilliant but quintessentially American touches of Disney imagination. Alice would be ruined by the introduction of false notes or false characters. For one thing, he thought Alice herself was a bit dull and suggested she be 'livened up' by giving her a companion with whom she could get into comic situations and gag routines. His idea was to bring in the March Hare for this purpose as a running character who would keep popping up at unexpected moments all through the film, lifting his top hat to Alice and saying: 'What ho!' and getting her out of scrapes. He was crushed when it was explained that he would be attacked for tampering with a classic. His advisers were equally condemnatory of his attempts to subordinate Alice to other Carroll characters. Thereafter, he edged away from the project altogether and gave his animators unexpected freedom to draw the characters as they saw them. They respectfully took a good deal of their inspiration from the original Tenniel drawings – with some brilliant variations. Frank Thomas, for instance, invented the famous doorknob sequence during which the comically animated doorknob remarks: 'You did give me quite a turn!' when Alice opens a door into Wonderland. Jim Macdonald achieved miraculous effects in creating the menacing but gossamer quality in the cobweb sequence, and Josh Meador drew what was possibly the most difficult sequence of all – Alice floating in the bottle, skilfully calculated to suggest her tiny size (she has shrunk) and the consequent ocean vastness of the water in the bottle.

But difficulties supervened and production was several times interrupted. When Walt did decide to examine the rushes he was dissatisfied. After four years' work and nearly 3 million drawings, he still had his doubts.

He decided to risk the wrath of the British critics and première the film in London. He wrote a note to his London office beforehand which hints at some of his apprehensions:

Alice is just about wrapped up and I think it is about as good as can be done with it. I think it is going to be an exciting show. While it does have the tempo of a three-ring circus, it still has plenty of entertainment and it should satisfy everyone except a certain handful who can never be satisfied.

He was hinting that he might be mauled by the critics. But when Alice opened at the Leicester Square Theatre on 26 July 1951, it was, on the whole, tolerantly received by the press, though one critic did suggest that it lacked 'any sense of summer peace, the comfortable drowsy Victorian quietude that used to brood over these magic stories'. Moreover, the reaction of the public was cool, and when it opened in New York a few weeks later, it did not exactly click at the box-office.

Roy Disney was appalled at the amount Walt was spending – and eventually losing – on *Alice*. One of their increasingly rancorous quarrels broke out. Roy centred his grievances on the folly of trying to make *Alice* at all, a project he had been against from the beginning. He accused Walt of deliberately trying to ruin the company for the sake of indulging his extravagant whims.

Alice's failure plunged Walt even deeper into depression. Losses were estimated at more than two million dollars, and more than wiped out the profits that *Cinderella*'s success was beginning to bring into the studio, and bit into the receipts being built up by the triumph of *Seal Island*. Nor did the release of *Peter Pan* in 1953 do anything to relieve the financial crisis. Once more Roy objected to the cost, and even the idea of the production. In any case, Walt's heart was no longer in it. Before the war, when he had first bought the rights to Barrie's play, he had thought the magic of this soaring boy who never grew up could be conveyed through the medium of the animated cartoon. But as he studied the story-line and the animated sketches accompanying it, his original enthusiasm leaked away and he was unable to find the vigour and determination needed to make the concept work. The truth was, he had reached a stage when he had begun to be bored with making animated cartoons and was not in the mood to be challenged into pioneering something new. He was therefore neither surprised nor too downcast when the première of *Peter Pan* failed to galvanize the critics or bring queues to the cinemas where it was shown.

The therapy that snapped him out of his dangerous depression this time was a hobby which was to stimulate, absorb and soothe his nerves for the rest of his life.

Way back in 1938, Ward Kimball had bought himself a full-sized railroad train.

'Those were the days,' he said later, 'when small western railroads were innocently scrapping their historical equipment and selling the scrap iron to Japan for its secret munitions build-up. Since I was already a train buff, I decided to buy an 1881 locomotive and passenger car for around 500 dollars and have it shipped down from Nevada to our two-acre backyard in San Gabriel (our place had once been part of an orange grove). With the help of friends, I restored the train to its original Victorian splendour. Walt came to one of our early steam-ups (in 1944) and when I invited him to take a turn at the locomotive throttle I noticed his expression was like a kid in a candy store. Walt, as it turned out, was secretly a railroad buff himself, having sold papers on trains in Missouri when he was a boy.'

Ollie Johnston, the animator, was another train buff around the studio. Now, while in the depths of his latest depression, Walt recovered some of his spirit when Kimball and Johnston told him about the latest craze among railroad hobbyists. Model-makers had begun building half-sized steam locomotives, and Walt decided to construct one of his own. It eventually became a one-and-a-half-inch-scale model for his estate in Holmby Hills.

'It was here that he started throwing his own railroad-type parties, inviting a few close friends to ride on his miniature train,' Kimball said. 'Sometimes he would ask me to come out and take care of running the train while he was busy making ice-cream sodas in his own full-sized soda fountain by the pool. I remember one party in particular because it had a rather bizarre guest list headed by actress Una Merkel, the agent Jules Stine (whom Walt kept calling the 'Octopus') and Salvador Dali, the surrealist.' (Dali was discussing an animated film project for Disney, but nothing came of it.)

So great did his fascination with trains become that when he began planning the building of Disneyland in California, he was determined it should have its own railroad. But what kind? Kimball recalled a trip he made to Los Gatos with Walt and Eddie Sargent to inspect some small-sized trains that had hauled people around the 1916 Panama-Pacific Exposition in San Francisco.

'Later, we all went to Trader Vic's in Oakland for an early dinner. This was before Walt began hosting his weekly Disneyland TV show, and most people had no idea what he looked like. The maitre d' at Trader Vic's didn't know Walt from Adam and wouldn't let him in because he wasn't wearing a tie. I kept saying, "Tell him who you are,

Walt, tell him you're Walt Disney!" "No, no, no!" Walt protested, "to hell with it – they just serve South Seas crap anyway." So we all drove to Jack's, a posh restaurant in San Francisco, where Walt, believe it or not, ordered his favourite dish, a plain old hamburger.'

But he was still seriously run-down, and his doctor kept warning him he was badly in need of a real holiday. To begin with, one thing the doctor advised to him do was stop coming into the studio on Saturday and Sunday when, Kimball recalled, 'he would snoop around to check up on how the work was coming along in the different story departments'. He was strongly urged to relax and spend more time with his family, get really enthusiastic over his hobbies.

'Walt had developed a lot of muscle tension in his neck, and it was becoming chronic,' Kimball said. 'Every evening at 5 p.m. the studio nurse, Hazel George, would go up to Walt's office and massage his neck muscles, after which he would take a couple of belts of booze and head for home. When Walt related to the nurse his doctor's advice about getting away from work, she told him about the big Chicago Railroad Fair she had read about in the papers. "Why not take a week off and go see it?" she suggested. "It would do you the world of good. Take Ward Kimball with you. He likes railroads too." '

So Walt called Kimball that evening and suggested that they make the trip together. By the following Sunday, Walt and Kimball were saying goodbye to their wives at Pasadena station and boarding the Santa Fe Super Chief for Chicago.

'After we had got settled in our rooms on the train,' Kimball said later, 'Walt rapped on my door. "How about a drink?" he asked and motioned me to a chair in his room. He then brings out this special cut-glass liquor decanter and glasses from his special travelling case and pours out three fingers in each glass. Now I never could stand whisky, in fact I hate it. I like "pretty" drinks like grasshoppers and stingers (Walt called them "diluted toothpaste"). He kept pouring more whisky, and I kept politely protesting. He would say, "Drink up, for Chrissakes, relax!" (This evening drinking bout was to be a regular occurrence for the whole trip, I soon found out.) By the time Walt had his fourth shot, I was still struggling with my second, and when he decided it was time to eat, the swaying train made my unsteady trip to the dining-car a nightmare to remember.'

Kimball was hungry, nevertheless, and had been looking forward to a famous speciality of the Super Chief's kitchen, the pot roast.

'We were going over the Cajon Pass,' he remembered, 'when the steward handed us the menus. Walt ordered the most expensive thing on the list, the big thick filet mignon steak. When I made it known I was looking forward to the pot roast, he couldn't believe it. "Pot roast!" he roared. "Why in the hell do you want pot roast?" He then turned to the steward and said, "He really doesn't want pot roast, tell the waiter to bring him the filet mignon." And that was that. Since he was footing the bill for the trip, I didn't complain.'

Things looked up the next day when the Super Chief stopped at Winslow, Arizona, and the conductor asked Walt if he and Kimball would like to ride in the cab of the locomotive.

'The invitation was courtesy of Mr Ripley, president of the Santa Fe Railroad, and Walt could hardly control himself. "Let's go, Kimball! Bring the camera!" What an experience! The engineer told Walt he could blow the whistle every time he saw a small sign with a "W" on it. Those were genuine moments of happiness for Walt as, grinning from ear to ear, he pulled the cord for the longest, most drawn-out locomotive whistling I've ever heard. After we returned to our car at Gallup, New Mexico, Walt just sat there, staring into space, smiling and smiling. I had never, ever seen him look so happy.'

Equally fulfilling was their stay in Chicago.

'We had the time of our lives,' Kimball said. 'The Chicago Railroad Fair was in full steam, a world's fair with trains. The highlight was a presentation of a three-times-daily pageant, "Wheels A-Rolling", which told the history of America through the progress of the country's railroads. Dozens of historic steam locomotives were taken out of museums, refurbished and put under steam for the show. Major Lenox Lohr, the director of the Chicago Museum of Science and Industry, gave Walt and me VIP treatment. Every morning after breakfast we would taxi down to the fair grounds on Lake Michigan, and the engineer in charge would let me and Walt try our hands (under supervision, of course) at running such famous locomotives as the Tom Thumb, De Witt Clinton, John Bull, and the New York Central's 999. Then we would have lunch and stay around for the afternoon show. Sometimes Walt would be invited to don period costume and take part in some of the historical episodes. I remember one in particular where he was part of the Santa Fe's Harvey House bit. Walt would watch the other actors and play it accordingly, all in pantomime. In the meantime, I was busy filming the whole show and Walt's cameo appearance from the orchestra pit. We were both acting like a couple of kids.'

The stage was gigantic, 200 feet wide with the lake as a

background. Once, when Walt and Kimball were both in costume for another crowd scene, they found themselves on the wrong side of the stage and had to get to the other side by going through the many subterranean dressing-rooms for the huge cast.

'It was August and very hot,' Kimball recalled. 'In the large crowded dressing rooms the female ballet dancers solved the sweat problem by stripping down to just their panties. I will never forget the crazy scene as Walt, in top hat and long coat, nonchalantly elbowed his way through a sea of bosomy female pulchritude with me tagging along, shouting, "Not so fast, Walt, what's the hurry?" Looking at me over his shoulder, he yelled back, "If you've seen one, Kimball, you've seen 'em all!"'

'I thought about Walt's comment later, when I recalled the long discussion we animators had with Walt during the making of *Fantasia* about what size the breasts of the Centaurettes should be, and when, and when not, to indicate the pink nipples.'

Tired and content, Walt talked most of the way back from Chicago about the amusement park he thought he might now build 'to give visitors from all over the world something to see when they come to Hollywood'.

'Disneyland was forming in his mind,' Kimball said. 'Of course, he thought such a showplace should have an almost full-sized steam train to carry the sightseers through the attraction, a train that he could have fun operating himself on days when the park was closed.'

A few weeks after their return from the railroad fair, Walt's wife, Lilly, met Betty Kimball at a party, and said: 'You know, Walt told me the trip he took with Ward was the most fun he ever had in his life.'

Kimball added, wryly: 'Unfortunately, his euphoria soon wore off, and he was back to his own unpredictable, grouchy self, shouldering all the studio's headaches and facing the return of his neck problem — which he hadn't mentioned once during our trip to Chicago.'

But his depression was gone. For the time being, anyway.

By the time the house was finished in the Holmby Hills, so was the miniature railroad system that Walt had been helping to build at the studio. Lilly had been horrified when she realized he proposed to run it through her new garden; so as a joking way of overcoming her apprehensions, he called in his lawyer, told him to draw up a formal agreement, and had his wife and daughters sign it, giving him the legal right to put a railroad round the house. In the end, to save some of his wife's shrubs, Walt made a tunnel under one part of the garden at great expense, and every weekend he invited guests to come over and ride in his new train.

Lilly hated it and never got used to the noisy contraption, filled with shrieking grown-ups, chugging around her beloved new garden and plunging into the tunnel below the lawn. She could hardly contain her delight when, one weekend, the locomotive turned over and Walt and his guests narrowly escaped serious injury. That's the end of that particular caper, she thought, and decided her husband would soon forget his obsession with nasty, smelly trains. Even the damage suffered by her plants was worth it if it meant the end of that. But then she realized that the spill had stimulated Walt rather than turned him off his hobby. It took some time, but slowly she came to accept the importance of the railroad as therapy, and became resigned – if never reconciled – to its brazen presence.

As for Walt: 'It saved my sanity,' he said later.

When Walt Disney celebrated his fifty-second birthday on 5 December 1953, the studio on Buena Vista had fully recovered from its postwar slump, and the organization was thriving again. *Cinderella* was still making money at the box-office. *Seal Island*, *Beaver Valley* and the other True Life Adventure movies were making surprising profits as public interest in wildlife – and Disney's startling close-ups of it – grew and grew.

By this time, the Walt Disney Studio had become an international operation. Studio accountants, worrying over the accumulating amounts of money in Europe, had stumbled at last upon the obvious way to utilize them. In Britain, particularly, there were enormous sums lying idle. So why not use them by transferring some Disney productions to England where there were plenty of actors, actresses and studios available? Taking Lilly, his daughters and a skeleton crew with him, Walt left for London and took over the D&P Studios to make a film of Stevenson's *Treasure Island*.

The change of scene and the fascination of being back in the production of films containing real people instead of cartoon characters was almost as magic a therapy as the discovery of railroads. *Treasure Island* was a big success, and both Walt and his family found the atmosphere in England congenial. The first film was followed by *The Story of Robin Hood*, *The Sword and the Rose* and by *Rob Roy*, and all made money.

Walt Disney still had his admirers but by now there were plenty of

Walt Disney talks to two 'inkers' on his staff in Burbank. Most of the members of the 'Ink and Paint Department', as it was officially known, were young women who painstakingly transferred the animators' drawings onto the 'cels'.

Walt Disney holds a conference with his storymen before starting the production of a new animated feature. Note the 'storyboard' on the wall. All sequences were illustrated before shooting began.

Walt Disney (right) watches as two of his artists mime an effect they are seeking for a new animated feature.

(© *Walt Disney Productions*)

Animator Ward Kimball and Walt Disney shared an enthusiasm for railroads. Here they are aboard one of Kimball's locomotives in the yard of his house in the San Gabriel Valley, California.

(*Ward Kimball Collection*)

Walt Disney looks on as Ward Kimball, one of his top animators, mimes an expression in a mirror.   (© *Walt Disney Productions*)

Walt Disney poses with his two most popular cartoon creations, Mickey Mouse and Donald Duck.

(© *Walt Disney Productions*)

Vince Jefferds took over the handling of merchandise for Walt Disney after the première of *Peter Pan* (1953), and subsequently his department made the company $50 million a year from Disney spin-offs. Here he is seen just before the *Peter Pan* opening with Walt Disney.

(© *Walt Disney Productions, photo from Vince Jefferds Collection*)

The orange groves in Anaheim, California, which were transformed into Disneyland by landscaper Morgan 'Bill' Evans.
(© Walt Disney Productions, Morgan Evans Collection)

The ornate landscaping at both Disneyland and Walt Disney World was done by a California landscape gardener, Morgan 'Bill' Evans, who transformed the orange groves of California and the swamps of Florida in order to bring Walt Disney's dream of a new kind of leisure park system to fruition. Here he is seen with Walt Disney making a tour of Disneyland, Anaheim, shortly after its opening in 1955.
(© Walt Disney Productions, Morgan Evans Collection)

Walt Disney shows the Indian leader, Pandit
Jawaharlal Nehru, around Disneyland in
Anaheim, California, in 1956.
(© Walt Disney Productions)

Hayley Mills (centre) with her mother, Mary
Hayley Bell, and Walt Disney during a break
from shooting at the Disney Studio in Burbank.
(© Walt Disney Productions, Hayley Mills Collection)

Matte-shot artist Peter Ellenshaw, who created effects for *Treasure Island, Mary Poppins,* and other
films, talks to Walt Disney.
(© Walt Disney Productions, Peter Ellenshaw Collection)

Peter Ellenshaw sketch for a scene with Julie Andrews and Dick Van Dyke and the children in *Mary Poppins*.

Julie Andrews poses for a scene in *Mary Poppins* against a matte-shot drawn by Peter Ellenshaw (below, centre).

Walt Disney studies plans for Walt Disney World and EPCOT in Florida.

The countryside which landscape gardener Morgan 'Bill' Evans had to transform to help build Walt Disney World in Florida.

(© Walt Disney Productions, Morgan Evans Collection)

Roy Disney (left) and Morgan 'Bill' Evans, landscaper (third from left), during the building of Walt Disney World in Florida.

(© Walt Disney Productions, Morgan Evans Collection)

All Aboard . . . Mickey Mouse celebrates his golden anniversary. As part of the festivities, Mickey and animator Ward Kimball embark on an Amtrak whistle-stop tour covering 18 states and 57 cities. Mickey retraces his roots with stops including Kansas City (where Walt Disney had his first studio), Chicago, the White House, and New York, where he first appeared on screen 50 years before.

people in Hollywood who were convinced he had developed an overweening ego and delusions of grandeur. With middle-age Walt had lost his boyish charm and had become something of a bully and a know-all. He would brook no opposition of any kind. In story conferences, if somebody argued with his line, he would shoot them down without a qualm, and be really tough about it. Even the veterans whom he liked had to be careful how they approached him.

'Sometimes we would try a little reverse psychology with Walt to get him to agree with our point of view,' said Ward Kimball later. 'If you praised something too much, he would automatically build up a negative attitude towards it. Likewise, if you took a critical stand on a point, you ran the risk of his taking the opposite view. For instance, there was a guy called Captain Iver who had spent years copying on to film stock the paper negatives of rare old films filed with the Library of Congress. From the 1890s up to around 1916, all films had to be copyrighted by filing these paper copies. Iver's task was monumental because many of the old motion pictures were made on odd-sized stock, necessitating the making of special printing machines for the different sprocket-hole systems used by the early film-makers before standardization. This collection represented hundreds of thousands of film footage from all over the world, actual war films, newsreels, dramas, fantasies, etc.'

At this time Disney had gone into television and was doing a weekly show on ABC, and they were constantly buying bits and pieces from Iver's collection at so much a foot.

'When I found,' said Kimball, 'that Iver might be agreeable to selling the complete collection for only 30,000 dollars, I approached Walt, ecstatically describing in detail what a great one-of-a-kind collection it would be for the Disney film library, and at what I perceived as a bargain price too. Walt listened patiently to my pitch. Then he slowly brought one of his eyebrows down in that penetrating Disney scowl I had seen so many times. He growled, "You like it, huh? You think it would be a good idea to have this film? You think it's a good price, huh? Well, forget it. We don't need that stuff, it's not worth the price." I was crushed. Had I caught him in one of his bad moods? No. I had made the mistake of praising the idea too much. I had turned Walt off. In hindsight, I should have proceeded to outline all the reasons why we should *not* have this film collection in our library, and then let Walt defend the idea – and maybe conclude we should buy. I had learned a hard lesson in reverse psychology.'

Walt Disney still tolerated union members inside the studio – he would have had another strike on his hands otherwise – but he was always surly and suspicious of any of their leaders, and could sometimes be heard muttering 'Goddamn Commies!' as he came away from policy meetings he was forced to attend with AFL leaders. He had become close to John Wayne and other right-wing actors and would have made alliances with Harry Cohn, Jack Warner and Louis Mayer and all the other pillars of the Republican Party in Hollywood if they hadn't all been Jews. For reasons of his own, which he was reluctant to discuss, he equated the Jews and blacks with communism, and did his best to cut them out of his personal and professional life. He was a firm supporter and contributor to all the extreme right causes, particularly cliques of conservatives like members of the Motion Picture Alliance for the Preservation of American Ideals.

'Roosevelt called this the Century of the Common Man,' he once said. 'Balls! It's the century of the Communist cut-throat, the fag and the whore! And FDR and his NLRB made it so!'

Yet despite this bitterness and malevolence, this fear and resentment of the workers who had once been his friends ('they were my responsibility, but they let me down!') he could still occasionally be humble and charming, and nothing brought out these qualities more than children. 'If all the world thought and acted like children,' he once said, 'we'd never have any trouble. The only pity is even kids have to grow up.'

One day at a movie show a small boy came up and asked him if he drew Mickey Mouse. Walt had to admit he didn't draw Mickey any more. At which the boy asked him if he thought up all the jokes and ideas in his movies, and he confessed that he no longer did that either. 'Then just what do you do, Mr Disney?' the small boy asked. 'Well,' said Walt, 'sometimes I think of myself as a little bee. I go from one area of the studio to another and gather pollen and sort of stimulate everybody. I guess that's the job I do.'

Now Walt had another flower he wanted to pollinate. He had been paying consultants for several months out of his own pocket to help him draw up plans for his fun park, and now he was ready to go. It would be so different from all the other fairgrounds he had ever visited he would not even use the word but would call it Disneyland instead – the first and only park devoted to thrills, fun, edification and leisure. He already had the area picked out where Disneyland would be built – a great tract of orange groves near Anaheim, California, where the growers were ready to sell.

He bustled into Roy's office and spread out his architect's drawings, plans and projections for a fantastic collection of exhibits and experiences, all of them based on the worlds he had built up in people's imaginations with his fabulous collection of films – Cinderella's Castle, Never Never Land, the African jungle complete with crocodiles, hippos and lions, the Pirate's Lair from *Peter Pan*. And a railroad.

His eyes were shining with excitement. 'Isn't it marvellous?' he said to Roy.

As Walt recalled it later, his brother grunted.

'How much?' he asked.

'Only a million dollars,' said Walt.

'And then some!' said Roy.

'We'll see, we'll see. But will you let me have the money?' asked Walt.

'You should know better than to ask that, Walt,' he remembered Roy saying. 'I'll have to consult the bank – and the shareholders. Had you forgotten this is a public company now?'

Next day he came into Walt's office, threw the plans down on his table, and said grimly that neither the banks nor the shareholders were ever going to let him do it. They would turn him down because it would cost too much, it was too risky an undertaking. Roy added that the bank had asked him whether or not he thought it would ever make money, and he had been sceptical. They had told him he was to use his discretion with his brother, but strongly hinted it might be better if Walt forgot his pipe-dream and got back to serious film-making.

'I think they're right. We could do with a good box-office smash,' Roy said.

At this point Walt angrily accused his brother of deliberately letting him down, saying that he could easily have persuaded the bank to let him have the money, but he hadn't really tried.

Roy admitted it. He hadn't tried because he was convinced it wouldn't work. He took some of the plans and riffled through them contemptuously. What kind of crazy crap was this, anyway? For a moment it looked as if Walt Disney would do something he had never done before, and punch his brother in the nose. Instead, he snatched the plans off the table, pointed at the door and told his brother to get out.

Just before Roy went, Walt said: 'You know I'm going through with this, Roy, don't you – even if I have to use my own money!' He had already seen his lawyer, Walt told him. He was cashing in all his assets, and would somehow find the money to make a down payment on the land purchase. He had already signed an option. He paused and took a deep breath: 'Roy, you'd better realize I'm serious,' he said. He was going through with this Disneyland project if it took every last cent he had.

'What did you call it?' asked Roy.

'Disneyland,' said Walt.

'What makes you think you can use the Disney name if the shareholders don't approve?' said Roy. 'They'll never let you get away with it. Walt Disney Productions doesn't belong to us any more – the shareholders own it.'

Chapter 18

DISNEYLAND

Aꜰᴛᴇʀ Walt's death, Roy Disney tried to persuade people that he hadn't really been against his brother over Disneyland, and that the real opposition had come from the banks and the shareholders. It wasn't true, of course. Walt was quite right in accusing Roy of letting him down; he could easily have convinced Disney's creditors and shareholders that Disneyland was a bold and promising enterprise, and one that well deserved to be financially supported. He failed to back his brother because he lacked vision and had lost his courage. He was terrified of losing more money, of putting the studio in jeopardy. So long as the company was still in debt to the banks, he was desperately anxious for Walt to play safe – something which, over the years, he should have learned was impossible for his brother to do.

'That was the trouble with Roy,' said one of his former employees later. 'He wasn't like Walt at all. When he took over after Walt died, everybody tried to foster the impression he was a genius just like his brother. He wasn't. He would like to have been, but he wasn't. Make no mistake, everybody liked Roy, much more than they liked Walt. They weren't afraid of him, as they often were of Walt. He was amiable and outgoing and sympathetic. But fundamentally, he was just a shrewd country boy who sometimes made a smart deal, and was always worried afterward whether he had done the right thing. When it came to big, bold projects, in fact, he wasn't even as good a businessman as Walt was. Right through their association together, he would take up schemes only after Walt had carefully thought them through – and he would still go on being hesitant, worried and reluctant even then, especially if there was a risk involved. And of course there always was. I don't mean to suggest Walt's schemes were always successful financially. Making money was never important to him, just grease to keep his wheels turning. But he was always challenging, original. On the other hand, Roy's instinct was to turn down any idea, no matter how fresh, that couldn't guarantee a profit from the start. He was against Disneyland, against Disney World and

217

against EPCOT, all of them. It was Walt who finally drummed up the money for them.'

There were plenty of outside investors willing to listen to Walt talking about Disneyland, but they proved reluctant when it came to giving him money. To a certain degree, that was because Roy had begun circulating stories that the banks were against Disneyland, and the shareholders were not even going to allow him to use the company name.

One of the members of Disney's promotional staff at this time was a remarkable character named Vince Jefferds. The former executive vice-president of a chain of New York stores, he had recently joined Disney to handle merchandizing and exploitation. Operating through the New York office, Jefferds had put together one of the most successful marketing programmes in the history of the movies on Walt's feature cartoon, *Peter Pan*. Now Walt called him in to help him drum up the money to finance Disneyland. In 1953, he asked Jefferds to join him at a meeting of a venerable insurance company in Philadelphia from which he hoped to promote a sizeable investment.

Jefferds had come from New York and had dressed for the meeting in a conservative charcoal suit and dark tie. Walt had arrived in the Hollywood uniform of sports jacket and slacks.

'We went into the boardroom, which was a mile long with huge portraits of all the directors from 1750 or something on the walls,' said Jefferds. 'The chairman of the board was, I would say, around seventy or seventy-five, ruddy-cheeked, short, robust, cheerful, eager, looking just like Edmund Gwenn. I had a feeling he liked Walt and genuinely wanted to do something for him if he could figure out a way. He was replete with good will and guffawed when Walt introduced me in my Wall Street clothes and said: "This is my representative from Forest Lawn." But wild rumours had reached the chairman too, and he obviously believed Walt had lost his senses and was trying to drum up money to get into the honky-tonk business – like Palisades Park or Coney Island when the Fleet came in. And *his* shareholders would never have stood for that. So eventually, but with obvious regret, he turned us down.'

Roy had spread the word thoroughly, and in other company boardrooms Walt was warmly welcomed and then sorrowfully rejected.

Walt had calculated that to carry out all his plans he would have to collect two million dollars. He had already spent most of his savings hiring architects and planners; he had travelled thousands of miles with them making surveys of amusement parks around the country, studying the rides and attractions and audience reactions to them. He went overseas, too, taking Lilly with him on a trip to the Tivoli Gardens in Copenhagen. The Danish amusement park impressed him and he immediately decided Disneyland should try to emulate its happy and casual air of relaxed fun. But as his savings were drained by fees and expenses, he picked up no really wealthy backers. In desperation, he went to his lawyer and told him to cash in his life insurance policy (from which he got 100,000 dollars). He briefly considered mortgaging his new house in the Holmby Hills, but finally resisted the temptation and signed over the property to Lilly instead.

Meantime, to circumvent Roy and the threatened interference from the shareholders of Walt Disney Productions (and, quite frankly, to keep them from sharing in any of the profits if and when his leisure park succeeded), he formed a new company to take control of Disneyland's affairs. He called it Walt Disney Incorporated, with himself as president and one of his planners as the sole vice-president. Since Roy was hostile and Lilly was scared, he asked neither of them to come in with him.

The moment Roy heard about the new company, he threatened legal action on behalf of the shareholders over the use of the Disney name. Walt was advised by his lawyers to change the title of the new company to WED Enterprises.

The breach with Roy was now so serious they were communicating only through each other's secretaries or wives. Roy Edward Disney Jr, who had developed into a cocky and self-confident young man, had recently come to work in the studio and one day, according to a story which eventually went the rounds in Hollywood, he approached Walt and said: 'Uncle Walt, is it true what my father says – that you're going to become a ringmaster for Barnum and Bailey's Circus?'

He giggled at his own joke, while Walt struggled for an answer and got red in the face.

Finally, his uncle said: 'It isn't true, Junior. But I'll certainly see about it if you and your father will join me as the company clowns.'

He was later to forgive Roy for his behaviour during this critical phase in his life, but he never did forget his nephew's insufferable attempts to be funny.

Disneyland was now no longer a joking matter where he was concerned. It had become a grim obsession, and he swore he would never do another thing at the studios until he had sufficient finance to get the project going. It had become the only thing in life that mattered to him, and even animated cartoons had, temporarily, lost their savour.

In an interview which he gave to the Hollywood *Citizen-News* at this time, he said:

The park means a lot to me. It's something that will never be finished, something I can keep developing, keep 'plussing' and adding to. It's alive. It will be a live, breathing thing that will need changes. When you wrap up a picture and turn it over to Technicolor, you're through. *Snow White* is a dead issue with me. I just finished a live-action picture, wrapped it up a few weeks ago. It's gone. I can't touch it. There are things in it I don't like but I can't do anything about it. I want something live, something that would grow. The park is that. Not only can I add things to it, but even the trees will keep growing. The thing will get more beautiful year after year. And it will get better as I find out what the public likes. I can't do that with a picture. It's finished and unchangeable before I find out if the public likes it or not.

In the end, he had to look outside the usual business channels for backing. But the idea of approaching television, which was what he eventually decided to do, was not something which came to him in a flash. Like many another Hollywood film man, Walt Disney both feared and was fascinated by the burgeoning television industry. He believed that the longer Hollywood refused to feed television with material and competitive ammunition, the more likely it was to collapse beneath the weight of its own mediocrity. At the same time, he knew both of the main television networks – there were only two in those days, NBC and CBS, with ABC a small upstart struggling to keep going – would give their right arms and lots of money to get their hands on some of the Disney cartoons and True Adventure stories. They were desperately short of movie entertainment and had several times offered substantial fees for the right to project Walt Disney productions. Not only was it general Hollywood policy not to sell movies to television, but Walt had long since decided that airing his cartoons through what he regarded as an amateurish outlet would do nothing but demean them. But now he was desperate. Not desperate enough to break the Hollywood taboo on selling theatrical products to television, but prepared to look for a way of circumventing the ban.

For instance, what if he made a series of films especially for television, and not for theatrical exhibition, and then offered them as a quid pro quo to the networks in return for finance for Disneyland?

That was the proposition he eventually made, and even Roy was taken with the scheme when he heard about it. He immediately made overtures to his brother and offered his help in pushing it with the networks. Walt suspected Roy was more interested in getting a new source of revenue for the studio than in procuring finance for Disneyland, which he still opposed. Nevertheless, he welcomed the offer as a gesture of reconciliation and took him up on it, whereupon Roy offered to go to New York and sell the proposition to the networks himself. To make sure he would keep money-for-Disneyland as the paramount priority in his mind, Walt called in one of his staff to write him a pamphlet about the leisure-park so that Roy could show it to the prospective backers. Meanwhile, he had bought the rights to the Zorro stories about a masked Mexican bandit (Douglas Fairbanks and Tyrone Power had played the character in cinematic versions). He told his script department to run up a series of draft scripts, which he would agree to make and deliver for television showing as part of the quid pro quo.

The pamphlet was written by Bill Walsh, a bear-shaped, cigar-smoking former gag-writer for the ventriloquist Edgar Bergen, who had joined Walt Disney Productions to do Mickey Mouse scripts and promotion films for Disney's British operations. He loathed television and when he heard Walt was contemplating making a deal with the networks, hastily scribbled him a note pleading with him not to do it. Typically, Walt promptly commissioned him to do the text of the pamphlet. Herbert Ryman, a former animator, was hired to do the drawings. It was obvious Walsh's heart was not in it.

The idea of Disneyland is a simple one [he wrote]. It will be a place for people to find happiness and knowledge. It will be a place for parents and children to share pleasant times in one another's company: a place for teachers and pupils to discover greater ways of understanding and education. Here the older generation can recapture the nostalgia of days gone by, and the younger generation can savor the challenge of the future. Here will be the wonders of Nature and Man for all to see and understand.

Disneyland will be based upon and dedicated to the ideals, the dreams and the hard facts that have created America. And it will be uniquely equipped to dramatize these dreams and facts and send them forth as a source of courage and inspiration to all the world.

Disneyland will be something of a fair, an exhibition, a playground, a community center, a museum of living facts, and a showplace of beauty and magic.

It will be filled with the accomplishments, the joys and hopes of the world we live in. And it will remind us and show us how to make those wonders part of our lives.

Apart from the last two paragraphs, it was a low-key, not terribly impressive presentation of Walt Disney's intentions, and the details that followed – setting out such Disneyland attractions as a True Life Adventureland, Rivers of Romance, World of Tomorrow, Lilliputia-land, Spaceship to the Moon – hardly gave a convincing picture, even with the illustrations, of the thrills to come. True, it also stated there would be a Tom Sawyer River Ride and a trip through Fantasyland, a moving walkway for the tired of foot, and, of course, a railroad from which people could see everything without walking a step. But neither Walsh nor Ryman conveyed the vividness of the concept bubbling in Walt Disney's mind, and the pamphlet made no impact whatsoever on the head of CBS. One of CBS's main sponsors, the pharmaceutical firm Johnson & Johnson, did agree to consider making an investment providing they were satisfied with the television entertainment Walt was willing to give them in return. They asked to see a pilot film of the Zorro series.

Roy shook his head. 'Walt doesn't do pilots,' he said. 'Never has. Says he never will. You know our track record. You'll have to judge us on that – and the draft scripts.'

'TV doesn't work that way,' the Johnson & Johnson people replied. 'No pilot, no sponsorship.'

David Sarnoff, head of NBC and the giant RCA Corporation, was rather more receptive, but each time his negotiators took over, the discussions bogged down on conditions. They too wanted to see a pilot of Zorro.

Roy came back from New York more than ever convinced Disneyland was never going to rise off the ground.

Then one morning in the spring of 1953, the telephone rang and a voice said: 'Walt, I hear you need money to build your fairground. If you will agree to let us put Mickey Mouse on our network, my directors are ready to advance you 250,000 dollars for it. Further-more, we're willing to come in on a joint venture with you and guarantee loans up to three million dollars.'

'For God's sake, how many times do I have to tell people it's a leisure park, not a fairground!' said Walt. 'Who is this anyway?'

'My name's Kintner,' said the voice, 'and I'm an executive vice-president of the American Broadcasting Corporation, otherwise known as ABC.'

'The peanuts network!' said Walt. 'What the hell good would it do me to work with you? You're the Little Orphan Annie of the TV airways, with hardly a station to call your own.'

'Give us Mickey Mouse, Walt, plus the Disney name,' said the voice, 'and I guarantee within two years we'll be one of the Big Three.' A pause. 'I hear you need the money real bad. A quarter of a million and a three million guarantee could be a great help, I figure. Is it a deal?'

Walt took a deep breath.

'Make it half a million in cash and a four and a half million dollar guarantee and Mickey is yours,' he said.

'Done,' said Kintner. Then, in a mock announcer's voice: 'And welcome to the TV airways, Walt Disney!'

In the summer of 1954, when the deal had been clinched with ABC president Goldenson, the first orange trees were torn out of the groves at Anaheim and work began on the building of Disneyland. Mickey Mouse was seen for the first time on television that autumn. A revolution had begun in the nature of television and leisure entertainment in the US, and soon, for Walt Disney, for ABC and for the American public, things would never be the same again. As Kintner had foreseen, Walt Disney turned ABC into a major network in the space of a few months.

During the opening ceremonies of Disneyland that August, after the first sod had been turned and the first bulldozer had butted its nose against a tree, Roy came over to talk to Walt. His son, Roy Edward Disney Jr, was with him, looking, to Walt's admittedly jaundiced eye, even cockier than usual.

'I just wanted you to know,' Roy was later reported to have said, 'that I've been talking to the board of directors – and they want in.'

Walt knew exactly what had been going on during recent days, but pretended to be obtuse.

'In?' he queried. 'What do you mean by in? In where?'

'In here,' said Roy. 'Disneyland. They like the concept. They like the way you've handled the deal. I've talked it over with them, and they're prepared to buy you and your share out for 500,000 dollars. Sign over Disneyland Inc. to Walt Disney Productions and the half million bucks is yours.' (During the negotiations with ABC, Walt Disney had formed an additional company to handle his Disneyland interests.)

According to onlookers, Walt pretended to give it deep thought. Finally, he said: 'I'll tell you what I'll do, Roy. You just go back to the board of directors and say I'll give them exactly 50 per cent of Disneyland Inc. for that half a million bucks.' Then he is said to have added: 'Or I'll cut that figure down to 25 per cent – on one condition.'

'What's that?' asked Roy.

Walt indicated his son, smirking away in the sunlight. 'On condition that your son, Junior, here, signs up to work at Disneyland once the park is finished.'

'That might be interesting,' said Roy. 'As what?' He put a fond arm around his son.

'As a clown,' said Walt. 'Did I tell you we plan to set up a circus side show in the park? Junior would do a real good job whooping it up as the back end of a horse.'

They finally settled for Walt keeping 17.25 per cent of the Disneyland holdings. He sold out the rest to Walt Disney Productions, who shared the investment henceforth equally with ABC, and Western Printing and Lithographing held 13.79 per cent.

As for Roy Edward Disney Jr, he continued to work at the Buena Vista studios, and never did make an appearance at Disneyland, and certainly not as a clown or the rear end of a horse. But neither did his relationship with his uncle improve in the years to come.

Chapter 19

ACOLYTES

AN English artist named Peter Ellenshaw had worked on three of the Disney live-action films made with frozen sterling funds in Britain, and it had proved to be the most formative experience of his life, simply because it brought him within the orbit and influence of Walt Disney.

Thirty years old in 1950, Ellenshaw had already worked with at least two giants of the film world (one recognized, the other comparatively unknown) during his short career in the movies: he had done the art work for some of Alexander Korda's most memorable epics, including *The Shape of Things to Come, Rembrandt, The Four Feathers, The Drum* and *The Thief of Bagdad*; and he had learned the art of matte-painting, at which he now excelled, from the pioneer and master of the craft, Percy (Pop) Day, whose immeasurable contributions to the refinement of aesthetic movie techniques would save the industry millions of dollars. Day's experiments with matte-painting began in France in 1910, and flowered in 1927 when he provided the simulated battlefield backgrounds for Abel Gance's classic epic, *Napoleon*. (The career of this often irascible perfectionist is full of rewarding incidents and discoveries, and it is to be hoped that some cineaste will one day write a biography of him.)

For Ellenshaw, even these two remarkable men diminished in stature when measured against Walt Disney, who left such an indelible impression upon him that even today he is apt to remark: 'What a wonderful thing to be able to say: "I once knew Walt Disney." '

Walt Disney used to tell an apocryphal story to the animators in the sweat-box at Buena Vista about how Ellenshaw came to work for him in America.

'I was in London, in Trafalgar Square, watching these pavement artists,' he would say, 'and there was a young man and he obviously had talent. So I asked him whether he would like to work for me, and he looked up from the sidewalk and said, "Oh, yes, guv!" And that was Peter.'

It was completely untrue, and because Ellenshaw had never been a

225

pavement artist in his life it made him squirm each time he heard it – which was probably why Walt was always repeating it. And since his staff never quite knew whether Walt was joking or not, they believed it. Ellenshaw would always be the ex-pavement artist to them.

In fact, he came into Walt Disney's orbit through quite legitimate movie channels. An Irish art director named Tom Morahan, well known in movie circles in London, was aware of Peter's work for Korda and of his reputation both as a serious artist and a talented pupil of Pop Day. He called him and said he wanted matte-shots for a movie of Robert Louis Stevenson's *Treasure Island* which Disney was about to make. The budget didn't allow for location trips, so Ellenshaw was required to simulate the real thing – and do it quickly.

'Painting matte-shots is a most tricky and meticulous art,' said Ellenshaw later. 'Let us suppose we are on location and need a castle on a hill. We have the hill but no castle. On a large glass, about six feet in front of a camera, we paint the castle. Through the clear part of the glass, the characters in the scene (or boats or other objects) go into action and are photographed at the same time as the background scene with castle is recorded. This is matte-painting in its simplest form.'

In this case, Ellenshaw had to visualize the sultry atmosphere of a tropical island as Stevenson had described it in his book, and painstakingly reproduce in exquisite detail matte-shots of every cove, cave, beach and forest glade specified in the script. Moreover, Walt Disney, who liked to follow through every stage in production, wanted to see his rough sketches.

'I took them along to his office every morning and there would be dozens of them,' said Ellenshaw. 'I soon discovered Walt liked drawings with dramatic back-lighting. It happens that I like back-lighting too, so that started us off with something in common. Subsequently, I had as many failures with him as I had successes, but in the main he liked what I did.'

Treasure Island was a great success and few film-goers realized the lush island setting of the film had been painted into the camera, or that Ellenshaw's graphic matte-shots had saved the company half a million dollars in location expenses.

Ellenshaw did more Disney films after that, and although Walt never once praised or thanked him, his two principal producers in Britain, Fred Leahy and Perce Pearce, admired his work so much they were always saying to him: 'Would you consider going to America?'

'Wouldn't I just!' said Ellenshaw, describing his reactions later.

Ellenshaw had met and married his wife while training as a navigator in the US during World War II. He then returned to Europe and served for four years in the RAF.

'You know what it was like in England in those days, just after the war,' he said. 'I had my young American wife, Bobbie, there with our three-month-old baby whom she had brought over from America in a troopship. We were living in one room because there was no accommodation available. Food was scarce. There was rationing. It was really a desperate time for Bobbie, and I couldn't wait to get out of the country.'

But Walt never personally invited him, nor did his producers ever offer him a specific job. In fact, whenever he tried to talk to them seriously about the prospects of working at Buena Vista, Leahy would always say, uncertainly: 'I can't say Walt thinks it would be a good idea. He's going to take a bit of persuading.'

And then, abruptly, Walt was bitten by the Disneyland bug and departed for America. His film operation in Britain came to a halt, and Ellenshaw was bereft. For weeks on end, he wallowed in miserable uncertainty, not knowing what to do, hoping against hope he would get a call from California to rejoin his boss. But no word came. The prospect of working with anyone else now seemed so bleak and unpromising, he could not bring himself to seek another job.

In the end, he decided there was only one thing to do. If Walt Disney did not send for him, he would go, unsummoned.

'We sold up everything we had in England, the tiny flat, the furniture, everything,' said Ellenshaw. 'And we came across the Atlantic by boat and across America by train, and since we were paying our own way and didn't have much money, it was dreadful. I had found out from Leahy we would probably be given a job once we reached Burbank, but it had nothing to do with Walt and the wage I was offered when we got there was very low. I took it. I'd have taken anything to get back into Disney.'

Once he was back in Walt's orbit, life was suddenly full of promise again.

'When Walt heard I was there on the lot, he called me into his office,' said Ellenshaw. 'He was sitting at this low desk. For anyone else it would have been chi-chi to have a desk that low. Instead of being perched up high, as the other movie moguls were, he was hunched down and looking up at you and smoking. He looked at me kind of half-pleased and said: "Well, Peter." Of course, I had got to know him quite well in England and when he was away from the

227

studio he had been quite free and open with me. But here he obviously had to be Walt Disney. The big guy. Chain-smoking. "Sit down," he says. "Now I'll tell you about the people you'll be working with. But I must say, I don't understand why you came. There aren't many mattes to work on, and I don't think you're going to find enough work to merit your being here." God, I'd sold up everything, burned my bridges, and he sounded as if he was about to send me back!'

Later on he concluded: 'He was making sure I didn't get an inflated idea of my own worth and start getting above myself. I think for the same reason, I was kept hanging around the studio for days on end, with no one telling me anything about what I was supposed to do. It was disconcerting, chilling, humbling.'

Despite the fact that Disney didn't mention a word about it, Ellenshaw could hardly have arrived at a more propitious moment. The Disneyland negotiations had gone into high gear and seemed certain to be successful. Walt had turned his attention back to movie-making and was fizzing with enthusiasm over his biggest and most expensive picture so far: a version of Jules Verne's *20,000 Leagues Under the Sea.* As if to celebrate his reconciliation with his brother, he was pressing Roy to agree a budget on the movie which had long since passed two and a half million dollars and was rising every week while Walt strove for effects that were more and more authentic, effective and expensive.

They were shooting underwater miniatures for *20,000 Leagues* on the back lot at Buena Vista under the direction of an old-time effects man named Ralph Hammeras, an eccentric character who sported a beard and wore a cloak. Like everybody else in the studio, Walt knew the special effects Hammeras was directing would make or break the movie. It was imperative they were dramatic and authentic. With nothing better to do, Ellenshaw would go to the sweat-box every evening to see the rushes of Hammeras's work for the day, and he was appalled.

'When I saw what was supposed to be the submarine, I thought: "My God, it doesn't have the scale! This looks like a little tin something going through the water. They're not lighting it from the back. It should loom up very big." '

He realized that this was his opportunity. Like everybody else, he had learned by now that Walt Disney was an inveterate snooper, wandering round the studio at night after everybody had left, riffling through papers on desks, opening drawers, reading letters or going through the contents of cubbyholes to find out what his staff were up to. Ellenshaw was not the first Disney employee to realize his boss's nosiness provided an ideal opportunity to plant things he deliberately wanted his boss to see. He was working on the top floor of the animators' building at this time, and he did a series of drawings – highly dramatized with heavy back light – of how he thought Captain Nemo's submarine should look as it cruised the murky waters. These he left spread carelessly over his desk.

A couple of weeks later, Walt called everybody into the sweat-box and said: 'We're going to run the rushes on how the underwater sequences have gone over the last two weeks.'

After the rushes had been showing for a time, Walt suddenly pressed the button and brought the screening to a halt. The lights went up and he said: 'Guys, this isn't working. We gotta start again.'

Everybody was looking at Ralph Hammeras. Whenever he was nervous, he had his script on his knee and he would shuffle through the pages, trying to appear busy. Suddenly, Walt turned.

'Ralph,' he said, 'I've seen some sketches of how these scenes should be lit, and these have been done by Peter Ellenshaw, and he's sitting right behind you.'

Hammeras glared malevolently at the blushing Englishman.

'You and Peter have to get together,' Walt went on. 'And you, Peter, have to stay with Ralph and make sure these scenes are going to be shot like your drawings from now on.' He looked at Hammeras's stony face and went on: 'You boys know this is the way we work here. We work together.' And then, clapping Hammeras on the back: 'I know you're in charge, Ralph, but I want Peter here to be with you there to help.'

Hammeras took the change very well, on the whole.

'He had been in the business since before the first war, but he was a sweetie really,' said Ellenshaw. 'He would ask me where I wanted the lights, and we worked as a team. We had to. Walt had his eye on us. But I did come in one day and I sensed Hammeras's attitude toward me had changed. We'd been shooting Captain Nemo's submarine hitting the hull of the pirate ship, the one that was carrying the munitions. I had kept it very low-key and all you could see was the blackness of the hull. I saw the warning signals on Ralph's face. He said: "I'm sorry, Peter, but I'm not going to be able to listen to you any longer. I just got the clips back from Technicolor, and they say there's nothing on the film. You've got me to light it too low-key and there's nothing on it, and I've got my reputation to consider . . ." '

Ellenshaw asked him to put the clips on the screen.

'I'd known what I wanted from the start,' he said, 'and when the scene came on it was just grey. Then out of the greyness comes this black shape and then the other black shape appears and then – bam! – it hits. True, there was only a feeble spark and it wasn't strong enough and we had to build it up later. But the scene did have a tremendous, uncanny, convulsive power. And it certainly caught the mood. I turned to Ralph and I saw he was sold on the scene, and to hell with what Technicolor said. But for me it had been a close one. From then on we worked harmoniously together, and you know the result.'

The collision of the submarine and the pirate ship and another underwater sequence featuring a giant squid, which was remodelled and reshot at a cost of 250,000 dollars, made all the difference to the movie's impact.

But so far as his relationship with Walt was concerned, Ellenshaw was still feeling for some sort of rapport. One day he heard Walt coughing his way along a corridor to a staff meeting he had called, and he came out of his cubicle and asked him whether he could end his collaboration with Hammeras and get back to matte-painting.

'I didn't have time to finish,' said Ellenshaw. 'He got mad at once. "For Christ's sake, Peter," he said, "what the hell's the matter with you? Don't you understand plain English? I told you to stay with old Hammeras, and I meant it. I'm not going to tell you any more times." I started to say something and he said: "I'm talking. You shut up." He cut me down as if he had a scythe in his hand. He swept on to the meeting with me trailing behind and I suppose the expression of my face betrayed just how miserable I was feeling, because he came across to me afterwards and said: "Don't take it to heart. But you see, you have to learn to work with the others." God, he could be rough with you! We had a writer and sketch artist called Don DaGradi, a wonderful fellow with a great feeling for the way scenes should be played, and one day Walt came up to him and said: "Have you been on the back lot today?" and Don said he hadn't. So then Walt said: "Look, I go down there every day to see how things are going. So how come you can't go down there? Get out and find out what's happening. For Christ's sake, don't hang around your office all day. Get your butt out of there." No matter how important you were, he'd rough you up.'

Slowly, painfully, surviving many an insult and wounding practical joke, Ellenshaw felt himself getting closer to his boss. Like everyone else who ever knew or worked for Walt, he never did achieve intimacy with him. But he did win back some of the friendliness he had experienced from him in England. He was soon working on matte-paintings for such successful films as *Darby O'Gill*, *The Castaways* and *Mary Poppins*. Later, he realized that the time when Walt seemed to relax and come closest to him was in London during the making of *Mary Poppins*. Ellenshaw did matte-paintings for many of the London scenes as well as hundreds of sketches for the cartoon sequences. Shortly after the company returned to California, they were shooting a number with the Chimney Sweep on the back lot, but when they saw it in the rushes it seemed to sag. Ellenshaw suggested to Bill Walsh, the producer, it might be lightened-up if the Chimney Sweep and all the Cockney characters round him did a song and dance number to the tune of 'Knees Up, Mother Brown', explaining to him it was a Cockney classic.

'I said it was a number that would get you thrown out of any pub in England,' said Ellenshaw, 'because the moment you started dancing it, everybody always stopped drinking and joined in. It was a wonderfully vulgar dance and Bill asked me to demonstrate it, and after seeing it said: "Great! Let's bring in Walt and get his approval to put it in." ' So Walt was summoned, and he watched a demonstration of the song and dance and agreed it should go into the sequence.

'And of course, it was infectious,' said Ellenshaw. 'Everybody joined in – Walt included. We linked arms and went charging across the room, roaring out "Knees up, Mother Brown"! The only trouble was, the dancers didn't realize this was the kind of dance you don't do in polite places, you have to get your knees really high up and you're not elegant at all, in fact you show so much of what you've got underneath you're downright rude. I had to keep telling everybody, Walt included, to "Get those knees up!" until we all collapsed, out of breath from laughter and exhaustion. But it made oh, such a wonderful clip in the film! And I suppose the whole episode excited me so much I didn't worry that when we finished singing and dancing, Walt, although he was laughing with the rest of us at the end of it – well, he didn't look too good. As if it had all been too much for him.'

But it certainly improved his relationship with Ellenshaw.

In the fifties, Disney had made a film about the US training ship *Eagle*, for which Ellenshaw had painted pictures. Now the *Eagle* had arrived in San Diego on an official visit, and Walt had been invited to take a trip in her. It was an indication of their improved relationship that Walt, via his secretary, asked if Peter would accompany him. It was a royal command, and Ellenshaw knew better than to refuse. All the same, he was somewhat disconcerted when he learned there was only one guest cabin aboard the *Eagle* and he and Walt would be sharing quarters. (The press covered the trip, but they were accommodated on another ship.)

They flew to San Diego and had an interesting day exploring the ship, and then had a slap-up dinner in the wardroom.

'Now as evening draws on, Walt's getting restless,' said Ellenshaw, 'and I'm getting restless too – at the thought that we both have to share this extremely small cabin – which was a little room for dwarfs. Almost immediately after dinner he said he was feeling very tired and he wanted to turn in. That was a signal for me to get lost while he got himself ready for bed, and he suggested I take a turn around the deck. I took several turns. When I calculated he should be tucked up in bed and sound asleep, I went down to the cabin.'

There he found Walt sitting on the lower bunk in his pyjamas, looking tired and drawn. Fixing Ellenshaw with his gimlet-eyes, he said: 'Now Peter, I'm here on this bed. But there's no reason why I should have it. I can sleep in the one up above.'

After some discussion he got into the lower bunk, and then he said: 'Peter, if you are going up there – you don't pee the bed, do you?'

Ellenshaw said, primly: 'I can assure you, Walt, I've never peed the bed yet, and I'm certainly not going to do it tonight.'

'Well, I was just wondering.' Another pause as he settled down. 'Some people do, you know.' And he launched into a long rigmarole about bed-wetters he had known.

Finally into his pyjamas and stretched out on the upper bunk, Ellenshaw tried to settle down.

'After what seemed hours – it was probably about forty-five minutes, really – he seemed to drop off to sleep, and I lay there thinking, if I miss a night's sleep it won't be a big problem. I'll catch up when I get home tomorrow. Because I certainly didn't feel like sleeping with this precious man beneath me. Then just as I was beginning to get a bit drowsy, there was a great bump below me. The head of my idol had hit the bottom of my bunk, solidly. I jumped a mile. I could hear him muttering below me. He climbs out with what he considers very great care, but he seemed to make a hell of a lot of noise as far as I was concerned. I was lying on my back with my eyes barely open, like when your mother comes to tuck you in, and he peers up. His great head comes over the edge of my bunk and he checks to see if my breathing's regular. Then he tiptoes across this tiny cabin, which had a tiny bowl in which you were supposed to wash yourself, and he gets a wet washcloth.'

By this time Ellenshaw was watching carefully and slowly realized Walt was in pain. He took the cloth, quietly ran hot water on it, and then held it against his face and neck.

'And from then on, every half hour or so all through the night, he would bang his head against the bunk, climb out of bed and wearily, groaning, swearing, he would go across to the washbowl and try and do something about his pain. I knew better than to show I was awake and aware of what he was doing, but it was agony to watch the poor man.'

When morning came, bright and early, Walt was awake and dressed.

'Well, Peter,' he said. 'How did you sleep?'

'I slept like a top,' said Ellenshaw. 'How about you?'

'Not bad,' he said, grinning. 'Not bad at all.'

'I didn't have the courage to tell him I hadn't slept a wink and I knew he hadn't either,' said Ellenshaw later. 'That was the trouble with Walt. People were so scared. Walt was such a private person you dare not show you knew he was ill and in pain. Even the doctors were scared of him. Examining him must have been quite a strain for his medical advisers because he hated it and them so much. His illness probably progressed faster because he didn't have himself examined in time. He didn't think doctors were any good – not for him, anyway.

'Of course, people, doctors, should have told him much earlier on to stop smoking those dreadful black cigarettes. He never for a moment thought they would do him any harm. They just made him cough, and he didn't worry about his cough. You could recognize him at Burbank by his cough. He coughed "Woof, woof!" and you'd hear it as he came down the corridor. And you'd think: "Oh, here's Walt coming to see me. Good." '

The opening of Disneyland on 17 July 1955 was a near disaster because nothing was ready in time. Some of the rides didn't work, and others weren't ready. Cement and tarmacadam hadn't dried, smearing clothes, wrenching heels off shoes, tempting small boys to leave footprints and rude messages. The gardens looked bare and ragged because too many orange trees had been bulldozed out of the ground. Press complaints were strident and unfriendly, concentrating particularly on a shortage of drinking fountains, which, they grumbled, forced customers to buy expensive Cokes when all they wanted to do was quench an honest thirst. Walt had his publicity department explain that a plumbers' strike had forced him to choose between free fountains and toilets. Meanwhile, he spent hours snooping around the park to watch how the visitors were treated by the staff and he had no hesitation in sacking an attendant on the spot for surliness or lack of patience.

'Always smile,' he ordered. 'Turn the other cheek to everybody, even the nasty ones. And above everything, always give them full value for their money. If a boat ride is supposed to last twelve minutes and they only get eleven minutes thirty seconds, they've a right to feel cheated. Thirty seconds shy, and they hate us for selling them short. Thirty seconds extra, and they feel they've gotten away with something. That's the way we want them to feel. Contented, even smug.'

He did not relax until everything was in order and his beloved railroad was running smoothly. The millionth visitor was clocked in before the end of the second month of operation, and twelve months later Walt Disney Productions was able to pay off nine million dollars in outstanding loans to the banks, and inform the shareholders the company was in profit. This was not entirely due to the success of the theme-park, of course. The television programme (also called Disneyland) was consistently top of the national ratings ahead of NBC and CBS and had, by the end of the first year, transformed ABC, its sponsor, into a major network.

Through his deal to put his products on television, Walt demonstrated both his inherent contempt for the medium and his shrewd knowledge of its capacity for propaganda and exploitation. So far as he was concerned, television was not an entertainment outlet but just another means of selling Disney to a wider public. His two first programmes were devoted to a guided tour of Disneyland and a film about the making of *20,000 Leagues Under the Sea*, which was due for release soon. Though expertly made, both had no purpose except to act as come-ons for potential customers for other Disney products. To handle the making of them and other programmes in the Disneyland series he assigned the talented Bill Walsh, who was, like Peter Ellenshaw, one of his most fervent disciples. In fact, so completely did Walsh regard Walt Disney as an all-knowing father-figure that when he met and fell in love with a beautiful ballet dancer, he took her to Walt first for his approval before proposing marriage to her.

Walsh loathed television and all it stood for. He regarded it as fundamentally meretricious, appealing to the shallowest of public emotions. Yet he had a natural instinct for knowing what images would excite the most public interest.

When Walt called him in and told him he had been given the job of writing the stories and producing the twice-weekly TV programme, he said: 'Why me? I don't know how to produce a TV show.'

'Who does?' said Walt, with a shrug.

So Walsh began 'by using a combination of glue and chicken wire' to cobble together clips incorporating scenes from Disney films past, present or in the making, all for the purpose of promoting them for future paying audiences at the cinemas.

'We promoted anything that moved in the studio,' he said. 'Walt felt that nothing we ever made should be left to stand by itself, so we always had to do something to help it along at the box office. We did a review of the year's product at Disney and it boosted the receipts when we put the old films in revival. The amazing thing is that nobody complained we were doing publicity movies. Far from it. Our *20,000 Leagues* documentary even won us an Emmy. *And* it brought in sponsorship for our programmes first from Coca-Cola and then from Johnson & Johnson.'

Sheer boredom with old Disney products, plus the ambition to do something a little more original, persuaded Walsh to branch out into productions of his own.

'I thought it might be a good thing to do a series on vaunted American heroes,' he said, 'and we mulled over subjects like Johnnie Appleseed, Daniel Boone, Winn Wagon-Smith, Big Foot Wallace and Davy Crockett. The first one we picked, by dumb luck, was Davy Crockett, who was someone at that time nobody had ever heard of.'

Walsh and a writer named Tom Blackburn researched their subject and produced a script, and because Walt would have to approve it first and understood pictures rather than words, they illustrated most of the action on story-boards which they hung round the walls of his office, showing Davy Crockett's progress from the Tennessee wilderness through his election to Congress and then to his death on the Alamo. Davy Crockett was drawn wearing a coonskin cap and fringed leather jerkin and breeches, and his huge body and facial features bore an uncanny resemblance to one of the Western film heroes of the day, James Arness.

Walt approved the idea but wanted the budget to be kept low. Arness would have cost too much money. In any case, when he ran one of Arness's movies, his eye was caught by Fess Parker, one of the minor players in the background.

Parker was by no means flattered when Bill Walsh approached him for the part of Davy Crockett. Parker hated Wild West roles but hunger had sometimes forced him into them and he found he was allergic to horses and loathed the dudes cowboys wore. His ambition was to appear in drawing-room comedies wearing lounge suits, and his lip curled in derision and distaste when he saw the drawings of Davy Crockett's outfit.

'You trying to make a Gene Autry out of me?' he asked, contemptuously.

'That'll be the day,' said Walsh.

Eventually hunger won out, and Parker signed up for the film. They had to teach him how to ride a horse first, and to do it without going down with a rash. His leather jerkins were specially sprayed before he wore them, and when he was out of camera range he shied away from them as if they were a bunch of poison ivy. For budget reasons and the time demands of television, there was no chance of going to Tennessee for location shots nor for matte-paintings from Ellenshaw to give verisimilitude to studio scenes, so action was bridged by drawings. By the time Walsh had finished the three segments of Davy Crockett's adventures, he had a sinking feeling he might have given birth to a turkey. Not only was the film long-winded but it was choppy, and the drawings were unsatisfactory in bridging the gaps in the narrative. Moreover, it ended with Davy Crockett dying on the Alamo. As one of the studio executives said after seeing the first rough-cut: 'Who the hell wants a hero who gets killed in the final reel?' Walsh gives credit to Walt for insisting on keeping the tragic ending. He also agreed that the segments needed some more satisfactory connecting link, and eventually suggested a theme song. Tom Blackburn, the scriptwriter, provided the subject matter ('Born on a mountaintop in Tennessee') and George Bruns, in the music department, came up with a tuneful and rollicking number. When Disneyland put the first instalment, *Davy Crockett, Indian Fighter*, on the ABC network just before Christmas in 1954, it was 'The Ballad of Davy Crockett' which gave it instant popularity. In a matter of days, the song was top of the hit parade and the programme soared in the network ratings. At which point, those viewers who also read newspapers learned the historical facts about Davy Crockett and were reminded he died fighting for his country on the Alamo. Letters descended upon Buena Vista from children of all ages pleading with Walt Disney to give history a twist and keep the hero alive at the end. There were so many of them that Walsh went to Walt and asked what he was going to do.

'You'll keep your word and let him die, won't you, Walt?' he asked anxiously.

'Hell, I suppose we'll just have to,' said Walt, glumly. Then he brightened. 'But I'll tell you what we're gonna do, Bill. You're gonna make a quick second series which we'll slip in before the last instalment called "The Further Adventures of Davy Crockett". And *then* we'll kick him off at the Alamo, the way he's supposed to.'

If ever there was an opportunity for exploitation by the Disney rights department, *Davy Crockett* was it, and Kay Kamen would have gloried at the chance presented to him. But Kamen had recently been killed in a plane crash and his widow had sold back his share of royalties to Walt and Roy. Roy had meanwhile appointed O. B. Johnson, an accountant, to take Kamen's place.

Failing to appreciate the spin-off potential in the Davy Crockett series, which he didn't much like anyway, Johnson signed away merchandizing rights to a manufacturing firm which was soon quietly making a brisk profit from reproductions. Belatedly, one member of the marketing staff at Disney did realize the possibilities in pushing replicas of Davy's coonskin cap, but enthusiasm waned when it was discovered American fur dealers had lost their expertise in manufacturing fur hats, and cheap and adaptable fur – or fake fur – was not easily available. But then the department had a stroke of luck. Someone came up with the information that there had once been a brisk trade in raccoon skins between the United States and China, but that since China had now gone Communist with the resulting imposition of a trade embargo by the US, the commerce in coonskins had come to an abrupt halt. But what about the American suppliers – and their coonskins? Had they found an alternative market, or did they have a lot of surplus coonskins lying around? They had indeed. It was shortly revealed that a small exporter in California had a whole warehouse full of the skins, and was so resigned to seeing them lie there until they rotted he was willing to let them go cheaply. A deal was made. A merchandize company dug out a veteran fur-hat maker from retirement, and a roaring trade began in Davy Crockett coonskin caps. Soon the warehouse was empty and still the demand for Davy Crockett hats mounted, until every amateur hunter in the country was shooting raccoons and shipping them to the manufacturer for a price which had climbed ten and twenty times in six months. For the first time, the future of America's most fecund wild animal was threatened.

Meanwhile, Walt had told Bill Walsh to cobble together the television series and cut and shape it into a full-length movie for the cinemas, and although industry experts were sceptical about its chances after so widespread a free coverage over the airwaves, *Davy Crockett, King of the Wild Frontier* became a smash hit. Its success stimulated a renewed demand for Crockett memorabilia, and this time it was international. So desperate were the cries of small boys everywhere for coonskin hats that they had to be made out of rabbit and squirrel skins. And not just small boys. One fur manufacturer in New York even produced a sable version for women with a price-tag of around 750 dollars, and it sold well.

By 1960, E. Cardon (Card) Walker, who ran promotion and exploitation at the Walt Disney Studio, had been appointed to the Executive Committee and named by both Walt and Roy as the man who would eventually become president of the company. Walt would retire first (though he left it vague when that would be), then Roy would take over for an interim period and soon afterwards hand the reins on to Walker.

In the meantime, Walker wanted Vince Jefferds to work with him and asked him to move from New York to California, where it was planned he would eventually take over the entire character-merchandising operation from O. B. Johnson. Jefferds accepted the invitation with mixed feelings, partly because his beautiful wife, Jean, was a successful model in New York and did not want to move to California, and partly because he did not relish working with O. B. Johnson, even temporarily. But Walker insisted and eventually persuaded him the move was in his own best interests. (Eventually, Johnson was kicked upstairs and Walker made Jefferds vice-president of merchandizing, then vice-president of the consumer products division, and finally senior vice-president of marketing.)

Appalled at Johnson's mishandling of the Davy Crockett spin-offs, both Walt and Walker decided Jefferds should be given a free hand to remedy the situation, and he lined up stores throughout the nation to handle Crockett posters, hats, jerkins, wooden rifles, all carrying the official Walt Disney logo and all paying royalties to Walt Disney Productions. It was the beginning of a new and massive source of income for the studio. At his peak, Kay Kamen had made Walt Disney Productions three million dollars a year in royalties. Jefferds increased that within two years to 12 million and when he resigned in 1983 it was bringing in a profit of 50 million dollars a year, after paying all his department's expenses.

No potential source of income escaped Jefferds. After *Peter Pan*, he had thousands of children all over the nation sleeping in nurseries – purchased from local furniture stores – exactly modelled after the one used by the Darling family in the Disney film. The furniture manufacturer and the store both, of course, paid royalties to the studio. Inspired by Davy Crockett's coonskin cap, he invented the first Donald Duck hat, a simple skull cap with a beak grafted on to it and plastic eyes, and it squawked when you squeezed it. In the first year eight and a half million copies were sold.

'I could make a good case,' Jefferds once said, 'that licensing of an article is more profitable than manufacturing it. I often made money out of movies that were a loss at the box-office.'

One thing was certain: Davy Crockett was as much a turning point in Walt Disney's history as Mickey Mouse or Donald Duck. It made the Disneyland television programme one of the most popular in the nation. It brought a flood of national advertisers to ABC, and changed the nature of its operation. Its signature tune stayed at the top of the charts for months, and persuaded Walt to go into the record business. And the movie's success at the box-office proved that a prior showing on the home screen enhances rather than diminishes its chances before a paying audience in the cinema. It also, incidentally, not only made Fess Parker into a big star but cured his allergy to leather. And if he never did learn to prefer fringed jerkins to lounge suits, there is no record that they ever gave him a rash again.

At the end of a hectic year during which Davy Crockett became the most popular television series in America, Walt Disney called Bill Walsh into his office and told him he was taking him off the twice-weekly programme.

'Thank God,' said Walsh. 'I'm exhausted.'

Walt grinned mischievously. 'I've signed with ABC for a new programme,' he said. 'It will be called The Mickey Mouse Club, and it will play for an hour every day. I want you to run it.'

Walsh fell to the floor in a simulated faint, and lay there, puffing furiously on his cigar. Finally, he climbed to his feet again, and said: 'Look Walt, if I do that, two things will happen. First, I'll be dead. Second, it will ruin my marriage.'

He was deadly serious. It was well known around the studio that Walsh was a diabetic who drank too much, smoked too much, and hated taking pills or dosing himself with insulin. From a health point of view, he was already a living time-bomb. Furthermore, his wife, Nola, had become increasingly resentful of her husband's devotion to Walt Disney and the way he allowed himself to be overworked by his boss. She hated, in particular, Bill's uncomplaining willingness to let Walt take all the credit for his achievements, even when Walt's contributions to them had been nil. Nolie Walsh was young, beautiful, sensitive, talented and devoted, and she knew Bill was deeply in love with her. But even at this stage in their marriage, she was often troubled by the prospect of what would happen if Bill was forced to choose between the wife he loved and the boss he worshipped. She had a feeling in her bones the choice would have to be made one day.

For the moment, however, that prospect was still over the horizon. Walt assured Bill Walsh he would be expected to work on The Mickey Mouse Club for ABC for a maximum of only two years, and then would be allowed to transfer to something he had always wanted to do, producing real films for movie theatres.

Under Walt Disney's name, of course.

Chapter 20

TEMPUS FUGIT

DIANE Disney was twenty years old in 1953 and considered by her tutors (at the Marlborough School, an academy near the Wilshire Country Club in Los Angeles) to be a bit of a rebel. High-spirited and tomboyish, she looked like a typical sunburned California blonde, but she was more sensitive and intelligent than her general behaviour would indicate.

Life at college had had its difficult moments for her. As the daughter of one of the nation's richest and most famous men, she had spent her formative years in a kind of familial cocoon. This was the time when celebrities feared for the safety of their offspring and – with the tragedy of the Lindbergh baby still vivid in their minds – had them closely guarded. In consequence, enrolment in college had been for Diane like release from a luxurious prison and, like any high-spirited girl, she savoured the sudden freedom from the silken ties with which her parents had bound her to them. It was hardly surprising that she instinctively rebelled – not against her new environment, where she anxiously tried to appear just like the other students – but against the establishment, against her parents and the respectable and conformist rules her famous father stood for. Particularly at fashionable colleges, it was chic to consider Walt Disney's movies corny and the sentiments he expressed in them sugary, blatantly commercial and out-of-date. Student comments about the character of Disney himself, whose conservative attitudes were well known, tended to be patronizing or insulting, and Diane, who loved her father, often felt desperately unhappy to hear these condescending opinions expressed. But she refrained from springing to his defence not simply out of fear of being jeered at, but because she guiltily agreed that many of his movies were indeed over-sentimental, and could only have been made by a man with the old-fashioned outlook young people despised. In any case, as a rich man's daughter deeply anxious to be accepted by her fellow-students as neither spoiled nor over-privileged but just like one of them, she felt she had to demonstrate beyond doubt that she shared their lofty contempt for the older generation and all that it stood for. These were the days before female American students began publicly espousing feminist causes, but the clarion call of sexual freedom was already being heard on campus. Diane knew her father would have been shocked at the thought of a daughter of his indulging in such shameless extra-curricular activities. He believed unmarried females should always behave like well-brought-up young ladies and never act 'cheaply' with men. He was of the opinion that no decent girl should ever marry before the age of twenty-five – and then not before consulting her parents – nor should she ever, no matter what her age, surrender her virginity to anyone outside wedlock, even if she had fallen in love.

So when Diane went with a party of her fellow-students to a football game in San Francisco and fell head over heels in love with a handsome college player named Ron Miller, she determined not to hurt her father unnecessarily. She brought the young man back home to Holmby Hills, introduced him to her parents, and firmly made it clear that she was going to marry him, no matter what. Lilly was pleased and Walt, although initially shocked – after all, Diane was still only twenty – reluctantly welcomed Miller, an amiable young giant, into the family.

The couple was married at an Episcopalian church in Santa Barbara in 1954. Diane's adopted sister, Sharon, came in from the University of Arizona, where she was a student, to be her bridesmaid, and tears streamed down Walt's cheeks as Miller slipped the wedding ring on his daughter's finger. It was normal behaviour for the father of the bride, but Walt seemed to feel it necessary to explain his overwrought state.

'I'm an easy weeper,' he whispered apologetically to those around him.

This was, indeed, the truth, for it had not escaped notice that practically anything seemed to bring Walt Disney to the verge of tears these days. If a strange mother thrust her child at him – which seemed to happen whenever, for instance, he walked around Disneyland – he would feel the tell-tale moisture welling in his eyes the moment he felt the weight of the infant in his arms. He rarely went to live drama performances any more because moments of tension on the stage made him audibly gasp or sob and often drew titters from other members of the audience.

There were certain events, however, which left him surprisingly dry-eyed. The year following Diane's wedding, before Disneyland got into its stride, Walt and Lilly had taken over the theme-park to celebrate the thirtieth anniversary of their wedding, on 13 July 1955. Hundreds of guests were invited and everything was free. A high point of the evening was the maiden voyage of the paddle steamer *Mark Twain* sailing down the Mississippi in the great Frontierland exhibit, with Dixieland bands playing, drinks circulating, everyone enjoying themselves.

Except Walt. He realized how far from finished his new theme-park was, and he was good and mad because, earlier in the evening, he had found the decks of the *Mark Twain* not clean enough for his satisfaction. Just before the first guests came aboard he and Lilly had taken brushes and tidied up the decks themselves. Diane's husband, Ron Miller, was doing his military service at a camp in northern California (they still had the draft in those days) but Diane had come down for the celebration, as had his adopted daughter, Sharon. Diane had already given birth to a son, making Walt a grandfather for the first time, and he knew he should be pleased and proud about it. In his youth, a fortune-teller had once forecast he would die before he was thirty-five years old, and here he was, still alive and kicking, fifty-four years old and a grandfather! He should be happy, but he wasn't. The messy, unfinished look of Disneyland appalled him.

After the trip on the *Mark Twain*, the guests adjourned to the Golden Horseshoe Restaurant for dinner and a cabaret, and soon all of them were on their feet acclaiming Walt and Lilly, with Diane at their side holding on to Walt's hand. In the circumstances, everybody would have forgiven him for becoming highly emotional. But the unfinished park and the unsanitary state of the *Mark Twain* had soured his mood. Furthermore, he hated this kind of thing: anniversaries, birthdays, commemorations, and the passing of time – such milestones only depressed him. Normally, he rarely took more than one drink in Lilly's presence, and certainly never allowed himself to get drunk. But on this occasion, it was noticed he was continually holding out his glass for refills. Once he gloomily speculated out loud whether the fortune-teller might have made a mistake. Could she have meant he was going to die at *fifty*-five and not *thirty*-five – next year, in fact? In any case, each time he looked at his smiling daughter and remembered she had made him a grandfather, he wondered why she had named her first son Christopher instead of Walter Elias, after his granddad. He had been deeply disappointed when he was told about it. It was not until 1961 that Diane got around to giving one of her sons her father's name: Walter Elias Disney Miller was the fifth of her seven children. ('At last,' murmured Walt, at the christening ceremony, 'you've named one after *me*.' And, of course, promptly burst into tears.) Altogether, it was an unhappy evening, and Walt, who usually preferred to drive himself, ended up, dry-eyed and drunk, being driven home to Holmby Hills by his daughter.

Though Walt later called Disneyland's official opening 'Black Sunday', he didn't feel half so bad after it as after his anniversary party.

Even though he had put no opposition in Diane's way, it could hardly be said his daughter's marriage had overjoyed him. Since Ronald Miller's only talents seemed to lie in his speed and capacity to take punishment on the football field, he fully expected to have to put him on the Disney payroll when he came back from doing his military service. It subsequently became clear, however, that Miller neither looked for nor needed a meal ticket from his father-in-law. After his release from the army, he was recruited by the Los Angeles Rams and did well for them as an end runner. Walt accompanied his daughter to several games and it was the agonizing expression on her face each time her husband was roughed up on the field below, rather than the bruises on his son-in-law's body, which moved him in the end to offer him a job at the studio. Miller worked on various television and movie units around the studio as an assistant director, and Bill Walsh took him in hand for a time. Then he was moved, on his father-in-law's orders, into the only sphere which promised real promotion at Disney so long as Walt was in charge – that of a producer.

For the first time, Miller came into close contact with Roy Disney's son, Roy Edward Jr, who was working on television shorts. Both were self-confident young men, only too aware of their family connections. It was antipathy at first sight.

This was the period when Walt Disney was not only troubled by morbid thoughts (though, of course, his fear of the fortune-teller's message was unfounded) but also by almost constant pain from his old polo injury. Even his most faithful employees often found him, as David Swift put it, 'at times tyrannical, dyspeptic and outright obstinate'.

To help him cope, Walt began making evening visits to Hazel George, the studio nurse he had employed in the early fifties, and she gave him regular massage and heat treatment. Mrs George was by no means a Florence Nightingale in her attitude towards her job, and most of the studio staff, who feared her salty tongue and rough ministrations, wondered how Walt could possibly put up with her. 'A hardened pockmark-faced bit of infelicity she was, indeed,' wrote David Swift in a letter to the present author. But Walt found her uniquely capable, not just of easing his pain but at the same time of talking to him frankly and fearlessly with hard common sense, as no one else in the studio now had the courage to do. She was soon the only person in the world who dared tell him when he was acting like a sourpuss or a fool. And no matter how roughly she talked to him, he listened to her every word and usually took notice of what she was saying. He also unburdened himself to her, made her privy to his innermost worries, grievances and secret fears, and she never let him down with her sometimes harsh but always practical advice. He came to rely upon her.

David Swift had been working for Disney, mostly in the animation department, since he came back from war service. But he was eager to change his status and get into directing. One of the schemes he had cooked up for persuading Walt to let him direct a movie was to do a draft script of *Pollyanna*. He had always considered Eleanor Porter's American classic (about a maddeningly perfect child) would make a splendid Disney film, and in his spare time he worked on the treatment, hoping Walt would let him make it.

'I couldn't get it right and I hated it,' said Swift later. 'Still, I sent it over to Walt, and a few days later I got a phone call from him. "I read it, Bud" (he always called me Bud), he said, "and I got a little tear there." I was surprised because I knew from the way he said it I was to go ahead and finish the script – with him looking over my shoulder, of course. Until the final script was finished, he sat in on everything, and always had a concept of how the movie was going to be, the music, the photography, the casting, the look of it.'

The only trouble was with casting Pollyanna. Not only did she have to be perfect in appearance, speech and behaviour, but she also had to be sympathetic too – 'or she would just make everybody who saw and heard her puke in their seats', said Swift. He auditioned scores of little girls but couldn't find anyone totally satisfactory. He finally narrowed down the choice to three, none of whom really satisfied Walt.

It so happened that one of Walt's senior producers, Bill Anderson, had gone to London to talk to the British director, Ken Annakin, about a film they were planning to make together. Anderson, who had joined Walt's staff from Lockheed during World War II, had advisory supervision over other activities at the studio and was aware of the search for a girl to play Pollyanna. He mentioned Walt's dissatisfaction with the choices to Annakin and his wife.

That night, the wives of the two men, Ginny Anderson and Pauline

Annakin, went to a West End cinema to see a new British film made by the Rank Organization called *Tiger Bay*. There was an important child's role in the film and it was played by a little blonde girl named Hayley Mills, daughter of a well-known British actor, John Mills, and his playwright wife, Mary Hayley Bell. Hayley Mills was a natural performer and gave such a moving performance that when the two women came out of the cinema at the end, Pauline Annakin said to Ginny Anderson: 'There's your Pollyanna.'

Ginny Anderson saw *Tiger Bay* again next day with her husband, who enthusiastically agreed with her judgement of Hayley Mills's performance. Despite the nine hours difference in time, he immediately telephoned Walt Disney in Hollywood and got him out of bed to tell him he had found the perfect Pollyanna.

'I tried to keep the enthusiasm out of my voice,' said Bill Anderson later, 'because I knew Walt was always resistant to sales talk and outside suggestions. He wasn't too pleased at being woken up, anyway, and I could hear the antagonism in his voice. He told me he thought he had finally found the right girl in Hollywood and was about to sign her up. I said: "Please, Walt, whatever you do, don't settle with anyone until you've seen Hayley Mills." '

Anderson then rushed round to the Rank Organization and told them he had to have a copy of *Tiger Bay* so it could be shipped to California immediately. All copies were out at the cinemas and only after Anderson had promised to buy an extra print and said he would pay all shipping charges did the British company agree.

In the event, he took the print back with him to Burbank and had it sent to Walt at once for screening.

'The first people I saw after that,' he said, 'were the director and producer of the Pollyanna film, and they were very angry. What the hell had it to do with me? They had found the girl and she had been approved. Why was I interfering? Luckily, just at that moment the telephone rang in the producer's office. It was Walt. He had just seen *Tiger Bay*. He thought Hayley Mills was wonderful. He not only considered her as the only possible Pollyanna but he thought she should be put under long-term contract with the studio right away.'

That was not quite as simple as it seemed. Since Hayley Mills was only twelve years old at the time, her mother took over the contract negotiations. Mary Hayley Bell (now Lady Mills) is not only a good playwright but she is also a very forthright woman who knows exactly how to handle affairs in the best interests of her family.

Some time later, Walt telephoned Anderson. 'He was in hospital with a bad case of laryngitis,' Anderson said, 'and he was so husky and his voice so high pitched I could hardly make out what he was saying. But he did manage to convey he was having difficulty signing Hayley to a long-term contract.'

Anderson was busy settling the cast for the film of *Swiss Family Robinson*, which he was going to make with Ken Annakin, and he informed Walt that Hayley's father, John Mills, had read the script and liked it.

'If that's the case,' said Walt, 'then for God's sake sign him up at once.'

Anderson did, and very soon afterwards arrangements for Hayley Mills to make *Pollyanna* were fixed.

The more he looked at the *Tiger Bay* film, the more fascinated Walt became with Hayley Mills. While the negotiations were still in progress, he flew with Lilly to London and stayed, as he usually did, in a suite at the Dorchester Hotel. And from there he asked that Hayley be brought to see him.

'I seem to remember I was taken out of school in order to meet him,' Hayley Mills recalled. 'I was well aware of who he was of course, and I was thrilled at the idea, although I only knew vaguely at the time he was interested in me for a film. It happened that we had recently been given a very small and sleazy Pekingese called Suky by Vivien Leigh. She had given it to Mummy because it peed all over her carpets, and it peed all over our carpets too. In our case, it just joined a lot of other dogs that were doing the same thing, so it really didn't matter. So I took this dog along with us and I met Walt Disney, who was lovely, very kind and very calm, and we spent most of the time on the carpet playing with the dog. My parents must have been terrified that it would start peeing there too, but fortunately on this occasion it didn't. Then he showed us the sights of London from his balcony, served some champagne and began talking to my parents. I didn't take much notice of that because, I suppose, it was all above my head. But shortly afterwards, I learned I was going to Hollywood to play in *Pollyanna*.'

She remembers it as the most eventful period of her life and still savours her arrival in Hollywood, where ('of course') they stayed at the Beverly Hills Hotel.

'I had a suite, my brother had a suite, and my mother had a suite,' she said, 'and there were televisions in every room, and the tables were piled high with mountains of fruits and candies and all sorts of goodies. And flowers! I mean you couldn't get into the room for all these things. I remember there was a great bowl of sweets from David Swift, and of course he went up in my estimation right away.'

For both Hayley Mills and David Swift, the making of *Pollyanna* was probably one of the happiest experiences of their professional lives. Swift doesn't recall a moment during the production when there was any friction. The crew was completely cooperative, and the three other stars of the movie, Jane Wyman, Brian Keith and Adolphe Menjou, took great pains to be helpful and friendly with the child star from Britain. In normal circumstances, once he was satisfied with the script and the director seemed competent and capable, Walt did not interfere with movies in progress on the studio lot – except to check up on the day's rushes. But in this case, he not only came frequently on to the set but regularly invited Hayley and her mother back to the Disney house in Holmby Hills.

'He had a small movie theatre in his home,' Hayley said, 'and he used to show us films. He had this soda bar in the theatre and all through the film you could hear the squirts and hisses as he would make those wonderful ice-cream sodas while we were watching. Then he had this big model train in his garden and he would take us for rides in it, driving it himself. And of course we had this most sensational launch into Disneyland – with him personally conducting us around everything, for two whole days. That was fun. He even took us to his private apartment at Disneyland over the fire-station, and I believe that was a special privilege. My father was there then, and my mother and my brother, Jonathan, who was nine, and we stayed at Disneyland overnight and it was absolutely wonderful. I've never done it since but I've been saving up the experience so next time I'm in Hollywood I can take my children there and let them realize what it's like too.'

They visited it together in the summer of 1984.

Hayley Mills has strange but affectionate memories of Walt Disney.

'He was so mild and nice and so eager to anticipate what would be pleasant for a young girl to see or experience,' she said. 'But then, of course, he could be a very tough person, too. Once while I was there he fired somebody on the set, and it shocked me because it was so sudden. He was wandering around in such a relaxed way, and he knew everybody there, Dick, Chuck, Wally, Fred, everybody. Then someone came up to him, and said: "Hi, Walt," and he replied: "Hi, Jim, you're fired." I never did find out what the man had done, or why he sacked him. It was done so abruptly and so casually. But I felt sure Walt had done it for the right reasons. I never felt he could be unjust. I always felt you could trust him.'

Her feelings towards him were warmly reciprocated, and more. For Walt, this shy, smiling, affectionate English child became his ideal thereafter of the perfect young lady, and for the rest of his life he was inclined to measure all other girls against her to their detriment. Certainly in his eyes neither his daughter Diane nor his adopted daughter, Sharon, possessed her modesty and charm.

'*Pollyanna* was Walt's favourite film,' said David Swift later. 'Because watching it would make him cry; of course, he would cry at the drop of a chord. I remember I showed him the rough-cut of *Pollyanna*, which ran two hours and twenty minutes, and I was surprised to see him crying, right there in the sweat-box. I hated it. But he had his handkerchief out and he was crying. I said: "Walt, we've got to take twenty minutes out of this," and he said: "No, no, no, don't *touch* it!" '

Hayley won a special Oscar for her performance in *Pollyanna*, but it was nearly two years before she made her second film, *The Parent Trap*. It too was directed by David Swift and was an even greater success at the box-office than *Pollyanna* had been. But Walt was seen less frequently on the set during the shooting of this one, and Hayley did not meet him as often. Swift remembers it as a time when he often found her curled up in a corner of the studio or hidden in her dressing room, sobbing her heart out, and her mother would ask the director to treat her gently 'because she's going through a bad time just now'. Swift put her distress down to the fact that Hayley was now fourteen years old and was struggling with the problems of puberty. Hayley herself remembers it as the time when she had a revulsion against herself and decided she was growing up into an ugly duckling; she resented her body because she thought she had 'no bosom', and hated her face so much she covered it up with a cloth when she cleaned her teeth in front of her bathroom mirror in the morning. Gradually she passed out of Walt's immediate ken, although she made several more films for Disney.

David Swift quarrelled with his boss and left the studio to work for 'those Jews' at Columbia.

'I was sorry about that,' Hayley said, 'because I think David Swift had a nice abrasiveness and a lovely quirky sense of humour. But like all other directors who worked for Walt, he had difficulty expressing his individualism. You had to direct exactly as Walt wanted the film directed. The usual Disney approach, where every movement and camera-angle is mapped out on the story-board, is all right for cartoon films. David Swift was very cleverly able to adapt it in such a way he didn't allow it to suffocate his own originality. But other Disney directors found it manacled them. I remember I was on Crete for ten weeks on location doing *The Moon Spinners* and we had terrible difficulty getting authority from Walt to change anything. Jimmy Neilson was the director and he had a lot of theatre actors in his cast, and theatre actors work in their own way. They get together and discuss things and they often come up with something quite different from the script – or, in this case, the story-board. We had Joan Greenwood and Irene Papas and Eli Wallach and they wanted to change things, and we would literally stop shooting for days on end while we waited for permission to make changes – and we rarely got it.'

But her memories of Walt's fond attitude towards her stayed with her long after her contract with Disney came to an end, and she will always think of him as one of the nicest and most sympathetic of men.

As for Walt, he never forgot her impact on him, either. 'Hayley – what a lovely young English lady!' he would often remark, and then add, nostalgically: 'What a pity they don't make nice girls like *her* any more!'

'Oh, Walt!' Lilly would say when she heard him voicing such sentiments, 'don't be so terribly old-fashioned!'

Chapter 21

TWILIGHT

By the sixties, Walt Disney Productions had paid off all its debts and had assets worth nearly 80 million dollars in the bank. It was now one of the most prosperous entertainment organizations in the United States. Yet, unless you counted Mickey Mouse and Donald Duck and the rest of the cartoon characters, it had no famous stars in its stable and picked up its name-players as and when the scripts demanded them. But then, it did not need to keep stars on its pay-roll, just as it did not need to boast of the glamour of those who, temporarily, joined the studio, or to make headlines by publicizing their life-styles. Disney's policy remained unchanged; it frowned on scandal and was still the sternest and most respectable studio in Hollywood, but, uninhibited by its moral stance, it was quietly becoming by far the most profitable. Every activity in which it engaged made money. As vice-president in charge of marketing, Vince Jefferds squeezed tens of millions of dollars out of the artifacts of its movie and television productions: Mickey Mouse and Donald Duck books and T-shirts, hats worn by Davy Crockett and absent-minded professors, 'magic' rubber (or flubber) playsets, squawking birds, snorting pigs, barking dogs, mouse costumes, duck costumes, dog costumes, Snow White wedding-gowns, Peter Pan pipes, Tinker Bell chimes, and a horde of other outrageous and often wildly eccentric souvenirs, all stamped with the Disney logo and all earning vast profits in royalties for the company every year.

The crowds were so thick at Disneyland in those days that Anaheim had become the entertainment Mecca of southern California, and all the citrus groves for miles around had been bought up by outsiders and besmirched with flashy motels, restaurants, bars, cabarets and junky fairgrounds cashing in on the theme-park's popularity. Walt cursed the poverty of a few years back which had prevented him from buying up more land and controlling the honky-tonk instincts of his rivals.

'Over there,' he was already saying, pointing east, 'is the rest of

251

America, yearning for theme-parks too. And some day I'll build them. But I'll not make the same mistake next time, because next time I'm going to buy up a whole state, not just a few orange groves. And no one is going to be allowed to cash in on me.'

Animated cartoon films were what had made Walt Disney famous but they had quite simply become too expensive to make by the sixties, particularly the shorts which were sold under restricted rental arrangements and could barely earn back their cost. The budget for *Sleeping Beauty*, completed in 1959, rose to six million dollars and lost the studio one million. *101 Dalmatians* cost nearly four million dollars. It fared better at the box-office, however, and did make a profit.

The studio no longer made many short cartoon subjects, and there were no more Mickey Mouse or Donald Duck series; the Silly Symphonies had long since been forgotten. True, Ward Kimball still went on making his own short subjects but then Kimball had a special relationship with Walt and was always the exception. In any case, he had already made an important breakthrough so far as animated cartoons were concerned. In 1951, Walt had assigned Kimball to direct the first Cinemascope animated film, *Toot, Whistle, Plunk and Boom*. Kimball had decided to gamble with a new graphic style that would lend itself better to the short's subject matter, the history of musical instruments.

'I got a lot of flack from old-timers at Disney when they saw some of the drawing techniques we were using in the picture,' Kimball said later.

These techniques were, in fact, so revolutionary that many of the animators and directors were convinced Walt would fire Kimball when he came back from a European trip.

'We had the picture about half animated when Walt finally screened our efforts,' Kimball said. 'I guess he surprised everybody by liking it. In fact, he even told some of the others to look at the picture because it had a lot of good ideas in it.'

Kimball's next departure was a direct result of the success of *Toot, Whistle, Plunk and Boom*.

'Around this time,' Kimball said, 'Walt was being interviewed on tape by Pete Martin for a series of articles dealing with Walt's life which appeared in the *Saturday Evening Post* [and subsequently as a book]. Called "My Dad, Walt Disney," it was supposedly dictated by Walt's daughter, Diane. By using this ploy, Walt avoided sounding too egotistical in the interview.'

When the articles appeared, one whole segment (and later a chapter in the book) was devoted to Ward Kimball. In the course of it, Walt stated: 'Ward is the one man who works for me I am willing to call a genius.'

Reading those words by his boss in a national magazine left Kimball in a state of mixed emotions.

'At first I was flattered, then alarmed at what might happen to the harmonious relationships I had with the people I worked with at the studio,' Kimball said. 'Fortunately, the good-natured heckling subsided, but the real problem developed from Walt. I began to realize there was method in his bestowing on me the genius title because whenever I would protest at being given too big a workload or an impossible deadline, Walt would interrupt, lower that famous eyebrow, and with a half-diabolic smile remind me, "What do you mean, not enough time? You're supposed to be a genius, aren't you?" '

But Walt saw to it that Kimball's life was never made impossible, and it was a time of happy collaboration for both of them.

'I had won the Academy Oscar for best animated short, *Toot, Whistle, Plunk and Boom*, and in 1954 Walt asked me if I would like to direct some space shows for the Tomorrowland segment of Disney's new weekly TV show. With a crew of young creative talent we did an impressive story-board on all phases of space travel. Walt was very excited about the idea of our working with such famous rocket scientists as Wernher von Braun. He insisted the shows had to be not science fiction but "science factual" and believable. I remember especially our first meeting with von Braun and Walt together. When von Braun outlined just how some day we would travel to the moon and the planets and even outer space, Walt listened wide-eyed, his mouth open in pure rapture at what he was hearing. I realized then how fascinated he was with things scientific and with the scientists themselves. After being around von Braun for only two hours, Walt became an instant "expert", his elephant-like memory quoting all the facts and figures he'd picked up in those brief conversational encounters with the wonders of space travel.'

The first of the Kimball shows, *Man in Space*, was aired on ABC on 9 March 1955, and the next day President Eisenhower called Walt to tell him how great the show had been. He asked for a print of the film 'to show all those stuffy generals in the Pentagon' how they should start planning for space travel.

'The second of our Tomorrowland shows,' Kimball recalled, 'was aired later the same year and was titled *Man on the Moon*.'

A few years later, when NASA's Apollo 8 actually made the successful flight to the moon, von Braun phoned Kimball and said: 'Well, Ward, it looks as though they are following our script.'

In December 1957, at a studio press conference at Disney after the preview of the third space show, *Wars and Beyond*, the critics told Walt they had loved the show.

'Walt put his arm around me and, in his joking style, started calling me "my son". This, I decided later, was as close as he ever got to complimenting me on my work.'

But otherwise, animated cartoons no longer kept Walt Disney Productions going. Some of the most talented of Disney's animators had already left the studio, not always under the happiest circumstances. Norm Ferguson, still dissatisfied with the share of the credit Walt had given him for his felicitous invention of Pluto and other cartoon characters, had gone to another studio but had shortly afterwards died of diabetes, alcoholism and, it was said, an acute case of Disney-deprivation. Fred Moore, once the bubbling uninhibited portrayer of nubile, unclothed nymphets, had been killed himself in a car accident.

Partly to relieve the atmosphere of gloom in which the animation department was wrapped these days, Walt had assigned several of its luminaries to design new features for Disneyland. Ub Iwerks began concentrating on Disneyland's technical problems, though he still advised on the company's major films. Kimball (and von Braun) had provided most of the inspiration for the Tomorrowland exhibit. Wally Reitherman and others first designed the tree house for the *Swiss Family Robinson* movie, and then reproduced it again in the theme-park. From another film directed by Ken Annakin, *Three Men on a Mountain*, which had been made in Switzerland, the animation department produced a scale model of the Matterhorn for Disneyland, with a hair-raising toboggan-ride down its steep slopes. This was officially opened at Disneyland by Walt's much-admired political friend, Richard Nixon, who rode in the first car down the mountain with Walt, Lilly, Diane and Sharon. Annakin, travelling in the car behind, sustained an injury to his back when it swerved too violently round a curve.

'Thank God it wasn't Dickie!' was Walt's reaction, when he heard about it. He ordered the ride halted and the public barred until the defect was found and cured.

Having lifted the ABC television network to national status, the

Disney channel ran into the inevitable resentment felt by a beneficiary towards its benefactor. Once it was no longer dependent upon Disney for its continued existence as a major network, ABC began complaining about the impact and ratings of some of its programmes. It then tried to impose onerous production conditions which persuaded Walt to look elsewhere for a television outlet.

Thanks largely to the benison of the Disney channel, the man who had originally given it a television platform, Robert Kintner, had since left ABC for better things at NBC where he was now president. Having brought him good luck and prosperity once, he was convinced Disney would do it for him again. The moment he heard the rumours, he indicated he would welcome Walt's television productions on his channel. ABC, however, though willing to agree to a divorce from Disney, wanted alimony for the separation and eventually, after some litigation, had to be compensated to the tune of seven and a half million dollars for their shares in Disneyland. The moment the papers were signed, Walt announced a tie-up with NBC and with it a significant step forward in the character of his television presentation. Though most of the programmes the Disney Studio had filmed for ABC had been in colour, they had, in fact, been shown on the small screen in black and white. But new technical developments were becoming possible on American television and, by the beginning of the decade, network engineers had made sufficient strides to begin national colour presentations. What competing networks now needed was the requisite material. With his usual foresight, Walt was ready to provide it in abundance for his new sponsors.

Walt Disney's Wonderful World of Color began its first transmissions over NBC on 21 September 1961, and a profitable new era in television began for both of them.

Bill Walsh had by that time already finished working as the principal programmer of the Disney television channel, and, true to his promise, Walt had switched him to a new career as a producer of live-action cinema films. Walsh made an impact from the beginning, and revolutionized the character of Disney's new generation of live-action movies.

One of the reasons for Disney's break with ABC had been the network's refusal to let Walt make a series out of a story called *The Hound of Florence*, written by Felix Salten, about a magic ring which changes a small boy into a dog. ABC thought the television-viewing public would never swallow such a far-fetched premise, and so when Disney moved to another channel, Walsh took the script with him and, with his boss's agreement, made a theatrical movie out of it called *The Shaggy Dog*.

'It brought Fred MacMurray back into films,' said Walsh later. 'It cost next to nothing and made an enormous amount of money, as well as making Fred MacMurray a bigger star than he had ever been before – especially when the movie was later turned into a TV series [for NBC, of course] as *My Three Sons*.'

He followed that with several other money-making films, culminating in one called *The Absent-Minded Professor*, also with MacMurray, which proved to be one of the most profitable movies Disney had ever made.

'Somebody had written some short stories for the old *Liberty Magazine*, and Walt bought them,' said Walsh. 'One was about rubber and one about flying cars and one about milk, and we combined them. A Professor Sumner Miller from El Camino College was brought in to supervise the laboratory sequences, and he helped to develop the idea of flubber, a sort of substance with the resilience of rubber and the malleability of plasticine.'

The Absent-Minded Professor made two and a half million dollars in profits for Disney, and subsequently exacerbated a growing crisis between Bill Walsh and his wife, Nolie.

Other Hollywood studios had been impressed by Walsh's skill and monetary success as a producer, and several attempts were made to woo him away from Disney. One of the most tempting was an approach from Darryl Zanuck at 20th Century-Fox who invited him to join that studio and start his own production division, with ample budgets, his own choice of subjects, stars and directors, and, of course, the credit he was not allowed to have on the films he was making for Walt. Walsh turned down this offer as well as all the others, and his wife was both irritated and depressed, because it confirmed her growing realization of the strength of the bonds between her husband and Walt Disney.

Nolie Walsh was a dancer who had appeared on the show when Walsh wrote and produced a television programme for Edgar Bergen in New York and she had subsequently married Walsh when she came to Hollywood. A long, lean, beautiful and ambitious young woman, she agreed with most of his admiring colleagues that her new husband was a highly talented showman who would one day be a powerful force in the film world. It was not, of course, simply his professional promise which had drawn her to him; like everybody else, she found Bill Walsh to be a charming giant of a man ('a cross between Clark

Gable and Ernest Hemingway,' was how she subsequently described him), and she loved being married to him. But one of the shocks of their life together was her discovery of how closely his life was tied up with Walt Disney's. Gradually, she became aware of the constantly increasing demands made upon Bill and their life-style by Walt Disney.

'He thought Walt was a genius,' she said later. 'He totally worshipped him. When I first met Bill I had the impression he could be like a Neil Simon. He had a wonderful sense of humour, a very sophisticated sense of humour, and I never realized that his whole career would be with Walt, that he absolutely adored him. Walt was only ten years older than he was, but it was like a father and son relationship between the two of them. Maybe that was because Bill was an orphan, and he was looking for a father figure. His mother had died of tuberculosis when he was ten years old and he had been shipped off to live with a sister, and I don't think they ever told him when his father died. So he was the outsider, looking for acceptance – and for a father. And there he was when Walt found him, ready to play apprentice to the Master, even though Bill already had a highly successful career in writing and public relations and was greatly respected in the industry. It was a shock for me to discover that his whole career hinged on Walt's approval and Walt's wishes. Obviously, Walt had great power over him – as he did over all the vastly talented people in the studio's inner circle. The brilliant artist, Peter Ellenshaw, a close friend of Bill, was in a similar situation. I'm sure that if someone had offered either of them six million dollars to leave Walt and go some place else, they wouldn't have done it. Walt had that charisma. He had very talented people who devoted their entire lives to him.'

Like most women, Nolie Walsh was never as impressed with Walt Disney as so many brilliant men, particularly his acolytes at the studio, seemed to be.

'Walt surrounded himself with men who were better than they themselves realized,' she maintained. 'Men whose tremendous talents in writing, producing and graphic arts were sublimated, repressed – sometimes totally lost as far as public recognition was concerned – because of the dominance of Walt himself. He was a master of playing people off against each other. He never praised, never made anyone feel secure. And he got people around him who obviously, psychologically, had that need to feel obligated to him.'

Ironically, though she increasingly resented his hold over her husband, Nolie Walsh felt no strain in her own relations with her husband's boss. It was obvious that he left her cold.

'Walt did not like women,' she said, 'particularly women with minds of their own. But I met him when I was nineteen and I was very shy, and I never made any pronouncements that would offend him. Even before we were married, Bill took me along to Walt's house to get the approval. Having looked me over, he said fine, so we got married. Subsequently, I went on location [for *Bon Voyage*] and Walt was there, and we talked about the weather, and that was about it. But I must say he was crazy about Diane and her children. We spent about three weeks in Paris and three weeks at the Hotel du Cap, at Antibes, and Diane had brought her three eldest children with her and was pregnant with her fifth, and on a day off we all went for a cruise on Fritz Loew's yacht, with Ron and Diane. And watching Walt I could see he was crazy about his grandchildren.

'Later, when I must have been twenty,' said Mrs Walsh, 'we were shooting in Mexico, and every morning I used to ride down to the location with Walt, and there was never a word spoken, and that was obviously fine with him because he didn't want women talking to him. And I didn't bother him. So we sat there, each of us in our silence.'

Though neither of them ever said a word to the other about it, the battle for possession of Bill Walsh was already beginning and would increase in bitterness over the years.

Almost all the films Walsh produced for his boss won acclaim and financial success. A chain of cinematic triumphs culminated in his production of *Mary Poppins*, which was both a critical and box-office smash. And each success resulted in new and better offers to Walsh from outside studios which Nolie Walsh, with increasing urgency, strongly advised her husband to take. It was no longer simple ambition for her husband's future which motivated her now. She was frightened of Walt's hold on him, unwilling to share him, afraid of what the relationship might eventually do to their marriage. She became obsessive in her determination to drag him free, but the more she pleaded with her husband to leave, the more determined he became to stay with the man he admired more than anyone else in the world.

She was no match for what she had convinced herself was Walt's malign hold over her husband. Eventually, realizing the struggle was futile, the bond between the two men unbreakable, she gave up the fight and broke up the marriage. It all ended tragically. There had never been any doubt about Walsh's deep attachment to his young wife, and her decision to leave and subsequently divorce him broke his heart. He was never quite the same again, and most of his zest for life went out of him. After the separation, and after Walt died, Bill Walsh's life and career seemed to go to pieces. So did his health. A chronic diabetic, he not only began to drink heavily but considerably increased his consumption of cigars, which had always been one of his weaknesses. There came a time when he began complaining the injections he was supposed to give himself and the increasing number of pills he had to take interfered with his mental processes. One day, on a trip to London with Vince Jefferds and Ron Miller, he declared it was better to live for a month with a clear and unimpeded mind than for a decade with his brain befogged by the effects of all this medication. In a dramatic (and drunken) gesture, he threw his pills out of the hotel window. He had his first heart attack shortly afterwards. Though she had ended their marriage, Nolie Walsh still felt responsible for him, and she saw him through that first attack. When he became seriously ill, some time later, she brought him into her home and nursed him until he died in 1975.

It cannot have given her much comfort to discover that even death did not break his attachment to Walt Disney. He made only one important stipulation in his will, and that was that he should be buried as close as possible to his beloved Walt. Nolie and his friends did their best to follow his wishes. There was a funeral ceremony, and despite the fact that he was a devout Roman Catholic, he was afterwards cremated and his ashes placed in a canister on a hillside at Forest Lawn, just below the memorial garden where members of the Disney family are buried.

No matter what the wives thought about Walt Disney, there was no doubt about his ability to bring out the best in the men who worked for him. Would they really have done better elsewhere, free from his selfish but catalysing influence?

In 1964, for instance, before the melancholy events recounted above took place, Walt and his three most faithful disciples – Bill Walsh, Peter Ellenshaw and Ub Iwerks – came together to work on *Mary Poppins*, and it proved to be one of the most prestigious and financially successful cinematic enterprises of the decade. Afterwards, most cinematic experts maintained that only Walt Disney could have brought it off.

Mary Poppins, a fantasy tale about a Victorian nanny who could fly, had long been a favourite book with children and grown-ups.

There was always a copy on Diane Disney's bedside table, and she had had it read to her by her mother as a child. Though it enjoyed enormous popularity as a cult book in many American homes, it had been written by Mrs P. L. Travers, an Australian living in England. Both Lilly and Diane read it over and over again and had often urged Walt to buy it and turn it into a movie back in the days when he was still making full-length cartoons. But when he tried to do so he found out the author had already been approached by practically every studio in Hollywood, all of whom she had turned down. She did not approve of the cinema. In the final months of World War II, someone mentioned to Walt that Mrs Travers was in New York with her son to escape the ravages of the London Blitz, and he sent his brother, Roy, to make yet another attempt to negotiate a film sale with her. She would not change her mind, even though she had heard of and did not disapprove of Walt Disney, but she could not conceive of Mary Poppins as a cartoon character.

It was not until 1960, fourteen years later, that Walt tried again. He met and talked to Mrs Travers at her home in Chelsea and exerted so much persuasive charm that she finally agreed to sell the book to him on two conditions, which, to everyone's amazement, Walt accepted. Not only did he pledge it would not be an animated cartoon but a live-action film with the character of Mary Poppins played by a real human being, but, most astonishing of all, he gave Mrs Travers approval of the script – something he had never done before.

The script was co-written by Don DaGradi, a Disney veteran, and Bill Walsh, who was also assigned to produce the film. Walt agreed to hire Robert Stevenson, an Englishman who had once had a nanny himself, to direct. And he brought in Peter Ellenshaw to do the matte shots of the London setting and to work closely with Ub Iwerks, who had invented a startlingly effective new matte process of marrying live actors with cartoon characters on the same screen.

But who was to play the crucial role of the flying nanny, Mary Poppins? As Mrs Travers had portrayed her in her book, she was a matronly, old-fashioned Victorian type of uncertain age, so unprepossessing that when Bette Davis was approached to play the role she flatly turned it down. It was just as well. Bill Walsh and Walt shortly afterwards decided the movie should have music and Mary Poppins would need to sing at least one number; and Bette Davis was no singer. Next, Walt became keen on signing up Mary Martin, but she was just about to retire from stage and screen and turned him down.

It was some time before they came around to the idea of trying out Julie Andrews, a young Anglo-American actress who had starred in *My Fair Lady* on Broadway and was now playing a leading role in the New York production of *Camelot*. Walt went to hear her in *Camelot* and, stirred by her bell-like voice and the humorously feisty nature of her stage persona, went round to her dressing-room and asked her to come to Hollywood and do a test for the part. He was sure he had found the star he needed. To his astonishment, Julie hesitated. Though he did not realize it at the time, she had lost her nerve, particularly about starring in the movies. After her triumph on the stage opposite Rex Harrison in *My Fair Lady*, she had done a screen test for Warner Brothers, who proposed to make a film version of the musical, and it had turned out badly. Someone told her she was unphotogenic. As a result, there was a strong rumour around that Warners would give the Eliza Doolittle role to Audrey Hepburn instead, and a depressed Julie Andrews had become convinced she was not the cinematic type. Moreover, she was pregnant.

Once Walt realized why she was holding back, he called in Walsh and Stevenson and told them to offer the part to Julie Andrews without giving her a test. Then he wrote to Julie, on 26 February 1962, asking her to come to Hollywood to listen to the music and talk over any problems she might have about the part. He added: 'We definitely feel in our own minds that, with your talent, you would create an unforgettable Mary Poppins, and we hope you will want to portray the wonderful character after you have seen the presentation which we can have ready for you in June.' [Disney Archives]

That November, Julie Andrews gave birth to a daughter, and was so euphoric over this happy event that the terrors of film-making paled into insignificance. She agreed to make the movie for Walt and arrived in Burbank in February 1964 with her then husband, Tony Walton, to begin work on the film. She made only one stipulation: if Warner Brothers did change their minds and consent to star her in *My Fair Lady*, she would be allowed to drop out of *Mary Poppins*. Walt was so sure Audrey Hepburn had already been signed for the role that he agreed.

At which point, Mrs Travers arrived on the scene, determined to defend the integrity of her book.

'She came over for a month or so,' said Bill Walsh later, 'and I don't think she was too pleased with us, to tell you the truth, because she kept saying things like: "Well, now, the rustle of Mary Poppins' skirt. There's a certain kind of sound it makes, and there's a drapery shop around the corner in Kensington and we must have that fabric." Walt would interject: "But Mrs Travers, we're not going to spend all that time looking up drapers' shops in Kensington Road." But by this time she would be off on something else. "And about the letter box," she would say, "you haven't got the right kind of red. There's a certain shade of red it has to be." She was always getting hung up on all these details. Meanwhile, what we were trying to do was get a reasonable story out of the book. The original was a series of little fragments with no story, just a sensational character and funny little bits of episodes. We needed a story to bring the whole thing together.'

Mrs Travers strongly objected to the idea of putting songs into the film.

'That was another hang-up,' said Walsh. 'And when Walt did persuade her to accept the idea that we had to have songs, she wanted us to use something like "Tarara Boom-dee-Ay" or "Greensleeves". So there were bumping of noses all the way along the line, until we finally got our way and things got going.'

Mary Poppins had its world première at Grauman's Chinese Theater in Hollywood on 27 August 1964, and was a huge public and critical success. While the thunderous applause was still roaring through the theatre, the severe figure of Mrs Travers was seen approaching and the smilingly happy Walt Disney felt a premonitory twinge.

Sure enough, she was not pleased.

'Julie Andrews is quite satisfactory,' she said. 'But then she is English. But how on earth did you allow the producer to use that Dick Van Dyke to play the sweep? He's all wrong – so American! And I just hate that dance number you've put in with those ghastly cartoon figures. You just have to cut them out, Mr Disney! When do we start the editing?'

Walt was too pleased with the reception of the film to be angry with her.

'Fortunately, Mrs Travers,' he said, smoothly, 'you only had approval of the script, not of the finished film. It goes out as it is. Wait till you've seen it again and read the notices. You'll just love it!'

At a celebratory dinner later that evening, Bill Walsh introduced a happy Julie Andrews to Jack Warner, who had just officially announced the casting of Audrey Hepburn in his film of *My Fair Lady*.

'Dear Mr Warner!' gushed Julie. 'Did you know I had a clause in my Disney contract allowing me to drop out of *Mary Poppins* if you chose me for Eliza Doolittle? How thoughtful of you not to allow me to do it and picking dear Audrey instead! I'll never forget you for giving me this chance!'

'Jack was absolutely furious,' said Bill Walsh later.

Chapter 22

THE WOUNDED BEAR

By the sixties the responsibilities and stresses of running the Disney empire were beginning to take their toll of Walt. The one-man operation method he had used to run the studio when he was younger and having fun with cartoon film-making was now inadequate to handle the added work-load of two Disney parks and the building of his future dream metropolis, EPCOT.

'There were so many things going on that even Walt, with his historical attention to all details, however small, couldn't find the time to cope with any more,' said Ward Kimball. 'Lord knows, he tried. He really was the last of the great rugged individualists. He had always had the final say on every script, every production, every hiring and firing, on the placement of every tree and the colour of every building – everything down to the smallest detail. All of this he still wanted to control, including the monumental plans for Florida and EPCOT. One Walt Disney was trying to be *five* Walt Disneys.'

Kimball added: 'His genius was being spread too thin, and we all knew it. And then came the shocking blow: his lungs were being eaten away with incurable cancer. For half of his life, there had been those awful, hacking coughs from chain-smoking. His doctors had continually warned him to give up cigarettes and maybe heavy drinking. During one of those last meetings I had with him, he broke into a long coughing jag that lasted for a whole minute at least. It was terrible. When I timidly asked him why he didn't give up smoking, Walt looked up at me, his face still red from the coughing, and rasped, "Hell, I gotta have a few vices, don't I?" '

He was always in a bad temper at these times, and in the studio they began calling him the Wounded Bear. Everyone took care not to cross him accidentally. When he got really angry, he would flatten his adversary without a thought, no matter who it was.

To Kimball and those who had worked closely with him over the years, it was obvious their boss was undergoing some sort of change – and even those who respected and feared rather than loved him were disturbed and saddened by it, the more so because they realized he was completely unaware of it.

One day in the mid-sixties, an animator named Charles Shows was in the hallway at Buena Vista when he realized Walt was just ahead of him.

'It was about six in the evening, after a hard day's work,' Shows said, 'and I guess Walt didn't realize there was someone behind him, because the rest of the hallway was absolutely empty. Normally, he moved with a jaunty youthful stride, but as if he realized he didn't have to pose for the time being, he abandoned all pretence. His head dropped on his chest, his square shoulders slumped, and I saw him age twenty years. As he shuffled down the hallway, his tired feet dragging his exhausted body, I had a dreadful gut feeling that I was looking at a man whose days were numbered.'

Then Walt heard the footsteps behind him and straightened up and shook himself, and it was as if the years and the weariness were being sloughed off like dust from his shoulders.

'I still contend,' said Ward Kimball, 'that the tension combined with trying to keep control of everything that was going on – even though Disney was at least twenty times bigger than when it started – all this, plus the beating his body was taking from the pain in his neck and all those cigarettes and booze, made him like a bomb waiting to go off. He may not have realized a fuse had been lit, but we did.'

He was in pain now for most of his waking hours, and the amazing thing is that he learned to live with it, and continued to be so active and look so cheerful. In truth, sometimes the only thing that got him through the day was the thought of the whisky Hazel George would pour out for him when she arrived for the evening therapy session. Nowadays, he no longer went to visit her at the clinic, where she had begun limiting the Scotch; she came instead to his office, where the supply of booze was ample and he could suck at it through a straw while she massaged his neck or treated the aching nerves to some heat.

But only Hazel George and a few close observers really knew the truth about how he was feeling, and to most of the others around the studio – even many of the veteran employees – he was the same tough and respected Walt Disney of old, full of energy and enthusiasm, ever the perfectionist, harsh and brutally critical of fools and slow-coaches and those who made errors. The difference was that in the past he had been prepared to forget and forgive when his excesses were pointed out to him. Nowadays, he was much harsher and relentless, and much more easily roused to anger by what he thought were attempts to poach on the precious preserves of his authority. For instance, when in 1960 the British director, Ken Annakin, set off for Tobago on location to begin shooting *Swiss Family Robinson*, the company took most of their wild animals with them: forty-eight monkeys, a baby elephant, a tiger and a lion, two anacondas and eight Great Danes. They were shipped from California to Tobago by plane, and the Los Angeles *Times* ran a story headlined: ANNAKIN'S ARK LEAVES FOR TOBAGO. Walt was furious when he saw it. Annakin had already made five successful movies for him, but he shouted: 'What the fuck is this? Who the hell is Annakin? It's not his ark – it's Walt Disney's ark!'

Annakin was hurt, but not too much, by Walt's comment. He had always considered that working for Walt Disney was the luckiest thing that had ever happened to his career. He had no doubt at all that Walt was a genius and always knew exactly what the public wanted and how to provide it. But like geniuses, he was apt to be temperamental.

'Of all the studio chiefs I have ever worked with,' Annakin said later, 'I have never known anyone who operated at conferences so magnificently as Walt. You would go into a story session with him, full of great ideas, and he would scratch his nose and say: "This is just from the top of my head, but I think we should do this and this . . ." And it would usually be like listening to a new fairytale, and we would break up the session happy and amazed that the solution to our story problems should be so simple – and different.'

Annakin forgave Walt Disney lots of things.

'Despite his tendency to be a dictator, he had a warm and generous side to his nature,' he said later. 'He once said: "You and your wife must be at a loose end this weekend. How would you like to use my box at Santa Anita [the race track]?" Pauline [his wife] and I jumped at the chance and we had a fabulous afternoon spending the gambling money Walt had secretly given us.'

During the first six months of preparations for *Swiss Family Robinson*, Walt had participated in all the production conferences, and when progress on the script was going well he usually invited Annakin and his wife to spend the weekend with him at his house at Palm Springs.

'Sometimes he would cook the meals for us,' Annakin recalled, 'and afterwards we would sit out under the stars discussing his ambition to build an entertainment park, or his passion for model railways. Sometimes he would take us down to Smoke Tree Ranch, where he would sit at the head of one of the big communal tables and invite discussion on any subject. But even here he could be touchy. Pauline once got into an argument about television. I think she said that British programmes were far superior to those in America. She got a thorough earful from Walt for that statement.'

At one point during the *Swiss Family* script conferences Walt had proposed a scene in which a tiger is caught in a trap by the pirates. He liked dramatic confrontations between animals and humans. Annakin remembers saying to Walt at the time: 'Does it have to be a tiger? Lions are much easier to work with.'

Walt immediately picked up the remark. 'Ah ha!' he said, 'Ken's afraid of a tiger, is he?'

From that moment, Annakin knew he would not only have to use a tiger in the film but make sure each shot was achieved exactly as sketched out with Walt – which, in one scene, meant that two of the Great Danes would actually have to make bodily contact with the tiger.

'I knew he would have reshot the sequence at great expense and effort to get it exactly as he had conceived it,' said Annakin. 'And he'd have got someone else to do it if I hadn't succeeded.'

John Mills, who was playing the role of Mr Robinson, his wife, Mary Hayley Bell, and their daughter, Hayley, flew down to the location with Annakin and the producer, Bill Anderson.

'We had a sequence where a zebra gets caught in quicksands,' Annakin recalled. 'The vultures are all around it and the Robinson boys try to save it. It wasn't too easy for me to shoot that. You make quicksands with a lot of bran, and, in this case, instead of struggling, the animal tended to stand still in it. So I had to give it what is technically known as a "hot shot". Of course, Pauline, the continuity girl and some of the others hated that, because they thought it was hurting the animal. It wasn't, not a prolonged hurt, anyway. But I knew perfectly well that unless I got the scene absolutely right, Walt would completely lose all faith in me. With him, you had to damn well do the impossible. Good training!'

The young Hayley Mills found it even more disturbing that the tiger had his sharp teeth filed down and his claws removed. Both the director and producer thought Walt might appear at any moment, and they were determined to make every scene with the tiger as graphic as possible.

'And we knew Walt would take exactly the same attitude as a circus trainer,' said Annakin. 'If you wanted to achieve something with a dicey animal, all right, he expected you to do what is necessary to get the scene. It was his picture and his conception, and you damn well did what was necessary to get what he wanted.'

It was their failure to remember that this was his production that caused trouble for them over *Swiss Family* and Annakin lived to regret it. As it happened, Walt was too busy with other projects to visit the *Swiss Family* location, and they never saw him from beginning to end.

'So perhaps we got the impression that he didn't come because he didn't think it was his film,' said Annakin. 'And I can remember Bill [Anderson] drawing up the credit cards and putting himself down, correctly, as the producer. Walt was angry, even though he hadn't been near us. And although *Swiss* became a popular success in the cinemas under the banner "Walt Disney Presents", both Bill and I had a lot of trouble launching the movie because Walt was sulking. The last thing we wanted to do was minimize his creative contribution, but the truth was he hadn't actually done anything to produce the movie after we left for Tobago. There was a certain small-mindedness about him at times – and this was one occasion when it showed up.'

Some time after *Swiss Family Robinson*, Walt and his wife came on a trip to London, and one night the Annakins invited them for dinner at their home in Onslow Square.

'There was a tentative idea I was going to make a film of *Westward Ho!* for Walt,' said Annakin, 'and we talked about it over dinner, while Pauline and Lilly chatted together separately. The time came to leave after a very warm, convivial evening. Six steps had to be negotiated from our apartment into Onslow Square, and Lilly slipped and fell on her butt. I rushed down and picked her up. Fortunately, she hadn't broken anything, but rather brusquely Walt took over and hurried her into the waiting limousine.'

After they were gone, Pauline Annakin, who has a shrewd insight into character, said to her husband: 'I have a strong feeling you're never going to make another film with Walt.' She was right.

'I never did make *Westward Ho!*' said Annakin. 'And though other projects came up at various times, Walt never came round to offering me another assignment. At one period I brought to Walt's notice the possibility of acquiring Kipling's *The Jungle Book* from the Kordas. I felt it would make a marvellous musical, and laid out the sequences as I saw them for Walt. We had some correspondence about it. Then he suddenly decided to make it as a cartoon movie. I've always thought he was swayed into that decision because he didn't want to be embarrassed working with me again. I had been witness to a piece of what he regarded was shameful behaviour on the part of a member of his family, and he couldn't face up to the fact that I had been there. Anyway, I never worked for him again.'

It was a sad confirmation of how Walt had changed – a year or two before, he would have laughed off the incident and forgotten about it.

In the early summer of 1964, mysterious strangers from out of state began buying up large tracts of land on the outskirts of the small central Florida city of Orlando. All efforts to track down the identity of the buyers were unsuccessful. The outsiders, who obviously had plenty of money and were willing to pay cash, made it a condition of the sales they effected that landowners did not divulge the identities of the buyers – who were using phoney names, in any case – and swore them to secrecy over the price and other details of the transactions. Local gossip soon had it that the US government was behind the purchases, and the wiseacres prophesied that Washington, already beginning operations on its space programme at nearby Cape Canaveral, would soon be moving into the Orlando neighbourhood and building a vast new complex to manufacture everything from intercontinental missiles to hydrogen bombs. Then someone let slip the fact that the famous Walt Disney had flown into the area twice recently from Hollywood in his private Beechcraft plane, and that a woman believed to be his wife had even been heard to remark, over a hamburger in a junk-food restaurant in Kissimmee: 'But it's just swamp, Walt! How could you possibly want anything here?'

Was it just a coincidence? It seemed so – especially when it was pointed out that Disney's father and mother had been married near Kissimmee, and it was plausible to suppose their celebrated son was simply making a sentimental pilgrimage. But the mysterious sales went on, and soon 30,000 acres had passed into the hands of the secret buyers.

It was at this moment that a young woman reporter named Emily Bavar, who edited the Sunday magazine of the Orlando *Sentinel*, quite fortuitously accepted a promotional trip to California to attend the tenth anniversary celebrations of the opening of Disneyland. Mrs Bavar, intrigued by what was going on in her own state, asked Walt Disney if he was buying up land in Florida to build another Disneyland. He did not bat an eyelid at her question, but replied: 'Who would ever want to build a theme-park in Florida – with the sort of climate, rivers and landscape you have over there!'

He reeled out a detailed list of reasons why you couldn't possibly open a Disneyland in Florida, and the more he talked the more Bavar got the feeling that Walt Disney was trying to bamboozle her.

So she looked him firmly in the eye and asked him to confirm or deny if it was his agents who were buying up all the land in Osceola County. Later, at lunch, she sat next to Walt and repeated her question to him. He nodded across the table towards Roy Disney and said all financial and investment matters were in his hands.

'In essence, his reply was: "I couldn't tell you even if I knew, because Roy is in charge." But,' said Emily Bavar, 'though I could just as well have been wrong, I just knew Walt was being evasive. But what made me particularly suspicious was the fact that he knew so much about Florida, its problems about rain, humidity and transportation. I didn't believe him when he denied my instinctive feeling. I decided to take a chance.'

That night she sent a story to the Orlando *Sentinel* positively identifying the Disney organization as the secret land-grabbers in Florida and predicting they would soon begin work on a new theme-park there. The paper's Sunday editor ran the story on an inside page, but that wasn't good enough for the *Sentinel*'s strong-minded proprietor/publisher, Martin Andersen. Shortly afterwards, when his reporter had returned and he had had a chance to talk to her, he ran another story from Mrs Bavar and prefaced it with an 'Editor's Note':

Emily Bavar, Editor of Florida Magazine, just returning from a visit to Disneyland at Anaheim, Calif., near Los Angeles, where she personally interviewed Walt Disney and was his guest along with other newspaper writers from Birmingham, Montgomery and Ft. Lauderdale, is firmly convinced the so-called 'mystery industry' to be located on the $5 million, 30,000-acre tract between Orlando and Kissimmee, is to be a second Disneyland. Or rather a similar attraction to the famous Anaheim attraction, but one, perhaps, with a new name and a new theme . . . The editors of *The Sentinel* are convinced that her Sunday piece was 'underplayed,' that it did not have the importance or impact it should have had, and that the new project is really going to be a new type of entertainment built by the world's greatest cartoonist, movie producer, showman and world's fair exhibit-maker.

After talking to Mrs Bavar, *The Sentinel* is convinced that the mystery industry's author, architect and builder is Walt Disney and that he will spend upwards of $30 million on it.

This time Bavar's story ran on the front page with a banner headline, and was confirmed on 15 November 1965 by a statement from Florida's governor, Haydon Burns, that work would soon begin on a new theme-park, to be called Disney World, near Orlando, Florida.

From Walt's point of view, all the secrecy was needed because he wished to avoid the mistakes he had made at Anaheim, and he was determined to buy enough land not to be hemmed in by honky-tonk rivals. Not only that. He had sent emissaries from Burbank to Tallahassee, the Florida capital, headed by the shrewd Card Walker, to make a deal with the local government before signing the final papers. In return for bringing such an enormous tourist attraction into the state, Walker asked for a quid pro quo on behalf of his boss, and the governor gave it to him. For the first time in Florida's history, control over all the territory to be included in the future Disney World was ceded to the owners. The new park would become what amounted to a self-governing community, with its own law and police services, hospitals, health and all necessary maintenance departments, plus a special tax rate, and no outside authority would be allowed to enter its territory without an invitation from the owners. Walt had an additional motive for secrecy, but this he was determined not to reveal until he was good and ready.

If anything could have enlivened and inspired him, Disney World was it. For a time, that is. Nothing in the history of leisure parks had ever been planned on such a scale before. The preparation of the ground at Disneyland in California had been entrusted to Morgan Evans, a landscape gardener from Malibu, known to Walt Disney as 'Bill'. He had prepared every man-made hill and planted all the trees. But the prospect Admiral Joe Fowler, Disney's construction boss, put before Evans when he showed him the Florida site for Disney World was daunting. They flew on an inspection tour out of Orlando. The territory stretched practically from horizon to horizon, and all Bill Evans could see were great tracts of bald cypresses and saw-grass, gashed every few hundred yards by drainage canals. He had seen the grandiose plans which Walt and his advisers had been working on over the past year, and he knew they included more facilities than there were in Disneyland, and each of them was to be substantially larger. How, he wondered, could his boss possibly imagine that out of this endlessly flat prairie wilderness below them, they could build a vast new city of entertainment, with multi-storeyed hotels, fairy castles, river-rides, prairie cow-towns, boating lakes, lawns and gardens and woodlands, not to speak of a giant monorail intended to whisk visitors from one end of the theme-park to the other? Even to his experienced eyes, which could normally see a desert transformed into a garden, this was a really dreary piece of landscape.

'Walt had paid 200 dollars an acre for the whole 30,000 acres, and that was all it was worth,' said Bill Evans later. 'It was no-good land. It wasn't even good as pasture land. After massive earth moving we probably had the world's worst soil in which to plant. But if I was fazed for a time, my boss certainly wasn't. He had inherited Walt's vision, and he could already see the jungle down there blossoming . . . And he wasn't too surprised or downhearted when we had nothing but grief at first. For instance, one of the features Walt had particularly wanted for Disney World was a real live jungle, not one of the kind you have in Florida, nor even like the jungles of Africa and South America, where the same old plants keep repeating themselves for mile after mile. He wanted a really dramatic jungle, full of sensational plants, and we picked elephant ears, ginger lilies, bananas, big ficus from Australia, Africa and Asia, all telescoped into a few hundred yards and giving more of an exotic jungle vision than you'd get in the real location without travelling hundreds of miles. But the first year, things went wrong with the planting, and a million dollars worth of exotic plants just died. This was before Disney World was open, and Walt was already dead, and when we confessed to Joe Fowler what had happened and why, he simply said: "Then you'll have to start all over again, won't you?" There was no question of abandoning what Walt had envisioned.'

In his last months, Walt had urged everyone transforming the Florida landscape to press on with the project at top speed, and damn the expense. Later on, some of his associates speculated that he must already have suspected that if they took too long about it, he would never live to see Disney World finished – as, of course, he didn't. In that last year he was impatient for the great new theme-park to be opened and operating, so his construction experts could turn their attention to the other project which he planned to build next to Disney World – the one he considered to be much more important. EPCOT.

The secret idea of EPCOT had first been revealed at the press conference of 15 November 1965, when the governor of Florida had announced the plans for Disney World, though its significance was overlooked at the time. Introducing Walt Disney to the reporters, Governor Haydon Burns had described him as 'the man of the decade, who will bring a new world of entertainment, pleasure and economic development to the state of Florida', and the attention of the press was on the details of the theme-park, which Walt described as 'the biggest thing we've ever tackled'. Most of the questions that followed were about its size, its cost, its potential for profit. Then, by chance, the plan beyond the plan got its first public mention. Someone asked where the huge working staff of Disney World would be housed once the park was operating, and Walt outlined his plan for building an enormous artificial lake in the grounds, and then using the 'fill' from all the dirt they would dig up to make a mountain.

'And inside that mountain,' he went on, 'we will build a small city for our employees, where they can eat, rest, swim, wash, sleep and breathe fresh, relaxing air which we will pump into the mountain's interior. It will be a sort of model community.' But that was not the only model community he was planning for Florida, he added. And suddenly the idea began to take root: 'I would like to be part of building something more than that,' he said, 'a city of tomorrow, you might say.' And he added: 'Here, in Florida.'

By the time the press conference was over, his enthusiasm for Disney World was already beginning to fade as a new and more exciting project began to occupy his mind. After all, what was Disney World anyway, except one more means of making millions? All he was building here in Florida was just another theme-park. But a city of tomorrow – that could be the last great challenge.

By this time the bulldozers were churning their way across Osceola County and the landscape of central Florida was undergoing a vast and convulsive transformation. If Walt Disney was beginning to be bored with it, the people in the area were certainly not. They already knew what had been wrought in Anaheim by the arrival of Disneyland, and if the ecologists shuddered at the thought of the radical changes that were being made to their environment, the officials of local government, the estate agents and the developers happily braced themselves for the challenges – and the profits – they knew were coming. The Orlando *Sentinel* put in an order for extra presses to cope with the increase in circulation they anticipated from the arrival of Disney World. The editors launched a campaign to construct a community centre big enough to handle all those conventioneers who would soon be coming in. In little more than a decade the population of Orlando and its environs, 30,000 in 1965, had swelled to a quarter of a million, and in spite of all the land Walt had bought to keep the honky-tonks at arm's length, Disney World still had to accept garish rivals a few miles down the road, if not immediately on its doorstep.

'They're really excited down there,' Card Walker reported when arriving back in Burbank from one of his trips to Orlando. But he and Roy Disney sensed from Walt's apathy that he had somehow been turned off, and from now on they knew better than to consult him too frequently about details of Disney World. It was not that he had lost his enthusiasm – but it was for something entirely different. He had a locked room at Buena Vista behind his office suite where no one else was allowed to go, except at his invitation. Some of the veteran animators joked about what it contained and called it Walt's Chamber of Horrors, and Ward Kimball even suggested it was the place where 'Walt keeps his dirty pictures'. It was, in fact, the repository of his hopes and dreams. No one except his secretary and two members of his immediate staff knew that this was the place where he was working out the details of his city of the future. One would have thought that the two who shared his confidence would have been chosen from among his acolytes, that Ub Iwerks and Peter Ellenshaw, perhaps, would be working with him on his new project. Instead, he left both men completely in the dark, and they knew nothing about EPCOT until its existence was common knowledge. His chief helpmates were two outsiders, General William E. Potter and Marvin Davis, one of whom was practically a stranger to him and the other a minor employee unsympathetic to his way of thinking and working.

General William E. Potter had retired from the army to become governor of the Canal Zone in Panama and, in 1964, had been appointed chief aide to Robert Moses in the construction of the New York World's Fair. Walt had been asked by Moses to give him some ideas for exhibits, and he had come up with the dramatic model of Abraham Lincoln which moved, appeared to breathe, and was so life-like when it arose and began to make a speech that it had proved to be a sensation. In the course of his many visits to New York Walt had several times dealt with Potter, found him bright and reliable, and eventually invited him to join his staff.

Marvin Davis (not to be confused with Marc Davis, a former animator) had also made his mark with Walt. The original idea had been to put both men to work on Disney World, but they had gradually become Walt's chief consultants, aides and confidants on his new preoccupation. As his representatives, they were now scouring the nation and the world, soliciting the aid of experts on future medicine, environment and city planning. They were authorized to pay highly for technical forecasts of what life could and should be like not in some idealized Utopia but in a carefully organized, expertly governed community of tomorrow. And only they really knew what was going on in Walt's mind.

Walt had piled the tables in his secret room in Burbank with the documents and surveys Potter and Davis had procured for him. The walls were covered with graphs, architects' drawings and landscape photographs scrawled with a jumble of heavily underlined comments. He had a name for it now, though he would not allow it to be pasted on the office door: EPCOT. He had come up with it during one of the many sleepless nights the pain in his neck now forced him to endure, which he passed in studying, reading and working in the annexe of his bedroom in the Holmby Hills. It was an acronym, he solemnly explained to his aides next day, and what it stood for was Experimental Prototype Community of Tomorrow; it had evolved from a phrase used to describe the project in one of the reports they had written.

But even now, Walt Disney could not keep his enthusiasm secret for too long. Soon he was willing to talk about what he was up to first to Roy who, as usual, was sceptical, and then to Lilly who, as usual, was scared.

In the autumn of 1966, at the end of a quite painful and miserable summer, he even gave a press conference and spilled out what was going on in his mind. For the first time he used the name of EPCOT in public, and tried to explain why he was going to build it, what its significance was, and what it meant to him.

One reporter afterwards commented that 'this famous man, who had looked so pale and lack-lustre when he first came into the room, suddenly began to glow with enthusiasm as he waxed more and more enthusiastic' and ended by resembling 'a born-again Christian at a revival meeting'.

EPCOT, said Walt, would be 'like the city of tomorrow ought to be, a city that caters to the people as a service function'. He went on: 'It will be a planned, controlled community, a showcase for American industry and research, schools, cultural and educational opportunities. In EPCOT there will be no slum areas because we won't let them develop; there will be no landowners and therefore no voting control. People will rent houses instead of buying them, and at modest rentals. There will be no retirees, because everyone will be employed according to their ability. One of our requirements is that the people who live in EPCOT must help keep it alive.'

How on earth had he stumbled into this project? he was asked; it sounded like one of those idealistic, socialistic communities of the early years of the nineteenth century. At which Walt violently shook his head, since the mention of anything to do with socialism was anathema to him.

'No way, no way!' he said, violently. 'It just happens that I am an inquisitive guy, and when I see things I don't like, I start thinking: Why do they have to be like this? How can I improve them? City governments, for example. We pay a lot of taxes, and still have streets that aren't paved or are full of holes. And city street cleaners and garbage collectors who don't do their jobs. And property owners who let dirt accumulate and help create slums.'

One of the reporters wondered aloud why he had let himself get involved in it. Was it really any use trying to change the world in such a radical fashion?

'Oh, you sound just like my wife,' said Walt, irritated. 'When I started on Disneyland, she used to say, "But why do you want to build an amusement park? They're so dirty!" I told her that was just the point – mine wouldn't be.'

Meanwhile, Potter and Davis began their research work on the latest medical discoveries in repairing failing human bodies and the prolonging of life. It was about this time that Walt Disney became acquainted with the experiments into the process known as cryogenesis. He was now in such pain that generous libations of whisky and massage and heat treatment from Hazel George failed to give him any comfort whatsoever. When he walked out to his car after one particular evening session, it was noticed he was staggering – not because he was drunk, but because he had lost most of the feeling in his left leg.

He decided to take Hazel George's advice and consult a doctor. Vince Jefferds recommended Dr Theodore Lynd, who discovered the condition of Walt's lung and advised him to have himself thoroughly examined. He made an appointment to see the surgeons at St Joseph's Hospital in Burbank, and they tested his heart, his blood pressure and his lungs. Then they sent him away, telling him he should try to keep to his many engagements, assuring him they would have a report ready for him in a day or two.

On 29 October he flew to Williamsburg, the model colonial settlement in Virginia, to accept an award. During the examination at the hospital, the pain in his neck and leg had suddenly ebbed away. But slowly, inexorably, it had come back again. And it was worse now.

'This pain is killing me!' he groaned, as the plane took off and pointed westwards for California.

It was indeed. Though he didn't yet realize it.

He came home to find the report from the hospital and, though it tried to be reassuring, he could take no comfort from it. They had found a spot on his lungs – only a spot – and he would need to undergo surgery to get rid of it. No need to worry, his doctor said. Just minor surgery.

On 2 November 1966, he called General Potter and Marv Davis in to see him and went over the plans they were getting together for EPCOT. He accused them of dragging their feet and listening to Roy's objections, but his real concern was that the operation might cripple him, make him helpless, even take his life away before he had a chance to finish EPCOT.

On 7 November 1966 he drove to the hospital in Burbank for his operation, and shortly afterwards the surgeons cut out his cancerous left lung.

'I've only got one lung now,' he told Lilly, grinning cheerfully, after he had regained consciousness, 'but otherwise I'm as good as new.'

But Lilly had talked to the doctors and knew it was much grimmer than that. What she did not know – and Walt did – was something he had no intention of revealing to her: the surgeons had taken away his diseased lung to examine it, and then were going to preserve it. Walt was pleased when he heard that. He knew enough about cryogenesis by now to be aware it was important to hold on to all the organs – just in case the surgeons needed to treat them before putting them back where they belonged.

Chapter 23

FINIS

WALT was so bored that, not many days after the operation, the doctors reluctantly let him out of the hospital. The first thing he did was cross the road to the studio, eager to find out what had been going on.

People were shocked when they saw him. He had never been overweight, except for a small paunch he had developed lately, but the flesh seemed to have run off him like melted butter, and he was gaunt and emaciated. What had always been one of his most charming features, his cheerful grin, now had the appearance of a grimace.

He spent some time with his secretary, Tommie Wilck (who had taken over from Dolores Voght on her retirement), dealing with his most urgent correspondence, talked to Marv Davis and then shut himself up in the EPCOT room. More reports had come in from the medical experts: projections about hospital improvements, organ transplants, post-mortem surgery. It was not until some hours later that he emerged and went down to the main studio.

Bill Walsh was in process of producing a film called *Blackbeard's Ghost*, directed by Robert Stevenson and starring Peter Ustinov.

'Suddenly I came on to the set and saw him sitting on one of those stools, and he was drinking coffee,' Walsh remembered later. 'I said: "Jesus Christ, Walt, I thought you were in hospital." He said: "Yeah, well, they cut away my ribs to get at something," and then added to Peter Ustinov, who had come up: "It's just some damn thing they're fooling around with." '

Both men were disturbed by his appearance but tried not to show it. In any case, Walt was particularly pleased to see Ustinov, whom he greatly admired both as an actor and an amusing and cultivated human being. He had already ear-marked him for the starring role in a film he had assigned Bill Walsh to make called *Khrushchev in Disneyland*. The Soviet leader had come to the United States some time before for an official visit and had been taken on a tour of the big Hollywood studios, but the special wish he had expressed to visit

Disneyland had been vetoed by the State Department on the grounds of security. Walt had been furious about that; he had planned to put old-fashioned cannons on his jungle and Mississippi river steamers, assemble them with his Jules Verne submarines from the *20,000 Leagues Under the Sea* exhibit, together with their replacements, and introduce the Soviet leader to 'the Disneyland Navy, the tenth largest battle fleet in the world'. Bill Walsh had already written the script of a live-action comedy about Khrushchev defying the State Department's prohibition and secretly visiting Disneyland, wearing some wild disguises as he dodged both US officialdom and anti-Soviet demonstrations. Ustinov, cast in the role of Khrushchev (who, he maintained, strongly resembled his mother) now told Walt he planned to shave his head for the role.

'I didn't know your Ma was bald,' joked Walt, his face cracking into a ghastly grin.

Both Ustinov and Bill Walsh privately decided that the surgeons must have opened him up, found something inside, and hastily sewn him up again.

'We decided he was doomed, but thought it would only spread gloom and despondency around the studios if we said anything, so we kept quiet about the visit,' Walsh said later.

Peter Ellenshaw was crushed when he heard Walt had been to the studio and he had missed him.

'I think he meant a lot to me because I'd lost my father at a very early age,' he said, 'and Walt, at a later stage in my life, became a very strong father-figure for me. He was always very demanding of me, but he was the sort of person I would appreciate as a parent.'

In some ways, Walt had resented the fact that Ellenshaw was leaving matte-painting behind and concentrating more and more on working on his own as an artist, and often, when he had asked for leave to go away and paint, Walt had given him homework to do that was calculated to take up most of his 'free' time. On the other hand, he liked Ellenshaw's pictures, and had taken to inviting him down to Smoke Tree Ranch, his cottage at Palm Springs, and encouraged him to do desert landscapes, which he found particularly dramatic and suited to Ellenshaw's style.

'The moment I heard he was in hospital, I wanted to go and see him,' Ellenshaw said. 'I'd run into him in the corridors before he went in and I said: "I see you're having difficulty in walking," and he had assured me: "It's just a polo injury in my back. I'm going to have it straightened." I thought: *God, if they mess with his back . . .* and I suppose I looked so concerned, he said: "Christ, Peter, if you go on looking like that, you'll really get me worried." So when he went in, I waited a bit, and then tried to see him. But he wouldn't see anyone. I gathered he had got so thin, he didn't want to be seen.'

But Ellenshaw was worried about his boss and longed to talk to him and encourage him. He tried to think up a way he could gain access to him in hospital.

'I finally thought: "I'll paint him a picture." I wanted to paint him something special just to show how much we all loved him – loved him like a father, I mean. And I painted him a smoke tree, because it was a smoke tree which had first introduced me to painting in the desert, after he had invited me and my wife down to Smoke Tree Ranch and let us work there. So I did this little picture for him.'

He took the painting into Tommie Wilck's office and said he would like to take it across the way and give it to Walt. But she said: 'But he won't see you, Peter. You'll only feel hurt. Why don't you just leave it with me and let me take it over?'

'So I left it with her, and he sent back word later how much he appreciated the picture. But he added: "Sorry I can't see you just now, Peter, but I'd rather you didn't come over. We'll get together just as soon as I'm all right again." '

But Ellenshaw never saw Walt, or the picture, again.

'It was quite a nice little work,' he said, years later. 'I often wonder what happened to it, but I think Lilly took it away.'

After Walt came out of hospital in mid-November, everyone assumed, thin and gaunt though he looked, he would soon be his old self again. Only Lilly, Diane, Sharon and Roy – who had had a succession of long consultations with the surgeons – knew the gravity of Walt's condition, and Roy strongly urged them not to say a word about it to anyone.

'The effect on the market could be disastrous,' he said. 'Christ knows what it would do to Disney stock!'

So everyone around the studio was assured Walt was getting better and no one realized – although some suspected – that his condition was inexorably growing worse. Not that it stopped him from working. Every day he came to the studio and did his round of the lots and labs, keeping tabs on the way work was going. His expression was grim and he was rude and short with most employees, but he had been like that for a long time now and so they didn't put it down to a deterioration in his condition. During each visit, he spent long hours inside his EPCOT room, studying plans for his city of tomorrow, and no one except General Potter and Marv Davis, perhaps, knew how desperate he had become to make sure not a single detail of construction had been overlooked, and, no matter whether he was there or not, EPCOT could go forward exactly as he had envisioned it – if his successors were willing to follow the instructions, that is. That was the snag, his aides realized – the worry which dogged him all through November and December 1966. Would those who came after him *try* to follow his plans? Were they even competent enough to carry them out? Above all else, was there really no way of making sure that once they had made a mess of it, he could come back from the grave and rectify their appalling errors and misjudgements? Once upon a time he had told Ken Annakin he didn't care what happened to Walt Disney Productions once he was dead. 'They won't be able to handle it, anyway,' he had said. 'So just let it fritter away.' But now he did care about what he was leaving behind, and the thought of what they would almost certainly do to EPCOT both angered and frustrated him.

This must have been the period, many of his associates now think, when he studied and consulted and sought most desperately for any method – transplants while he was still alive, cryogenesis when he had ceased to breathe – by which he might avoid or postpone the dreadful consequences of such a tragically ill-timed death.

At the end of November he was in such pain he had to be taken to hospital again, and though a succession of distinguished surgeons concentrated their attention on him, there was little they could do to prevent the rapid change in his physical condition. He was too weak for transplants and his heart was already failing to pump sufficient blood. Under the circumstances, it was amazing how cheerful and optimistic he continued to be despite his physical deterioration. It is true he sometimes burst into tears, and was particularly upset when Hazel George came to see him.

'Fancy being remembered around the world for the invention of a mouse!' he said to her, mournfully, tears rolling down his cheeks.

'You're better off than Hitler,' she told him. 'All they remember about him is he killed all those Jews! I don't think you ever killed anyone.'

'No, but I wanted to,' he said. 'Donald Duck, for instance! There were times when I really wanted to wipe out that little monster!'

They both laughed. But when she embraced him to say goodbye, the tears were already rolling down his cheeks again.

By 5 December his state was so low that even though Lilly, Diane and Sharon came along he was in no condition to celebrate his sixty-fifth birthday.

Roy was the last to see him alive, on the night of 14 December, and they talked for nearly an hour together about EPCOT. Roy faithfully promised to see it through, but assured his brother he would be up and about again soon, and would look after the project himself – 'as you know you always do'.

When the surgeon came in to see him just before ten o'clock the following morning, Walt Disney was dead.

Walt himself had asked Roy Disney to keep his illness secret, but more surprising was the manner in which the world was apprised of his death. If the news had not been quite so stunning, more people might have speculated about the reasons behind the concealment.

Need there have been an interval between his actual death and the official announcement? Did dealers on the New York Stock Exchange need time before they were allowed to learn the news? Was the delay really intended to avoid a panic selling of Disney holdings – especially since, when the news was finally made public, the value of Disney shares did not collapse but went up considerably? Did he have to be rushed into the ground so precipitely and privately – and into a plot already filled with family ashes from which the public would always be barred? Even today, Disney veterans still wonder about that. Many of them are convinced the gap between Walt Disney's death and the revelation of his secret cremation and interment had special reasons behind it.

'Is old Walt really buried out there in Glendale?' asked one of his old associates. 'I don't believe so. I think he's someplace else, waiting.'

'When Disney fans ask me if it's true that Walt's body is kept frozen for future resurrection,' Ward Kimball said, 'I answer the question by pointing out that Walt was always intensely interested in things scientific, and he, more than any person I knew, just might have been curious enough to agree to such an experiment.'

'My information is that he *is* frozen down,' said Ken Annakin. 'There again, that's Walt, interested in everything. He probably didn't believe in cryogenesis at all, but thought: "Well, maybe there might be just a chance of coming back, so I'll try it."

'Of course, if he has had himself frozen and he does come back, there's going to be hell to pay at Disney. He wouldn't approve much that's gone on at the studio, except on the animation side. He'd like that. He was always great on improvements in technique. But the stories and the way they've been handled, no.'

'He's going to be good and mad at what they have done to his city of tomorrow,' said another old associate. 'When he comes back, a lot of heads at Disney are going to roll, that's for sure.' He added: '*If* he comes back. If he's still around to come back, I mean. Maybe all the rumours are wrong, and he was hurried into the ground in all that secrecy because that's the way he wanted it. Maybe he really is dead. But I don't know. There are too many people who believe otherwise. In any case, how do you *prove* he's dead? Even if you got an order to dig up Walt from the Disney Memorial Park at Forest Lawn, can you be sure what you find is the one and only Walt? How do you tell his ashes from those of Elias and Flora and Ruth and Roy, who are also down there?'

Annakin prefers to believe that Walt is in a strange refrigerated tomb somewhere else, waiting for medical science to deal with him so that he can come back one day and clean up the mess his successors have made of Disney – and particularly of EPCOT – since he went away on 15 December 1966.

EPILOGUE

WHAT do you do when the king is dead and there is no heir worthy of taking his place on the throne? In medieval times there were conspirators, usurpers and plots. In modern America, the greedy financiers emerge armed with takeover bids.

In the days following the announcement of Walt Disney's death, the company's shares rose by ten points and more, not because anyone thought Walt Disney Productions and WED would be better without Walt's guiding hand, but because there was money to be made in tearing his creation to pieces. There was a golden backlog of animated cartoons, nature films, live-action movies to be exploited and a fortune to be made from selling off the landholdings in Anaheim and Florida for the rich rewards of mindless expansion. From the moment they knew he was dead, the money vultures began to hover over Burbank, Anaheim and central Florida.

'Everybody at the studio started to jockey for position,' said Ward Kimball, 'to consolidate his own little kingdom in the new pecking order. Name plates were added to the desks. Personal notepads multiplied. Framed full-colour portraits of Walt magically appeared on the office walls of the many self-appointed executives, seemingly to give assurance of Walt's silent blessing to whatever questionable decisions might be made at the desks below. When Walt was alive he was the total boss. No one moved an inch without his final word. Department heads who had never before had to make decisions for themselves now had to strike out on their own. It was tough for some, easy for others.'

Kimball watched the organization slowly coagulate into a corporate structure where decisions, good or bad, were now made by committees instead of by the one man upon whom they had all depended so heavily in the past.

'Of course,' Kimball said, 'there were some rather stupid executives who tried to establish creative niches for themselves by making such asinine remarks as, "Now I am sure this is the way Walt would do it".

284

They knew full well it was impossible ever to predict what Walt would have said or done when he was in charge.'

Roy Disney seriously tried to take his brother's place. His main achievement was to keep the vultures at bay. Thin as a skeleton, his head like a skull with skin stretched over it, he was already a tired, sick old man of seventy-three when control passed to him after his brother's death, and his only concern was to see Disney World finished and in operation, Walt Disney Productions out of debt and in profit, and then he would thankfully retire. A bent and melancholy figure, he spent weeks at a time wandering over the Disney World site in central Florida and hated every moment of it, complaining aloud at the 'goddamned madness that got into Walt when he decided to make a theme-park out of this awful swamp'. As his brother had rightly surmised, he had no enthusiasm whatsoever for EPCOT and ignored the plans for the project Walt had left behind him. 'It's a money-loser, anyway,' he said, contemptuously, tossing Walt's cherished studies aside.

On his money-raising trips to New York to finance the continuing work for Walt Disney World (he announced the addition of his brother's first name to the theme-park shortly after his death 'so people will always know this was Walt's dream'), he was careful to keep the subject of EPCOT out of his conversations, deciding the banks would never advance him the money if they thought he would fritter part of it away on his brother's utopian project. Even so, he paid well beyond the going rate for the money he borrowed, much to the dismay of his associates, who felt it betrayed his basic lack of faith in the legacy Walt had left behind him.

These were unhappy days at the studio. To help him in his task of running the organization, Roy Disney had appointed a committee to advise him. It consisted, in part, of Bill Anderson, the producer, who was put in charge of filming activities; E. Cardon (Card) Walker, a brilliant visualizer and advertising man; Bill Walsh, Ron Miller and Roy E. Disney Jr and others. Roy Disney Sr believed that competition between the members of this group, each one of whom, he surmised, cherished ambitions to succeed him, would eventually produce a leader whom he could name as his successor when he retired. But it didn't work out that way. Bill Walsh would have seemed the logical man to take over the film division, and he might not only have revived Disney's flagging movie production programme but also have snapped the veteran members of the animation department out of the sullen and resentful stupor into which they had fallen over the years – ever since Walt had lost his enthusiasm for cartoon films. But Walsh himself had lost his dynamism. Crushed and dispirited by Walt's death, he was all flab and misery, the ambition drained from him, and the last thing he wanted was responsibility. He left all decisions about filming to Bill Anderson, who was no good at galvanizing anyone. Walsh shared his sorrows with Ub Iwerks, who was also bereft by Walt's death, and neither could resist making sour comments to all and sundry on the paucity of Anderson's imagination. Naturally, this stirred ill-feeling. Ron Miller, now promoted to executive producer, had begun flexing his muscles. Long constrained by Walt's mild contempt for his abilities, he felt released by his father-in-law's demise, and, bolstered by the knowledge he had his mother-in-law Lilly and his wife Diane behind him – and they were now the most powerful shareholders in the company – he was tempted to throw his weight around. The one he proceeded to hustle was his *bête noire*, Roy E. Disney Jr. In many ways Roy Jr took after his father, which meant he was good at figures and investments but unimaginative when it came to innovations. As a film-maker, he was short on flair and expertise, and Ron Miller made sure his dullness did not go unnoticed around the studio. So far as Roy Jr was concerned, in fact, life at Burbank was just like old times only worse. He had always resented being pushed around by his temperamental uncle, genius though he might have been, but he was damned if he was going to take the same treatment from Walt's son-in-law. Relations between the two men became so bitter, in fact, that if Miller hadn't been such a hulk of a man they would undoubtedly have come to blows. As it was, Roy Jr stuck it out as long as his father was in charge of the studio, but then quit after a blazing quarrel with Miller. He stayed on the board of Walt Disney Productions and clung to the shares his father had left him. Hugging rancour to his bosom, he vowed one day he would come back to the studio – but only after he had got rid of Ron Miller. There were those around Burbank who were convinced he cherished another ambition too: to eliminate his uncle's name and influence from the Disney organization altogether. So far as he was concerned, it was his father, Roy, and not Walt, who had done all the work of making Disney rich and famous.

On 1 October 1971, Walt Disney World opened at last in Florida. Walt would have made it a gala occasion by inviting famous artists, singers, stage and movie stars to celebrate the occasion with him; and even if Stokowski was now too old, at least von Karajan might have been brought in to do the musical honours. Roy, however, hired

Arthur Fiedler to conduct the so-called World Symphony with 145 musicians representing sixty-six countries in a concert of theme tunes from the famous cartoon movies, popular classics and patriotic music. They were all there – Lilly, Roy and Edna, Diane and Ron Miller, Sharon and her husband, William Lund, Roy Edward Disney Jr and his wife Patricia, plus fourteen grandchildren. It was a highly sentimental occasion. Down a ramp in front of Cinderella's Castle, to the sounds of 'When You Wish Upon a Star', Lilly was led by an employee dressed as Mickey Mouse to join Roy, on the platform in front of the tearfully sentimental crowd. Turning to Walt's widow, Roy waved his hands across the trim walks and fairytale landscape of this new Disney kingdom and cried: 'Lilly, you knew all Walt's ideas and hopes as well as anybody. What would Walt think of it?'

Wiping away her tears, she replied tremulously: 'I think Walt would have approved.'

Well, maybe. He would certainly have approved of the magnificent, billion-dollar job his builders and landscape artists had done in creating the theme-park, for they had transformed a hostile wilderness into a vast tamed terrain of lakes, beaches, hotels, river-rides and shiningly spotless communities, its flat monotony broken by artificial hills, rivers and wide roads, all linked by a super-modern monorail system, an overhead chair-ride, and an old-fashioned steam-locomotive network. Walt had always enjoyed a sentimental occasion, and he would have loved the moving moments of the opening ceremonials, even if Roy had pinched pennies in their details. But it is also just as likely that he would have had some crisp comments to make about the one unmentioned subject in all the vast number of speeches: EPCOT.

As he had rightly suspected during those last days in hospital, the moment he was off the scene, *nothing* had happened about EPCOT. When Roy had taken over, he had forgotten all his promises to his brother. EPCOT was awaiting what an official statement from his office described as 'a practical approach to its complexities', which meant, as far as Roy was concerned, finding some way to make a profit out of it. He never did get round to solving that problem, nor did he worry too much about it. As far as he was concerned, he had carried out his brother's wishes by seeing Walt Disney World brought to fruition, and the moment it was opened he decided that his obligations had been fulfilled and his task was over.

Roy Disney died in 1971, at the age of seventy-eight, shortly after the opening ceremonies of Walt Disney World, and, some time later, Card Walker took over as president. Walker had started working for

Walt Disney as a messenger boy back in the days when he had first come out to California from Idaho, and he had always been one of Walt's most dedicated admirers. Card knew what EPCOT meant to Walt Disney, and he was determined to do something about it.

'Card knew how much Walt wanted to see EPCOT rise in Florida,' said his associate, Vince Jefferds. 'He saw a lot of his boss in those last days before his death, and he knew EPCOT was taking up all his ebbing strength and attention. Walt realized EPCOT was going to be monstrously expensive, but he said he didn't care about that. He felt he could get the money from American industry and perhaps even from the US government (for developing a prototype city).

'Walt always felt there was no point trying to reclaim slums. He felt it was better to start anew with perfectly-planned cities in fresh locations – cities that would enable the designer to combine urban and suburban advantages in a single plan. That was part of his conception of EPCOT. He died before he completed his blueprint, of course, particularly from a standpoint of economic feasibility. But we all knew he would have gone for broke on this project, as he had on all his earlier projects. In the end, all his ventures paid off. It would probably have been true for EPCOT. Anyway, we all realized that if Walt lived he would have built it, even if it risked bankrupting the company. Risks didn't scare him. And I think he would have gotten away with it.

'Walt Disney did things that made other people do things, too, things that didn't seem possible on paper. He had a way of bringing out the best in people, of lifting them to their highest level of performance. I think he could have evolved a plan that worked. But I also believe that in order to get the money from industry to build EPCOT, he would have had to incorporate an exhibit area into it for them – like the present EPCOT.'

But would he? Others who knew what Walt Disney had in mind believe he would have fought savagely and successfully to prevent any such commercialization of his plan.

In any case, Card Walker was dedicated to doing something that would come somewhere near Walt's ideas. After Walt's death, he asked his associates to give him their ideas of how EPCOT should be built.

'In 1974,' said Jefferds, 'the Disney design group [WED] presented a project costing 35 to 40 million dollars which would add some shops and annexes around the Contemporary Hotel [inside Walt Disney World]. Card showed it to me and I said I thought it stunk. He reacted angrily to that. "You're such a smartass, you know about everything," he said. "Give me a constructive idea instead of criticism." '

Jefferds, who is also an artist in his spare time, spent a week going over the terrain around Walt Disney World and putting his ideas on paper. The result was an entirely new area which Jefferds called 'Interworld'. Unlike Walt's original design, which would have been a single, self-contained city, Interworld would combine exhibits of industrial giants and foreign nations inside a new land-and-water complex.

At Card Walker's suggestion, Jefferds presented his plan to the key vice-president of Walt Disney World, and the board subsequently voted for it unanimously. It was obviously a commercially viable proposition.

At this point, Card told Jefferds to take it back to the WED design group and have them rework it closer to Walt's original EPCOT concept. WED took Jefferds's plan and separated the industrial exhibits from those of the foreign countries and put them into two concentric circles.

'It would be a showcase for American industry,' said Jefferds, 'but, of course, not in the context of an operating city-complex as Walt envisioned. Still, we lined it up with a monorail at a cost of a million dollars a mile, and Card personally sold most of the 350 million dollars in contributions from major US corporations. Sale of pavilions to foreign governments was disappointing, but we pressed on.'

So the post-Walt Disney EPCOT came into being. It began to make money from the start, and thousands upon thousands of visitors flocked to gape at its wonders. But if it was a slick and fascinating exposition, it was not the city of the future; it was not the EPCOT Walt Disney had envisioned. He would have hated it.

Howard Means wrote in the Orlando *Sentinel* (10 December 1982):

Disney conceived EPCOT originally as a single city, completely climate-controlled, on different levels, with deliveries below and a hotel above. In fact, it is few of those things. Certainly it is not a module of a city complex, a community of souls living a quarter of a century into the future, while the rest of us watch on. More's the pity, too, because extraordinary things could have been learned from such an idealized laboratory city.

But more's the shame, too, because if anyone in this century could have pulled off a successful Utopia, it would have been Walt Disney . . . Disney's future world wasn't going to be built on the shifting sands of ideology. It would have lifted up the founding rock of future-tech. Utopias for all their charm are often the work of misanthropes, people unsuited to their times and place. But Disney, in a way that no other American of this century did, tapped the mainstream of American hopes, desires and dreams. Whatever flaws he may have had in his private person, the public Walt Disney was loved in a rare and special way.

To say that EPCOT would have survived and prospered as a Utopian community is not to say that one would have wanted to live in it nor even that those who chose to live there would have been in any way representative of the rest of us. EPCOT would, I think, have been very much like the contemporary city of three million people that Le Corbusier proposed in the Radiant City.

Unfortunately, in both cases, the proposition never came to pass, and the messy community at Chandighar and the travesty of EPCOT are their only legacies.

There is still a mystery about whether or not Walt Disney is entombed in some isolated refrigerator in a Californian university hospital waiting for medical science to clean him up, thaw him out and deliver him back into life, so he can return and put things in order. But does it matter any more? It is too late for him to do any good, anyway, to what his successors have wrought with his heritage. All his talented artists are either dead or have disappeared into the obscurity of old age, and even Mickey Mouse and Donald Duck nowadays are animated on computers. The studio has abandoned Davy Crockett, flying autos, magic rubber and absent-minded professors in favour of 'adult' films featuring half-naked mermaids. The toughest money-men in Hollywood have taken over the lot on Buena Vista and the whole nature of Walt Disney Productions has changed. Furthermore, Roy E. Disney's dream seems to be coming true. He has forced the resignation of Walt's son-in-law, Ron Miller, as president of the company, and the cynical story going around Burbank is that he may soon be getting rid of Walt's name too. Not that Walt would care very much about that. The only thing that must be really troubling him now – wherever he is – is what they have done to EPCOT.

He certainly wouldn't like to have Walt Disney's name on *that*.

APPENDIXES

A. WALT DISNEY'S FILM HISTORY

NOTE. This section has been checked by Disney archivists who point out that they 'try to dignify the animated features by not calling them cartoons, a term usually reserved for the short films'. I have decided to adopt the Disney usage below.

1920-23: Kansas City. Animator/director/producer of Laugh-O-Gram series. Founder of Laugh-O-Gram Film Company Inc. with Ub Iwerks. First of Alice comedies series (live action/animated cartoons featuring six-year-old Virginia Davis, created and animated by Walt Disney and Ub Iwerks).

1923: Company goes bankrupt. Moves to Hollywood.

1923: Hollywood. New Alice comedies series featuring Virginia Davis (later replaced by Margie Gay plus live dog). Animated by Walt Disney assisted by brother, Roy Disney, until Ub Iwerks rejoins Walt from Kansas City to do principal animation.

1927: Oswald the Lucky Rabbit all-cartoon series (created by Walt Disney, animated by Ub Iwerks and others) supersedes Alice.

1928: Loses control of Oswald the Rabbit character. Forced to find substitute.

1928: Creates Mickey Mouse.

1928: First two Mickey Mouse cartoons – *Plane Crazy* and *Gallopin' Gaucho*, both silent – completed (animated by Ub Iwerks).

1928: *Steamboat Willie*, first Mickey Mouse cartoon with sound completed and shown in New York (principal animation by Ub Iwerks).

1929: *The Skeleton Dance*, first of the Silly Symphony series, completed (principal animation by Ub Iwerks).

1928-34: Characters of Minnie Mouse, Donald Duck, Goofy and Pluto added to Disney's cartoon company.

1933: Silly Symphony *The Three Little Pigs* completed and shown.

Song from cartoon, 'Who's Afraid of the Big Bad Wolf?', becomes a hit.

1934: Work begun on first Disney feature-length animated film *Snow White and the Seven Dwarfs*.

1935: First Mickey Mouse cartoon in colour.

1937: Première of *Snow White*. Smash hit.

B. WALT DISNEY AS PRODUCER OR EXECUTIVE PRODUCER, 1940-66: A SELECTION

1940: *Pinocchio*; *Fantasia* (animated features)

1941: *The Reluctant Dragon*; *Dumbo* (animated features)

1942: *Bambi* (animated feature)

1943: *Saludos Amigos!* (animated feature); *Victory Through Air Power* (animated and live action); and other films, made mainly for the armed services and US government

1945: *The Three Caballeros* (animated feature)

1946: *Make Mine Music* (animation); *Song of the South* (animation with live action)

1947: *Fun and Fancy Free* (animation and live action)

1948: *Seal Island* (first True Life Adventure)

1949: *Melody Time* (animation); *So Dear to My Heart* (live action with animation); *The Adventures of Ichabod and Mr Toad* (animated feature)

1950: *Cinderella* (animated feature); *Treasure Island* (live action directed in England by Byron Haskins)

1951: *Alice in Wonderland* (animated feature)

1952: *The Story of Robin Hood* (live action directed in England by Ken Annakin)

1953: *The Sword and the Rose* (live action directed in England by Ken Annakin); *Peter Pan* (animated feature); *The Living Desert* (True Life Adventure); *Toot, Whistle, Plunk and Boom* (Oscar-winning cartoon directed by Ward Kimball)

1954: *Rob Roy: The Highland Rogue* (live action with Richard Todd and Glynis Johns); *The Vanishing Prairie* (True Life Adventure); *20,000 Leagues Under the Sea* (live action directed by Richard Fleischer, starring James Mason, Kirk Douglas)

1955: *Davy Crockett – King of the Wild Frontier* (live action produced by Bill Walsh, script by Tom Blackburn, starring Fess Parker); *Lady and the Tramp* (animated feature); *The African Lion* (True Life Adventure); *The Littlest Outlaw* (live action)

1956: *The Great Locomotive Chase* (live action); *Davy Crockett and the River Pirates* (live action); *Secrets of Life* (True Life Adventure); *Westward Ho the Wagons* (live action)

1957: *Johnny Tremain* (live action directed by Robert Stevenson); *Old Yeller* (live action produced by Bill Anderson, directed by Robert Stevenson); *Perri* (True Life Fantasy)

1958: *The Light in the Forest* (live action); *White Wilderness* (True Life Adventure); *Tonka* (live action)

1959: *Sleeping Beauty* (animated feature); *The Shaggy Dog* (live action produced by Bill Walsh, directed by Charles Barton, starring Fred MacMurray); *Darby O'Gill and the Little People* (live action); *Third Man on the Mountain* (live action directed in Switzerland by Ken Annakin)

1960: *Toby Tyler* (live action); *Kidnapped* (live action); *Pollyanna* (live action directed by David Swift, starring Hayley Mills); *Jungle Cat* (True Life Adventure); *Swiss Family Robinson* (live action directed by Ken Annakin, produced by Bill Anderson); *Ten Who Dared* (live action); *The Sign of Zorro* (live action)

1961: *101 Dalmatians* (animation); *The Absent-Minded Professor* (live action directed by Charles Barton, starring Fred MacMurray); *The Parent Trap* (live action directed by David Swift, starring Hayley Mills); *Nikki – Wild Dog of the North* (live action); *Greyfriars Bobby* (live action); *Babes In Toyland* (live action)

1962: *Moon Pilot*; *Bon Voyage*; *Big Red*; *Almost Angels*; *In Search of the Castaways*; *The Legend of Lobo* (all live action)

1963: *Son of Flubber*; *Miracle of the White Stallions*; *Savage Sam* (all live action); *Summer Magic*; *The Incredible Journey*; *The Sword in the Stone* (all animated features)

1964: *A Tiger Walks*; *The Three Lives of Thomasina*; *The Moon Spinners* (all live action); *Mary Poppins* (live action and animation, directed by Robert Stevenson, produced by Bill Walsh, songs by Robert and Richard Sherman, starring Julie Andrews and Dick Van Dyke); *The Misadventures of Merlin Jones*; *Emil and the Detectives* (both live action)

1965: *Those Calloways*; *The Monkey's Uncle*; *That Darn Cat* (all live action)

1966: *The Ugly Dachshund*; *Lt Robin Crusoe – USN*; *The Fighting Prince of Donegal*; *Follow Me Boys!* (all live action)

1967 (appeared after his death in 1966): *The Jungle Book* (last animated feature over which Walt Disney presided); *The Happiest Millionaire* (live action)

C. THE ANIMATORS

NOTE. I should point out that the list below is necessarily incomplete and inevitably omits the names of some important animators who did valuable work for Walt Disney. Some Disney archivists feel these omissions are likely to cause ruffled feelings among some of the veteran animators who are not mentioned, and feel I should list all or none. Since neither is practicable, all I can do is extend my apologies to those who have been overlooked, and stress that I have taken expert advice on those names I have included. Here again I have run into difficulties. Except in some obvious cases, I have found that opinions differ, even among the experts, over the achievements for which the animators I have named should be particularly saluted. As I mention below, since each animated film was always a joint effort, there is considerable confusion even among the animators themselves over who invented specific characters and over who was responsible for certain remarkable sequences. It is for this reason that I have had to adopt a general consensus and cite those characters and sequences for which the animators specified are likely to be best remembered.

It should be emphasized that Walt Disney not only catalysed the ideas of his staff but sat in on the shaping of every character which appeared in his cartoons. However, Frank Thomas and Ollie Johnston stress in their authoritative book, *Disney Animation*, that everyone who has worked on a picture feels that his or her personal contribution made the cartoon special. The story-man, the animator, the director – 'To all of them he is their character,' write Thomas and Johnston, once animators themselves.

It is certain that Walt Disney, for instance, conceived and produced Mickey Mouse, gave him his voice and developed him, but Ub Iwerks drew him first and animated many of the early cartoons, and Mickey's shape, mobility, even character, were taken in hand by many other animators, particularly Fred Moore. Moore considerably altered Mickey's appearance over the years and was the first to give Mickey 'eye movement', which made such a difference to the impression he created on the screen. As the earlier part of this book recounts, that brilliant animator Norm Ferguson insisted he had 'invented' Pluto, the lovable but gormless hound, but Thomas and Johnston point out that if Walt Disney had not acted him out for Ferguson's and the other animators' benefit, mimicked his character and foibles, demonstrated his habits and facial and bodily movements, Pluto could easily have turned out to be too dull a dog to put on the screen. So if Ferguson maintained he was the mother of Pluto, then Walt Disney could plausibly claim fatherhood. (As, indeed, he did; it was Walt's insistence on *sole* parenthood of *all* the famous cartoon characters which particularly disgruntled Ferguson and other Disney animators.)

So all I can do here is append a list of some of Walt Disney's most brilliant and effective artist/animators and indicate in brackets alongside their names in which characters, effects or cartoons they played a significant role. Though none of them can justifiably be given sole credit for any particular character, included are those who have surely won a place for their names on the Disney Roll of Honor for particular contributions. An asterisk indicates those veteran studio animators dubbed the Nine Old Men by Walt Disney.

Ed Arnall: Volcanic effects in Rite of Spring segment of *Fantasia*
James N. Algar: Deer in *Snow White*
Ken Anderson: *Snow White*; *101 Dalmatians*
Art Babbitt: Nutcracker Suite segment of *Fantasia*; development of Goofy; work on Dopey in *Snow White*
Mary Blair: *Alice in Wonderland*; *The Three Caballeros*; *Song of the South*
***Les Clark:** Minnie Mouse; Sugar Plum Fairies in *Fantasia*; dance sequences in *Snow White*; animation of Mickey Mouse in the Sorcerer's Apprentice segment of *Fantasia*
Claude Coats: *Cinderella*
Jim Coleman: *The Fox and the Hound*
Don DaGradi: Tinker Bell in *Peter Pan*
***Marc F. Davis:** *Bambi*; *Sleeping Beauty*; Cruella in *101 Dalmatians*; eagle and octopus scene in *Victory Through Air Power*
Al Dempster: *The Jungle Book*
Norm Ferguson: Pluto; Wicked Witch in *Snow White*; animator on *Dumbo*; *Pinocchio*; *Frolicking Fish*; *Fantasia*
Hugh Frazier: *Mr Toad*
Bernard Garbutt: *Bambi*
Vance Gerry: Sir Hiss in *Robin Hood*; *The Sword in the Stone*
Hardie Gramatky: tugboat sketches and story of *Little Toot*
Don Griffith: *The Fox and the Hound*; castle scene in *Robin Hood*
T. Hee: *Victory Through Air Power*

John Hench: *Cinderella*
Hugh Hennesy: layout artist on *Snow White*
Dick Huemer: *Lullaby Land*
Ralph Hulett: *The Rescuers*
Albert Hurter: Dance of the Hours segment of *Fantasia*; Huntsman sequences in *Snow White*; preliminary sketches of dwarfs in *Snow White*
Ub Iwerks: Mickey Mouse animation in *Steamboat Willie*
Wilfred Jackson: *Song of the South*
***Ollie Johnston:** work on *Bambi*; Mr Smee in *Peter Pan*; Dopey in *Snow White*; Mowgli in *The Jungle Book*; *101 Dalmatians*; *Robin Hood*
***Milton Kahl:** work on *101 Dalmatians*; *Pinocchio*; *Robin Hood*; Medusa in *The Rescuers*
Glen Keane: *The Fox and the Hound*
Richmond Kelsey: *Trees*
***Ward Kimball:** *The Three Caballeros*; Captain Hook in *Peter Pan*; wins Oscar with original cartoon *Toot, Whistle, Plunk and Boom*; Lucifer the Cat in *Cinderella*; Tweedledee and Tweedledum and Mad Hatter's Tea Party in *Alice in Wonderland*; circus train in *Dumbo*; animation of *It's Tough to Be a Bird, Victory Through Air Power, Man and the Moon*; dwarfs and other characters in *Snow White*
***Eric Larson:** Figaro in *Pinocchio*; *Melody Time*; flying horses in Beethoven 6th Symphony segment in *Fantasia*
Rico Lebrun: *Bambi*
J. Gordon Legg: Toccata and Fugue segment of *Fantasia*
***John Lounsbery:** the alligator, Ben Ali, in the Dance of the Hours segment of *Fantasia*; *Bambi*; *Victory Through Air Power*
Dick Lundy: early development of Donald Duck
Don Lusk: stag in *Bambi*
Ham Luske: animator of *The Tortoise and the Hare*; several characters in *Snow White*
Josh Meador: bottle scene in *Alice in Wonderland*
Fred Moore: development of Mickey Mouse; character creations and drawings in *Pinocchio, Bambi*; Maid Marian in *Robin Hood*; dwarfs in *Snow White*
Kay Nielsen: Night on the Bare Mountain segment of *Fantasia*
Ken O'Brien: *Bambi*
William Peet: Mowgli, Bagheera and the tiger, Shere Khan, in *The Jungle Book*; *The Sword in the Stone*

Martin Provensen: drawings for Peter and the Wolf segment of *Fantasia II*

*__Wolfgang (Woolie) Reitherman:__ Goofy; *Cinderella*; Rite of Spring segment of *Fantasia*; *The Rescuers*; *Aristocats*

Art Riley: *Bambi*

Joe Rinaldi: Ichabod Crane in *Ichabod and Mr Toad*

Bill Roberts: *Alpine Climbers*

Retta Scott: *Bambi*

John Sewell: *Bambi*

Mel Shaw: *The Rescuers*

John Sibley: *Ichabod and Mr Toad*

Gustaf Tenggren: sketches and layouts for *Pinocchio*

*__Frank Thomas:__ *Bambi*; *Sword in the Stone*

Vladimir (T-bone) Tytla: Doc, Dopey, Grumpy in *Snow White*; *Dumbo*; Stromboli in *Pinocchio*; Devil in Night on the Bare Mountain segment of *Fantasia*; chief animator of *Snow White*

INDEX